BERLIN
IN THE
EAST-WEST STRUGGLE
1958-61

INTERIM
HISTORY

E 70

BERLIN
IN THE
EAST-WEST STRUGGLE
1958-61

Edited by Glen D. Camp, Jr.
Dept. of Political Science
Long Island University (Brooklyn, N.Y.)

FACTS ON FILE, INC.   NEW YORK

BERLIN
IN THE
EAST-WEST STRUGGLE
1958-61

Library of Congress Catalog Card Number: 70-159689

ISBN 0-87196-198-9

9 8 7 6 5 4 3 2 1

PRINTED IN THE UNITED STATES OF AMERICA

320.943
C 186

CONTENTS

INTRODUCTION

A NYONE PUBLISHING ANOTHER BOOK on Berlin must answer the question "why?" Quite simply because we found no handy account in English that offered both a sampling of the relevant documents and a completely objective narrative of the events that would show how Berlin fared in the East-West struggle in the period 1958-61. This is the troubled period culminating in the building by the Communists of the wall separating East Berlin from West Berlin.

The material used is largely drawn from FACTS ON FILE plus the major documentary collections and studies of Berlin. The documentary sources include HMSO (British), *Selected Documents on Germany and the Question of Berlin, 1944-61*; (U.S.) *Documents on Germany, 1944-61*; and (West German) W. Heidelmeyer and G. Hindrichs (editors), *Documents on Berlin, 1943-63*; *ibid., Dokumente zur Berlinfrage, 1944-62*; W. Hubatsch *et al.* (editors), *The German Question*; and the definitive volumes by Heinrich Siegler, *Dokumentation zur Deutschlandfrage.*

Major studies drawn on include John Mander's brief *Berlin: Hostage for the West,* Jean Edward Smith's *The Defense of Berlin,* W. Philips Davidson's *Berlin Blockade,* Hans Spier's *Divided Berlin* and Philip Windsor's *City on Leave, a History of Berlin 1945-62.*

The following have afforded an authoritative Soviet view: G. Tunkin's "Berlinskii voporos v svete mezhdunarodnogo prava," in *Mezhdunarodnaya Zhizn'* No. 2 (Feb.) 1959, pp. 45-56; *ibid.,* "Nezadachlivye tolkovateli mezhdunarodnogo prava," reprinted with West German replies in *Internationales Recht und Diplomatie,* Heft 3/4 (1960), pp. 564-6. Helpful in obtaining an East German view has been Herbert Kroeger's "Adenauers 'Identitaetstheorie' und die voelkerrechtliche Stellung der DDR," in *Deutsche Aussenpolitik,* Heft 5 (May 1957), pp. 353-64.

Many of the translations into English are those of the editor, who accepts responsibility for any errors of fact.

The editor would like to thank Long Island University for a research grant that assisted in the preparation of this book.

1

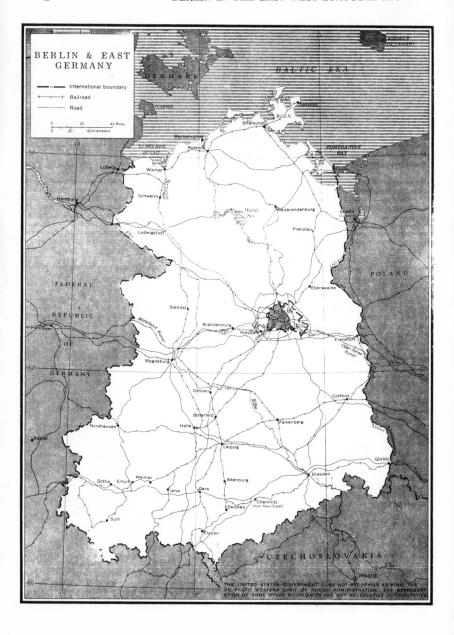

BERLIN & EAST GERMANY

- ▬ ▪ ▬ International boundary
- ┼─┼─┼─ Railroad
- ────── Road

0   20   40 Miles
0   20   40 Kilometers

DENMARK

BALTIC SEA

FEHMARN

RÜGEN

Stralsund

Warnemünde

LÜBECKER BUCHT

Rostock

POMERANIAN BAY

Lübeck

Wismar

Hamburg

Schwerin

Müritz See

Neubrandenburg

Stettin (Szczecin)

Ludwigslust

Prenzlau

POLAND

FEDERAL

Eberswalde

REPUBLIC

Stendal

BERLIN

Hannover

Mittelland Kanal

Brandenburg

Potsdam

Frankfurt (Oder)

OF

Spree Kanal

Oder

GERMANY

Magdeburg

Dessau

Elbe

Cottbus

Bitterfeld

Falkenberg

Nordhausen

Halle

Neisse

Kassel

Leipzig

Görlitz

Gotha

Erfurt

Weimar

Altenburg

Dresden

Jena

Gera

Suhl

Chemnitz (Karl-Marx-Stadt)

Zwickau

Plauen

CZECHOSLOVAKIA

Elbe

PRAGUE

THE UNITED STATES GOVERNMENT DOES NOT RECOGNIZE AS FINAL THE
DE FACTO WESTERN LIMIT OF POLISH ADMINISTRATION. THE REPRESENT-
ATION OF SOME OTHER BOUNDARIES ARE NOT NECESSARILY AUTHORITATIVE

BACKGROUND

World War II Agreements

The joint occupation of Germany had been agreed on in principle by the Big 3 at the Moscow Conference Oct. 19-30, 1943 and confirmed at the Teheran Conference Nov. 28-Dec. 1, 1943. The Moscow Conference established a European Advisory Commission (EAC) to develop occupation zones for Germany and occupation sectors for Berlin.

The first major agreement reached by the EAC was the London "Protocol on Zones of Occupation and Administration of the 'Greater Berlin' Area," issued Sept. 12, 1944. It was based on clear Soviet acceptance of the idea of Allied joint occupation of a special "Berlin area." This acceptance appears to conflict with the assertion of the USSR in its Berlin blockade note of July 14, 1948 that "Berlin ... is a part of the Soviet zone."

The 2d major agreement reached by the American, British and Soviet EAC delegates in London was the "Amending Agreement on Zones of Occupation and Administration of the 'Greater Berlin' Area" Nov. 14, 1944. It left the Berlin sectors unchanged. A French sector of Berlin and zone of occupation in Germany were added in an agreement signed July 26, 1945. Finally the EAC Nov. 14, 1944 concluded its "Agreement on Control Machinery in Germany," with French participation added May 1, 1945.

Charles (Chip) Bohlen's minutes for the Yalta session of Feb. 5, 1945 indicate that Franklin D. Roosevelt handed to Joseph Stalin a map that clearly showed Berlin well within the Soviet zone but that was marked "Joint Zone," whereas the enclaves of Bremen and Bremerhaven, well within the British zone, were clearly marked "U.S. Zone." Stalin's acceptance indicated that Berlin was not considered by the Soviets as part of their zone of occupation despite their arguments to the contrary in Stalin's blockade notes of 1948 or Nikita S. Khrushchev's notes of 1958.

The effect of the EAC's London agreements was shown when U.S. and British forces halted their advance at the end of Apr. 1945. Before the Western Allies linked up with the Red

3

Army, more than 1/3 of the future East Germany had been conquered, only to be given up when the Western troops retired to the EAC zonal borders. The areas given up included the most populous and industrialized areas of Thuringia, West Saxony and Saxony-Anhalt, with more than 8 million people and about 13,000 square miles of territory.

On the basis of the EAC agreements and the Truman-Stalin correspondence of June 14-19, 1945, the Western powers withdrew partly, in exchange for the right to occupy their sectors of Berlin. That occupation included "provision of free access for United States forces by air, road and rail to Berlin from Frankfurt and Bremen."

In order to implement the exchange of territories in Germany as outlined in correspondence exchanged by Stalin and Pres. Harry S. Truman, the 3 commanders-in-chief or their representatives (Lt. Gen. Lucius D. Clay represented Gen. Dwight D. Eisenhower) met at Soviet Marshal Georgi K. Zhukov's headquarters in Karlshorst, Berlin June 29, July 7 and July 10, 1945. During their July 7 meeting they established the Berlin Kommandatura "for the purpose of exercising the joint administration of Berlin." They agreed that orders of the Kommandatura "must be obeyed in all zones of the city" of Berlin. Just as each zonal commander in Germany had ultimate control over "his" zone, so each Berlin sectoral commandant "was to have full authority over his sector of occupation." Policy instructions came to the Kommandatura from the Allied Control Council, however, not from the Soviet military governor, and the Kommandatura was to "direct jointly the administration" of Berlin—not administer Berlin itself. Contrary to later Soviet arguments, the Kommandatura, therefore, was intended to be a lower level policy organ, not just a governing and administrative organ.

The Karlshorst meetings made no permanent commitments on Berlin access. The vital June 29 agreements (in which the conferees made temporary arrangements for one main highway, one rail line and 2 air corridors to Berlin) were oral, and no protocol was issued. Nor did the Potsdam Agreements directly affect Berlin very much. Perhaps the most important Potsdam agreement affecting Berlin access was II.B.14, which said: "During the period of occupation Germany shall be treated as a single economic unit." Other Potsdam agreements affecting Berlin were II.A.7 (control of education), II.A.9 (decentralization and local responsibility), II.A.9(I) and II.A.9(II) (local self-government and rights of democratic political parties to organize throughout Germany). All these provisions were as valid in Berlin as in other parts of Germany and all were apparently violated by the Soviets from the earliest days of the occupation.

Most of the ACC (Allied Control Council) agreements which provided the detailed regulation of Western rights of Berlin access have not been published. This is true of CONL/P(45)27, approved by the ACC Sept. 10, 1945, establishing the technical arrangements for supplying coal and food to Berlin. It is also true of CORC/P(45)128, establishing the Air Safety Center. (The ACC was the central governing agency for Allied control of Germany.)

Berlin Blockade (1948-9)

The Berlin blockade is generally reckoned as lasting from the first day of total embargo until Gen. Vasily Ivanovich Chuikov lifted it, *i.e.,* from June 23, 1948 to May 12, 1949. The Allied airlift, which broke the blockade operated from June 26, 1948 to Sept. 30, 1949. The North Atlantic Treaty was signed Apr. 4, 1949, and the 3 Western foreign ministers Apr. 8 signed the "Washington Agreements" establishing "Trizonia." An Allied High Commission replaced the military governors with civilian authority, and an "Agreed Minute Respecting Berlin" attached to the Washington Agreements promised that the 3 Western sectors of Berlin would be governed as a unit "as far as practicable."

The New York Agreement is the name usually given to the 4-Power Communique signed May 4, 1949, which lifted the blockade. Under the accord, the 2 sides agreed to remove by May 12 all restrictions on communications, transportation and trade imposed since Mar. 1, 1948 between the zones and Berlin.

The Paris Agreement is the name generally given to the communique issued by the Council of Foreign Ministers June 20, 1949. Part I, Point 5 reaffirmed the validity of the New York Agreement but went well beyond it, for it required each occupation authority in its own zone to take the measures "necessary to ensure the normal functioning and utilization of rail, water and road transport for ... movement of persons and goods and ... communications by post, telephone and telegraph." East and West were therefore pledged *not* to reintroduce traffic or communications restrictions on interzonal or Berlin-zonal trade. However, a "creeping blockade" was instituted by the Soviets almost as the ink was drying on the Paris Agreement.

The Western powers extended their official support to the hard-pressed Berliners during the "creeping blockade" through several acts of the London 3-Power Conference held May 11-15, 1950. In the so-called "London Statement on Allied Rights in Berlin," issued May 13, the 3 Western foreign ministers pledged their countries to "continue to uphold their rights in Berlin."

This was the situation in Berlin when Khrushchev threatened to abrogate Western occupation rights in Berlin by signing a "peace treaty" with the East Germans. Western rights in Berlin were based on the right of conquest. Legally, they were rights of occupation, and the rights of access were derived in law and fact from the prior rights of occupation. There was political irony in the fact that the occupiers in Berlin protected the Berliners against the former friends of the occupiers. The Soviets often pointed this out, just as Western observers pointed out that Khrushchev appeared to be trying to enforce his policy at the risk of igniting World War III.

2d Berlin Crisis (1958-61)

The first Berlin crisis lasted intermittently from 1948 through 1949. Although Western costs in men and material were not inconsiderable, the first Berlin crisis was regarded by most observers as a significant propaganda defeat for the Soviet bloc.

The 2d Berlin crisis lasted from 1958 to 1961. Although not a disaster for the Western powers, it was generally regarded as a significant defeat, culminating in the unchallenged construction of the "Berlin Wall" beginning Aug. 13, 1961.

This 2d Berlin crisis never reached the point of blockade of land, sea and air access routes into Berlin. The threat of such a sanction, however, was clearly stated. Many Western observers felt that the 2d crisis was much more carefully managed than the first and that it developed incrementally. No attempt was made to emulate Stalin's 1948 all-out attempt to swallow all of Berlin at one gulp. Rather, Berlin apparently was to be swallowed in bites, beginning with the Soviet sector. If the 3 Western sectors proved indigestible, they would be left for later.

The 2d Berlin crisis can be divided into 3 main phases:

First, a long preliminary phase of Eastern statements with more or less co-ordinated Western replies.

2d, ultimata from the East with the threat of blockade more and more clearly expressed. This phase culminated with the Soviet diplomatic notes of Nov. 27, 1958, which formalized the explicit Soviet threat to blockade Berlin and which implied the threat of war.

The 3d phase was marked by a gradual relaxation of the blockade threat in exchange for agreement to hold a series of East-West meetings. These meetings included a foreign ministers' conference in Geneva and "summit" meetings between Pres. Dwight D. Eisenhower and Soviet Premier Nikita S. Khrushchev at Camp David and in Paris.

The end of this 3d phase came with the relaxation of the blockade threat and the construction of the Berlin Wall beginning Aug. 13, 1961. Gradually West Berlin became a city walled off from its traditional hinterland. Located 110 miles from the West German border, Berlin became an island city in the middle of Communist East Germany. The Wall reduced the flood of refugees into West Berlin to a trickle. Berlin, the "city in the middle" of the German Democratic Republic, was isolated.

Glossary

ACC—Allied Control Council (established by wartime Allies to govern post-war Germany)

ADN—official East German news agency

autobahn—German superhighway; some connect West Germany with Berlin

Bundesrat—upper house of West German parliament

Bundestag—lower house of West German parliament

CDU—Christian Democratic Union (one of 2 major political parties in West Germany)

CP—Communist Party

DPA—unofficial West German news agency

EAC—European Advisory Commission (established at Moscow Conference to work out occupation zones for Germany and occupation sectors for Berlin)

FRG—Federal Republic of Germany (official name of West Germany)

GDR—German Democratic Republic (official name of East Germany)

IAEA—International Atomic Energy Agency, a UN specialized agency

NATO—North Atlantic Treaty Organization, established Apr. 4, 1949 to protect West against Soviet expansion

New York Agreement—name given to 4-Power communique of May 4, 1949 ending Berlin Blockade

Paris Agreement—name given to communique issued by Council of Foreign Ministers June 20, 1949 reestablishing the pre-Blockade status quo

Potsdam Agreement—World War II agreement between the Big 3 (U.S., USSR, Britain)

SED—Socialist Unity (Communist) Party of East Germany

SPD—Socialist Party of Germany (West German social democratic party)

Tass—telegraph agency of the Soviet Union (official Soviet news agency)

1958

YEAR OF THE 2d CRISIS

The first 6 months of 1958 were marked by dispute and petty hindrances to traffic bound to and from Berlin. Then Walter Ulbricht, head of the East German Socialist Unity (Communist) Party, demanded the "normalization" of the Berlin situation. His demand was made in a speech delivered July 10 with Soviet Communist Party chief Nikita S. Khrushchev in the audience. Observers were inclined to dismiss Ulbricht's speech, however, until he repeated and hardened his demands in another speech delivered Oct. 27. In this speech he threatened to cut off all traffic except that needed by the Western garrisons and to shift control over Allied traffic from Soviet to East German armed forces.

Any doubts as to whether Ulbricht spoke for the entire East bloc or just for the East Germans were removed when Khrushchev demanded Nov. 10 that the Western Allies leave Berlin. Khrushchev said that if the West refused to give up what he regarded as remnants of the occupation regime in West Berlin, the USSR would hand over its responsibilities to the "sovereign" East German government. The threat was apparently backed by Soviet armed forces, since if the Western powers tried to force their way through East Germany, the USSR could aid its ally under the Warsaw Pact. Thus World War III was a distinct possibility if the West refused to bow to Soviet demands.

Khrushchev's speech was followed by formal Soviet diplomatic notes delivered to the Western Allies Nov. 27. The Soviet government granted a 6-month delay before turning over its occupation responsibilities to the East Germans. The *notes suggested that West Berlin be turned into a "free city," independent of its Western protectors.*

During the remainder of the year there were, alternately, Soviet threats of war and indications of a Soviet desire for peaceful solutions. Despite some apparent differences between the Western Allies, the Western replies, issued Dec. 31, demonstrated considerable unity. The Western notes had, in fact, been coordinated and approved by the NATO Council. In the notes, the Western powers rejected Soviet demands for the liquidation of Western occupation rights and opposed the "free-city" idea. The Allies did suggest renewed East-West negotiations to settle the Berlin question as part of an overall German and European settlement.

Communist Protests & Traffiç Harassments

A verbal sparring match between East and West over the status of Berlin took place during the first half of 1958. The USSR led Jan. 6 with a protest from its UN delegation to the UN Secretary General. The Soviets objected to the naming of Berlin as a *Land* (or state) in international treaties and agreements to which the Federal Republic of (West) Germany, or FRG, was a party. Berlin had a "special status in international law" and was "the capital of the German Democratic Republic" (GDR or East Germany), the Soviets argued.

U.S. State Secy. John Foster Dulles replied to this Soviet protest indirectly. At a Washington reception held Feb. 10 in honor of West Berlin Lord Mayor Willy Brandt, Dulles assured Brandt of complete U.S. support for Berlin's freedom. Dulles reiterated that U.S. policy was to assure unimpaired access for both people and goods to and from Berlin as guaranteed in the New York and Paris 4-Power Agreements of May 4 and June 20, 1949.

During a visit to Berlin, Dulles read a statement May 8 before the Berlin House of Representatives. Noting that he spoke "with the express authority of Pres. Eisenhower," Dulles reaffirmed U.S. support of the 3-Power (U.S.-British-French) Declaration of Oct. 3, 1954. He said: "The security and welfare of Berlin and the maintenance of the position of the 3 powers there are regarded by the 3 powers as essential elements of the peace of the free world in the present international situation. Accordingly, they will maintain armed forces within the territory of Berlin as long as their responsibilities require it. They therefore reaffirm that they will treat any attack against Berlin as an attack upon their forces and upon themselves."

Dulles told West Berlin leaders that their divided city was a "lively exhibit" of the USSR's refusal to honor pledges for the reunification of Germany and of its violation of international agreements as a "legitimate technique" for advancing Soviet interests.

The GDR Apr. 24 had raised canal tolls for ship traffic between West Berlin and the FRG to compensate for what it described as increased costs of water conservation construction projects at Geesthacht in the GDR. The FRG assumed the additional costs as a contribution to the West Berlin economy.

Barge traffic to West Berlin from West Germany through East Germany was suspended May 5 because East Germany had applied transit taxes of 3 Deutschemarks (71¢) per ton on traffic through the Elbe River and Mittelland Canal. The tax, which would cost up to $750 per barge trip and total $6 million annually, was in retaliation for West German plans to dam the Elbe River 20 miles southeast of Hamburg. (In 1957 barges had brought to West Berlin 2.5 million tons of cargo, 30% of the city's requirements.) The West Berlin barge traffic was resumed May 13 despite the newly imposed transit taxes. The U.S., British and French ambassadors to West Germany protested to Soviet Amb.-to-East Germany Mikhail Pervukhin May 16 against the new taxes on barge traffic to West Berlin.

The Soviet embassy in Washington protested to the U.S. State Department Aug. 11 against the extension of the statutes of the International Atomic Energy Agency (IAEA) to West Berlin. The Soviet note asserted that a statement by an FRG spokesman that IAEA statutes "also apply to West Berlin" could not be accepted. The note stated that Berlin currently enjoyed "international status" and that Berlin was not a part of the FRG. Therefore, the note declared, the FRG was not competent to extend the coverage of international agreements to West Berlin. The State Department agreed in a note to the Soviets Aug. 20 that Berlin was not subject to the governing power of the FRG. However, the U.S. note continued, the FRG was competent to declare the application of the IAEA statutes to Berlin with the agreement of the Allied Kommandatura. The note further insisted that the application of these statutes to Berlin was thoroughly consistent with the international legal position of Berlin.

The East Berlin deputy mayor, Waldemar Schmidt, had demanded Mar. 15 a "normalization" of the Berlin situation, particularly in the capital of the GDR (East Berlin). The exact conditions of this normalization were left unclear. Walter Ulbricht, secretary of the Socialist Unity (Communist) Party (SED), repeated the demand July 10 in an address before the 5th SED Party Conference. In the presence of Soviet CP First Secy. Nikita S. Khrushchev, Ulbricht indicated the new policy line on Berlin by also demanding "normalization" of the Berlin situation. Like Schmidt, however, Ulbricht refrained from saying exactly what he meant by "normalization." Most observers at the time did not attach too much importance to Ulbricht's address even though Khrushchev's presence might have suggested the possibility of a change in East-bloc policy toward Berlin.

Ulbricht Claims All of Berlin

"Normalization," however, was apparently a slogan for a policy *demarche* by the East bloc. This became evident when Ulbricht indicated more precisely what he meant by the term. In an address delivered at the Friedrichstadt Palace in East Berlin Oct. 27, Ulbricht stated that the "position of Berlin as capital of the GDR is based on its inseparable connection with the other areas of the GDR." All of Berlin, therefore, was part of the sovereign GDR territory, he declared. In 1945 when the different occupation zones were created, Berlin was not made into a 5th zone, Ulbricht declared. It remained a constituent part of the Soviet zone, he argued, a zone in which the troops of the Western powers participated by joint occupation of the city.

Ulbricht insisted that the Allied Kommandatura had never been granted supreme power over Berlin, merely the power of "administration of the area of greater Berlin." Since both West Berlin and the island of Quemoy were misused as centers of provocation, he contended, both had been illegally separated from their hinterland and constituted integral parts of their respective countries—the GDR and the People's Republic of (Communist) China. The Soviet-GDR treaty of Sept. 20, 1955 applied also to Berlin, Ulbricht contended. Therefore, in the "democratic part of the capital of the GDR" (East Berlin), the "control and supervisory powers of the occupation period no longer existed."

Ulbricht also delivered an attack on the Western position in West Berlin. He argued that the continuation of the occupation regime in West Berlin contradicted international legal documents that the 4 powers had agreed on. The purpose of the Western powers' presence in Berlin was, together with the USSR, to use their occupation and administration of Berlin to liquidate Nazism and to democratize the city, he said. The Potsdam Agreement required this and also required the maintenance of Berlin's unity as the capital of a unified peace-loving Germany. Therefore, Ulbricht maintained, the Western powers had undermined the legal basis for their presence in Berlin as well as any legal claim or moral-political basis for their further occupation of West Berlin.

The occupation power of the Western allies in West Berlin was still a fact "at present," Ulbricht noted. The GDR, which recognized no limitations on its sovereignty or its territorial boundaries within and for Berlin, proceeded from this real situation in developing its policy. Therefore, Ulbricht concluded, the GDR agreed that for the time being the control of troop and goods traffic between West Germany and West Berlin needed to supply the garrisons of France, Britain and the U.S. would be exercised by Soviet armed forces. Such an arrangement, Ulbricht warned, did not exclude the competence of the GDR—as a sovereign state in every respect—over these questions. Traffic between the GDR and the Western sectors of Berlin and traffic inside Berlin were not treated by any agreements. This applied also to overflights of GDR territory in the air corridors between the FRG and Berlin insofar as such flights were not connected with the provisioning of the West Berlin garrisons of the 3 powers.

The sanctions threatened by Ulbricht were explicit: the possible shift of control over Allied traffic from Soviet to GDR armed forces; also a cutting off of all traffic, including air flights to and from West Berlin, except those needed by the

Western garrisons, *i.e.,* a resumption of the 1948-9 Berlin blockade.

Willy Brandt, as lord mayor of Berlin, replied Nov. 5. He argued that the "Protocol ... on Zones of Occupation ... and Administration of 'Greater Berlin,'" signed by the victorious Allies Sept. 12, 1944, clearly divided Germany into 5 areas. These 5 areas were 4 occupation zones and a Berlin area. Brandt rejected Ulbricht's contention that Berlin had not been an independent occupation zone as of 1945. He also rejected Ulbricht's view that Berlin belonged to the Soviet zone and that the Western powers were present in the city in fact but without international legal justification.

Speaking to the workers of a large West Berlin industrial firm, Brandt asserted that the reason the Soviets alone had occupied Berlin was solely military. Like the American occupation of Thuringia and part of Saxony, Soviet occupation of Berlin had no political ramifications, Brandt said. The Americans transferred these areas, which they had conquered, to Soviet control just as the Soviets transferred the 3 Western sectors of Berlin to Western control. In all these areas the occupying power had transferred its trusteeship authority by means of valid international legal agreements. In Berlin, for example, the transfer was made by the USSR to the Allied Kommandatura. Brandt emphasized that these agreements still existed. The fact that the planned administration of Berlin no longer functioned was not the fault of the Berliners, for the city was split Nov. 30, 1948 when the Soviets established an East Berlin City Council *(Magistrat)*.

"Berlin does not belong to the so-called 'GDR'! The East zone rather belongs to Germany, and the capital of all Germany is and remains Berlin, all of Berlin!" Brandt asserted.

Brandt also disputed Ulbricht's views on the sovereignty of the GDR. He noted that the GDR had declared its willingness to permit the control over traffic of troops, personnel and goods of the Western powers to Berlin to be exercised by Soviet armed forces. Brandt declared that this said a good deal about the Ulbricht thesis that the sovereignty of the GDR was unrestricted and that the GDR was therefore competent in questions of traffic between Berlin and West Germany.

Such traffic questions were also regulated according to international legal agreements between the victor powers, Brandt continued. An example of such agreements was the American-Soviet agreement of May 4, 1949, which provided for ending traffic, trade and transport restrictions between Berlin and the Western zones. This agreement was further confirmed by the 4-power agreement at the Paris foreign ministers conference of 1949. These agreements were still valid and could not be unilaterally rescinded, Brandt said. In any event, he concluded, these 4-power agreements were not subject to the arbitrary interpretation of the GDR power elite.

State Secy. Dulles also replied to Ulbricht's July 10 and Oct. 27 speeches. At a news conference in Washington Nov. 7, Dulles was asked if he saw any potential danger in the "propaganda campaign" of the East German Communists, who "have begun to say repeatedly that West Berlin belongs to East Germany." "No," replied Dulles, "I see no danger in it because ... we are most solemnly committed to hold West Berlin, if need be by military force." "That is a very solemn and formal 3-power commitment to which the U.S. stands bound," he observed. "I think as long as we stand firm there, and the Communists know we will stand firm, that there is no danger to West Berlin."

Khrushchev Demands that West Quit Berlin

Many diplomatic observers in the West still had doubts that Ulbricht's statements represented Soviet policy. These doubts were largely removed when the USSR demanded that the West leave Berlin. Soviet Premier Khrushchev called on the U.S., Britain and France Nov. 10 to "give up the remnants of the occupation regime in Berlin and thus make it possible to create a normal atmosphere in the [East German] capital." Khrushchev said that the USSR, "for its part," would "hand over those functions in Berlin which are still with Soviet organs" to the "sovereign" East German government.

Khrushchev's demand carried an implied threat that the USSR would terminate its Berlin military mission and thus force the Western powers to deal directly with the East German regime on matters normally handled through Soviet occupation authorities.

Speaking at a Moscow rally for visiting Polish United Workers (Communist) Party First Secy. Wladyslaw Gomulka, Khrushchev charged that the West had taken advantage of the 1945 Potsdam agreement fixing Berlin's 4-power occupation to create "a kind of state within a state" in Berlin as a base for "subversive activity" against East Germany. He asserted that the Western powers had consistently violated the Potsdam agreement and thus had "abolished the legal basis on which their stay in Berlin rested."

Charging that the rearmament of West Germany had been achieved only through an encouragement of German militarism specifically forbidden by the Potsdam accords, Khrushchev chided the West for its observance of those sections of the treaty permitting it to hold "sway in West Berlin." He noted that the U.S., Britain and France "enjoy the right of unhampered communication between West Berlin and West Germany by air, rail highways and the water" belonging to an East German state "which they do not even recognize."

Khrushchev suggested that the Western powers "form their own relations with the [East German government] and come to an agreement with it if they are interested in certain questions connected with Berlin," presumably those involving Western access to the city. He asserted that the USSR would maintain its "obligations" to East Germany, particularly those "which stem from the Warsaw Treaty." He made clear that an attack on East Germany would be considered an attack on the entire Soviet bloc. He stressed that the Soviet obligations included defense of the Oder-Neisse frontier, the post-World War II border between East Germany and Poland.

Khrushchev indicated that the USSR planned to transfer to the GDR control of all traffic to and from Berlin. If the West tried to break a Berlin blockade, he warned, this could mean war, and modern war "would be fatal to West Germany and would bring untold calamities to the peoples of other countries." Khrushchev suggested that these unpleasant results could be avoided if the West would merely recognize the GDR as a state and deal with Ulbricht: "Let the United States, France, and Britain themselves build their relations with the German Democratic Republic. Let them reach agreement with it themselves if they are interested in any questions concerning Berlin."

Western reaction to Khrushchev's Nov. 10 ultimatum was swift. U.S. State Department officials called attention Nov. 10-11 to the Nov. 7 statement in which Dulles had called the West "committed to hold West Berlin, if need be by military force." These officials also expressed doubt that Khrushchev's statement would lead to a renewal of the Berlin blockade.

A West German statement approved Nov. 12 by Chancellor Konrad Adenauer's cabinet warned that Soviet abrogation of the 4-power Berlin statute would "constitute a threat to the freedom" of Berlin and would increase "the already tense situation in the world." The Bonn declaration, issued by government spokesman Felix von Eckardt, asserted that the implementation of the Soviet proposal "must impair German-Soviet relations" and presumably would cause a diplomatic break. Von Eckardt warned that any Soviet effort to turn control of Berlin air corridors over to East Germany would constitute a "threat" to West Germany. Mayor Willy Brandt of West Berlin had asserted Nov. 10 that there were not "the slightest grounds for Berliners to feel uneasy." "We have confidence in the security guaranty of the Allies," he said.

A White House spokesman pointed out Nov. 13 that the rights of the Western powers to stay in Berlin as well as enjoy free access to Berlin were not based on the Potsdam Protocol of Aug. 1, 1945. The Allies came to Berlin and remained there as a military occupation with a right of occupation based on their victory over Nazi Germany. The White House spokesman declared: The zones of occupation were delineated in the European Advisory Commission communique issued in London Sept. 12, 1944; the 4-power occupation system in Berlin was created by declaration of the 4 commanders in chief, which referred to occupation zones and the control apparatus in Germany; the Berlin occupation system was also created by agreement of the 4-power administration of Berlin July 5, 1945.

The White House spokesman insisted that the Western powers' right of access to Berlin proceeded from their right of occupation and was confirmed by many 4-power agreements. The rights of the Western powers were confirmed not only by the New York Agreement of May 4, 1949 and the Paris Communique of June 20, 1949 (which re-established the *status quo ante* blockade) but also by practice, which had remained constant.

Spokesmen from the British Foreign Office and the French Foreign Ministry also stated Nov. 11 that the presence of the Western forces in Berlin was based on the right of occupation and not on the Potsdam Agreement.

The U.S. State Department told the USSR Nov. 13 that the Western allies possessed "the right of occupation" in Berlin "based on their defeat of Nazi Germany and a series of subsequent Allied agreements in which the Russians participated." The department said Khrushchev had been "confused" in thinking that Western occupation rights were derived from the Potsdam Agreement.* It reminded the USSR that its 1948 Berlin blockade had been defeated by the Western airlift.

A U.S. State Department statement Nov. 19 rejected Soviet charges that West Berlin was being used as an espionage base against East Germany. It declared that the USSR itself was "guilty of massive interference in German affairs expressed in its effort to maintain by armed force domination over a large part of the German people." It pointed to the USSR's Nov. 1957 declaration of intent to "use Communist and workers' parties throughout the world in attempts to install the 'dictatorship of the proletariat' in all countries."

The East Germans appeared to retreat Nov. 12. Premier Otto Grotewohl of East Germany indicated Nov. 12 that the USSR and East Germany were not ready to terminate the Soviet military role in Berlin or to launch a major campaign against the Western powers' continued presence in the city. In a markedly softened statement on the Berlin question, Grotewohl asserted that it was "becoming increasingly difficult for the Western powers to prove their claim for special rights in Berlin." He urged the Big 3 to realize that "their remaining in Berlin is not in the interests of the German people." He added that Berlin was "not the main problem" in the overriding question of "an understanding among Germans." A Grotewohl comment that indicated the USSR might withdraw its Berlin

---

* General terms for the occupation of Germany were fixed in the Yalta agreement in Feb. 1945. The 4-power Berlin occupation legally was established by an agreement, signed June 5, 1945 by U.S. Soviet, British and French military commanders. This accord provided that "Greater Berlin shall be occupied by troops of each of the 4 powers" and "an inter-allied authority ... created" in order to "administer the area jointly." The Berlin accord was confirmed later by the Potsdam Agreement.

forces before the West did so later was revised to make clear that Soviet troops would remain in Berlin as long as Western forces were there.

(3 U.S. Army trucks and their crews were detained by Soviet guards at the Babelsberg checkpoint outside Berlin Nov. 14 but were released after 8¼ hours. The drivers had refused to let Soviet officials search their cargoes. Other military and all civilian truck, rail and air traffic to Berlin remained normal.)

Chancellor Konrad Adenauer of West Germany issued his own warning Nov. 15. He said that Soviet threats to blockade Berlin had created an "extremely dangerous situation" for West Germany and the entire world. He told newsmen that Bonn did "not want to take up the Berlin challenge" but might be forced to do so by events.

USSR Plans Berlin Withdrawal

A new element of urgency was added to the situation with reports that the Soviets were arranging with the East Germans the logistics of the Soviet withdrawal from Berlin. Press reports also suggested the possibility of a split between the Western powers, with the British prepared to accept East German control over Western military traffic to Berlin.

A Soviet-East German commission met in East Berlin Nov. 21 to begin discussions on the transfer to East German control of Soviet functions in the 4-power administration of Berlin. The commission was said to have reached agreement on a number of questions presumed to affect the U.S.-British-French presence in Berlin and the Western powers' rights to air, road, rail and communications access to Berlin from West Germany.

East Berlin reports that Soviet personnel were beginning to evacuate the Red Army headquarters compound in Karlshorst were denied Nov. 21 by the Soviet embassy in East Berlin.

Soviet Amb.-to-West Germany Andrei A. Smirnov had met with West German Chancellor Adenauer in Bonn Nov. 20 to inform him of what the Soviet embassy termed "steps that the Soviet government planned to take to realize its aim of ending the occupation status of Berlin." Smirnov, who refused to reveal what took place at his meeting with Adenauer, told newsmen Nov. 21 that the USSR would "give Berlin back to the Germans" in time for "a peaceful Christmas."

First Deputy Premier Walter Ulbricht of East Germany asserted Nov. 24 that Soviet troops would be withdrawn from Berlin and that East Germany would assume control of all Berlin matters currently handled by Soviet authorities. Ulbricht, interviewed by the London *Daily Mail,* insisted that a Soviet withdrawal would force the Western powers to open "normal" talks with East Germany on access to Berlin. Ulbricht said: "Whoever uses the territory of East Germany does *de facto* recognize the existence of East Germany, no matter whether he uses it by water, by land or in the air."

Berlin reports had said Nov. 20 that reported Allied differences centered on British willingness to negotiate with East Germany on continued access to Berlin if the USSR carried out its threat to withdraw from the city's administration. The U.S. and France, backed by West Berlin and West Germany, were said to have insisted that East German officials be barred from any control over the Allies' military traffic to Berlin from West Germany. The French Foreign Ministry said Nov. 21 that France was "determined to stay in Berlin ... to guarantee the will to freedom of the West Berliners."

State Secy. Dulles, returning to Washington Nov. 24 from a 5-day Canadian vacation, denied reports of growing Western disagreement on how to reply to the Soviet pressure against Berlin. Dulles told newsmen that there was "no evidence at all as to disagreement between the principal Allied powers" on the Berlin question. Bonn dispatches reported Nov. 25 that Western diplomats in West Germany had received specific instructions on dealing with any Soviet steps to end its occupation of Berlin. The orders were said to have been agreed on in intensive U.S.-British-French-West German negotiations following Chancellor Adenauer's meeting with Soviet Amb. Smirnov Nov. 20.

Mayor Willy Brandt had told the West Berlin Parliament Nov. 20 that Berliners were prepared to undergo a new Soviet blockade rather than surrender to East German controls and eventual Communist rule. Brandt, who asserted that "Berlin was, is and will remain the capital of Germany," warned the USSR that an attempt to seize Berlin could provoke World

War III. A joint communique issued in Berlin Nov. 22 by Brandt and West German Foreign Min. Heinrich von Brentano told Berliners that the Western powers had pledged to defend their continued presence in Berlin as a guarantee of the city's freedom.

In a statement issued through Press Secy. James C. Hagerty, Pres. Eisenhower Nov. 22 reaffirmed that the U.S. "firm intentions in Berlin remain unchanged." Hagerty said that the President's statement referred to U.S. pledges to "maintain the integrity of West Berlin" in the face of Soviet threats. Hagerty made clear that Mr. Eisenhower's statement had been worked out in close consultation with the British and French governments.

The issue of exactly what role if any East German officials should play with regard to Western military traffic to and from Berlin was discussed at a press conference in Washington by State Secy. Dulles Nov. 26. Many diplomatic observers thought his use of an "agent" theory indicated that the U.S. had tempered its refusal to recognize East German authority in Berlin and "might" permit the East German government to act as a Soviet "agent" in administering Western communications to Berlin. Dulles said that the primary question involved in the Berlin dispute was whether or not the USSR could legally renounce its "explicit obligation" to assure the "Allied powers" and "the world generally normal access to and egress from Berlin." He indicated that in the event the USSR reaffirmed its Berlin obligation, the U.S. "might" be willing to accept East German government functions in Berlin provided it did not involve "acceptance of the East German regime as a substitute for the Soviet Union in discharging the [Berlin] obligation of the Soviet Union."

Dulles expressed the opinion that the USSR's motive was not "to drive us out of Berlin or to obstruct access to Berlin but to try to compel an increased recognition and ... increased stature" on the East German government. He made clear that U.S. acceptance of East Germany as an "agent" of the USSR would not be intended as U.S. recognition of the "puppet" East German regime. He noted that the Western powers and West Germany had "in certain practical matters" dealt with "minor functionaries of the [East German government]."

(Trade agreements signed Nov. 21 by the East and West German governments provided for the sale of 200,000 tons of West German steel and for the exchange of one million tons of East German brown coal and 50,000 tons of wheat for one million tons of West German hard coal. The agreements were made conditional on the maintenance of "existing relationships" in Berlin and other matters.)

Vice Pres. Richard M. Nixon, during a visit to Great Britain, issued a clear warning to the USSR not to misjudge U.S. intentions on Berlin. Nixon had left Washington with his wife Nov. 24 for a 4-day ceremonial visit to England. Arriving in London Nov. 25, Nixon asserted in an address that U.S. forces would "remain in [Berlin] ... until a German settlement acceptable to the German people has been achieved." He said Soviet Premier Khrushchev "could make no greater miscalculation than to base his policies on his professed conclusion that our recent election reflected a lack of confidence in the foreign policy leadership of the President [a view expressed by Khrushchev Nov. 7] and might therefore bring about a weakening of our determination to resist his aggressive tactics."

Soviet Notes Detail Berlin Plans

In notes handed by Soviet Foreign Min. Andrei A. Gromyko to the U.S., British, French and West German ambassadors in Moscow Nov. 27, the USSR proposed that West Berlin be made "an independent political entity—a free city"—demilitarized and separate from "either of the existing German states." The USSR suggested that the free city be given "its own government" and be permitted to "run its own economy, administrative and other affairs." Russia conceded that East and West Berlin should be joined as "a single city" but expressed doubt that unity would be obtainable due to differences between "the way[s] of life in the [city's] 2 parts."

In its notes, the USSR said that it was prepared to negotiate 4-power Berlin guarantees similar to the Austrian neutrality agreement. It pledged that West Berlin would be "given the right to establish a way of life at its own choice ... based on private capitalist ownership." It called on West Berlin to purge itself of alleged subversive activities directed against

East Germany and promised that the USSR would "ensure the stability and prosperity ... of the free city" by adequate supplies of needed "raw materials and foodstuffs on a commercial basis."

The Soviet notes called on the U.S. and other countries concerned to open negotiations on the establishment of Berlin's free-city status. The USSR said that it "would have no objection to the United Nations also sharing ... in observing" Berlin's new status. It pledged a 6-month delay in East German assumption of control over Allied military traffic into Berlin but stressed that if the free city proposal were "not acceptable" to the U.S. and the other Western powers, "there is no topic left for talks on the Berlin question by the former occupying powers."

The USSR warned that it would turn all Soviet occupation functions over to the East German government at the end of the 6-month period if the Western powers had not accepted the free city proposal. It specifically renounced the Allied agreements signed Sept. 12, 1944 and May 1, 1945 providing for 4-power occupation and control of Greater Berlin. It made clear that Soviet military authorities would cease their Berlin duties at the end of 6 months and that the East German regime then would "fully control ... its sovereignty on land, on water and in the air."

To many Western observers, the arguments in the Soviet notes were familiar. They had been raised before by Khrushchev, Ulbricht and other Soviet-bloc leaders. 3 items were new: The first departure was the use of formal diplomatic notes. Most Western observers agreed that this procedure formalized the Soviet threat to Berlin by emphasizing its seriousness. By making their diplomatic retreat more difficult, the Soviets increased the credibility of their threat. The 2d item was the 6-month delay granted by the Soviet government before it turned over its occupation functions to the East Germans. The introduction of this delay "defused" the situation to some extent by providing the Soviets with some diplomatic flexibility. The 3d new item was the proposal to turn West Berlin (but not East Berlin) into a "free city" independent of its Western protectors. The possibility that West Berlin might not long remain "free" but be added to the territory of the East German government was noted by most Western observers.

Western reaction was immediate, partly because the Soviet threat developed slowly enough to permit thorough consultation among the Allies and partly because the threat itself was so serious. From the Western point of view, the ejection of the Allies from Berlin would have constituted a major psychological defeat. Therefore, without formally rejecting the new plan, the Allies made it clear that they would not accept such a defeat by altering Berlin's 4-power occupation status.

The U.S. State Department warned Nov. 27 that the U.S. would not "enter into any agreement with the Soviet Union" that "would have the result of abandoning the people of West Berlin to hostile domination." A statement said that the Soviet note would be studied but that the U.S. would "not acquiesce in a unilateral repudiation by the [USSR] of its obligations and responsibilities ... in relation to Berlin" It stressed that the U.S., Britain and France were "solemnly committed to the security of the Western sectors of Berlin."

Pres. Eisenhower pledged Nov. 30 that the U.S. would not "embark on any course of conduct" that would result in "abandoning the [U.S.'] responsibilities ... for the freedom and security of the people of West Berlin." The President's statement, issued by State Secy. Dulles after a White House meeting on the Berlin question, was considered to be aimed at negating Dulles' earlier indication that the U.S. would permit the East German government to act as the USSR's "agent" in Berlin. Dulles disclosed that the U.S., Britain, France and West Germany had begun close consultation on the Berlin problem and had reached "a general harmony of views." In a joint French-West German communique, issued in Bonn Nov. 26 following talks between Chancellor Adenauer and Premier Charles de Gaulle, the 2 leaders had pledged to continue the maintenance of Berlin's current occupation status. The British Foreign Office said Nov. 27 that Britain was "not likely" to accept a revision of its "present position" in Berlin. British Prime Min. Harold Macmillan told Parliament Dec. 2 that he had informed Soviet Premier Khrushchev in a personal message Nov. 22 that Britain would "uphold its rights over Berlin."

(Gen. Henry I. Hodes, U.S. Army commander in Europe warned at a Berlin news conference Nov. 30 that any hostile action against the 4,000-man U.S. garrison in Berlin would be "an action against the U.S." Hodes asserted that he would consider any denial of Western access to Berlin as an "infringement" subject to U.S. military action.)

The Soviet proposal of free-city status for Berlin was denounced by Major Brandt Nov. 27 as an "unbearable" attempt to split the city from West Germany and make it dependent on the "Eastern bloc." Brandt charged that the Soviet plan aimed at the eventual absorption of Berlin in East Germany. He declared that any revision of Berlin's status not based on German reunification would be opposed by Berliners and the Western Allies. Brandt said in a radio broadcast Nov. 30 that the acceptance of the USSR's free-city plan would make Berlin a "temporary concentration camp."

Chancellor Adenauer told West Berliners in a Bonn statement Nov. 27 that West Germany would do "everything" to preserve their "security and freedom" and "free right of passage between Berlin and West Germany." Adenauer, who met with Chairman Erich Ollenhauer of the Social Democratic Party and other opposition leaders Nov. 30, appealed to all West German political parties Dec. 2 for "a united front in the face of the Soviet threat" to Berlin.

(West Berlin financial sources reported Dec. 2 that 25 to 30 million Deutschemarks [$6 to 7 million] had been withdrawn from Berlin savings banks and that many Berlin firms had begun transfer of surplus assets to West Germany during the past 2 weeks.)

In reactions to the statements of the Western powers, Soviet spokesmen indicated a tolerant, even jovial attitude. Khrushchev, for example, expressed his desire Nov. 29 to "drink toasts again with our wartime allies." The East German reaction, however, was tougher. Ulbricht asserted that the Western powers would need East German permission to use access routes to Berlin after the 6-month deadline.

Khrushchev had said at a Moscow news conference Nov. 27 that Soviet leaders were "realistic people" who did not believe the "fantasy" that West Berlin or West Germany could be converted to communism. Khrushchev, who described occupied West Berlin as a "cancerous tumor" in East Germany, asserted that the USSR was willing to negotiate a revision of the city's status gradually so that it would not be "painful" to the West. He said the USSR would not ask West Berliners to accept free city status for "eternity" but only as long as they wished.

Speaking at an Albanian Embassy reception in Moscow Nov. 29, Khrushchev reportedly called for a "round table" East-West conference on Berlin. He was said to have indicated that the USSR would be satisfied if Berlin negotiations were begun within the 6-month Soviet timetable for settling the problem. (Soviet embassy spokesmen in East Berlin said Nov. 28 that the USSR would be willing to delay the transfer of its Berlin functions to the East German government if East-West talks showed promise of agreement on a free city of West Berlin.)

Ulbricht warned Nov. 29 that any Western attempt to renew an airlift to West Berlin would be regarded as a "military threat" to East Germany. He told the *N.Y. Times* that within 6 months East Germany would "have all the powers" currently exercised by Soviet occupation authorities. He also rejected suggestions that proposed Berlin negotiations be broadened to consider German reunification.

Communists Rebuffed in West Berlin Election

Elections held in West Berlin Dec. 7 assumed the character of a plebiscite on Soviet policy. Instead of regarding the balloting as merely local elections for a city House of Representatives and 12 borough councils, Western leaders made it plain that they considered the elections a test of West Berlin's attitude toward Communist plans.

The results were decisive. Socialist Unity (Communist) Party candidates won less than 2% of the votes cast. The Social Democrats, headed by Lord Mayor Willy Brandt, won 52.1% of the vote, up 7.5% from their 1954 vote. The Christian Democratic Union of Chancellor Adenauer remained the 2d largest party with 37.3% of the West Berlin vote.

Final returns Dec. 8 showed that a record 93.1% of West Berlin's 1,757,152 registered voters had cast ballots. Party totals (1954 results in parentheses): Social Democrats—849,883, or 52.1% (44.6%); Christian Democratic Union—608,927, or

37.3% (30.4%); Free Democrats—61,054, or 3.9% (12.8%);
German Party—53,899, or 3.8% (4.9%); Socialist Unity
(Communist) Party—31,520, or 1.9% (2.7%); Free German
People's Party—10,657, or 0.7%.

West Berliners had been called on to make the election a
demonstration of their resistance to Communist rule. Adenauer
had arrived in the city Dec. 4 for a 3-day visit, and he told
Berliners that West Germans "stand behind" them. Adenauer,
whose plea for West German party unity on the Berlin question
was rejected Dec. 3 by opposition Social Democrats, snubbed a
meeting Dec. 5 with Brandt, a Socialist. However, before
leaving for Bonn Dec. 6, Adenauer urged Berliners to back
"any of the democratic parties" as "a vote against the Soviet
[free city] plan."

East German Premier Otto Grotewohl warned West
Berliners Dec. 8 that their elections could not "be taken as some
sort of decision on the question of the Soviet note" demanding
an independent and unoccupied Berlin. He said that all of
Berlin belonged to East Germany and eventually would be
controlled by it. The 400-member East German Volkskammer
(parliament) declared unanimously Dec. 3 that it would
"conscientiously" assume Soviet military functions in Berlin.

West Firm Against Red Demands

Lord Mayor Brandt of West Berlin, strengthened by his
party's election victory, called on the Western powers Dec. 9 to
refuse any negotiations on the basis of the USSR's
"ultimatum" for their withdrawal from Berlin. Brandt thus
aligned himself with Adenauer in refusing any compromise on
Berlin or German unity. Brandt and Adenauer had been
reported at odds over Brandt's previous willingness to accept
East-West Berlin talks as a way to reopen the entire German
unity question with the USSR.

The most important immediate reaction to the Nov. 27
Soviet notes was probably that of Pres. Eisenhower because it
was generally accepted by both East and West that the
Americans provided the only real military protection for
Berlin. In what was regarded as a preliminary reply to the
Soviet note to the U.S., Eisenhower publicly reaffirmed Dec. 10
that the U.S. and its Western allies would "stand firm on the

rights and the responsibilities that we have undertaken" in Berlin. He made clear that the West's responsibilities included "maintaining the freedom of the western part of Berlin."

Speaking at his first news conference since Soviet Premier Khrushchev had demanded an end to the 4-power occupation of Berlin, Eisenhower said Dec. 10 that the West would continue to honor East-West accords specifying allied rights in Berlin and pledging eventual German reunification through free elections. He noted that these agreements, although prepared by the Allies' European Advisory Commission in 1944, confirmed by the Yalta and Potsdam conferences in 1945 and reaffirmed by the Geneva conference in 1955, had been "quickly repudiated" by the USSR.

Eisenhower refused "to even talk about a program that did not contemplate peaceful methods for the reuniting of Germany ... by means of free elections." He warned that perpetuation of the division of Germany was "detrimental to the peace of the world." He asserted, however, that German reunification without freedom would mean "abandoning people that have a right to ... the kind of cooperation that we have promised."

A personal message from Khrushchev was delivered to Eisenhower Dec. 9 by Sen. Hubert H. Humphrey (D., Minn.). The message, known to center on current U.S.-Soviet friction, had been given to Humphrey during an 8-hour Kremlin interview with Khrushchev Dec. 1. Humphrey told newsmen that the Soviet move in Berlin had been designed "to get the Western powers out of Berlin and ... set them quarreling among themselves over the question of Berlin." He did not currently see "any room for a compromise" of conflicting Western and Soviet positions on Berlin, Humphrey continued, but he believed that "legal questions [of Western occupation rights] will have to be tempered with prudent judgment."

A Soviet statement Dec. 11 attacked the "speeches on a 'right of occupation'" that "now sound strange, not to say senseless" almost 14 years after the end of the war. It said: "2 sovereign German states now exist which do not need occupiers, especially occupiers who claimed to speak for Germany and whose right of occupation is unlimited in time." The statement held that Western occupation rights in Berlin "long ago ceased to exist." "How many decades do the occupiers wish to sit in Berlin under cover of this so-called 'right of occupation'?" the statement asked. The statement repeated arguments of the Soviet notes on the alleged misuse of West Berlin for propaganda incitement and subversive activity. It reiterated the assertion that the Potsdam Agreement laid down "precisely fixed" goals for the occupation of Germany. The Western powers had turned West Berlin into a "bridgehead of the NATO military bloc," and the purpose of the occupation was the "preparation of war" against the USSR, the statement charged. All this constituted "direct mockery" of the principles agreed to by the 4 powers at Potsdam. The statement reiterated that "any attempt to break through to Berlin with tanks would be considered an attack on East Germany and the Warsaw Pact powers." The statement warned that such an attack "would be rebuffed by all the Warsaw Pact powers" and could lead to a general nuclear war.

The U.S. State Department Dec. 12 published a reply to the Soviet statement. The reply noted that the Soviet remarks "appeared to repeat" the arguments contained in the Soviet note of Nov. 27 but with an "increasingly threatening tone." "The viewpoint of the Western Allies on the Berlin question was well known," the U.S. reply asserted. "They cannot accept the unilateral annulment of obligations which the Soviet Union undertook toward the Western Allies during the war and which were confirmed in 1949 and 1955. The United States, which had issued no threats, would not allow itself to be frightened away from the defense of its own rights and from the fulfillment of its responsibility toward 2.25 million free men in West Berlin."

Khrushchev had warned Dec. 11 that any Western attempt to force entry into an isolated Berlin "means war." Khrushchev, in an interview for the Munich newspaper *Sueddeutsche Zeitung,* said that Western leaders had considered using tanks and troops to keep open Allied traffic routes into Berlin but that he did not believe "the West will pick a war" in this way. A personal message from Khrushchev to British Prime Min. Harold Macmillan Dec. 1 had restated the intention of the Soviet Union to end its occupation of East Berlin within the 6 months stipulated in the USSR's Nov. 27 note.

Soviet notes to the 15 NATO powers Dec. 13 renewed demands for settling the Berlin question by the creation of a free city of West Berlin.

A joint statement issued in Warsaw Dec. 15 by Polish United Workers' (Communist) Party First Secy. Wladyslaw Gomulka and East German SED (Communist) Party First Secy. Walter Ulbricht asserted that Poland and East Germany were united in support of Soviet proposals for settling the Berlin crisis and for East-West summit talks to avert the danger of a new war. The declaration, made public at the end of a visit to Poland Dec. 9-15 by Ulbricht, charged that Western violations of the Potsdam Agreement had prevented the formation of a "unified ... and democratic German state with Berlin as its capital." It condemned West Germany for "expanding its militaristic position" in the Baltic and charged that West Germany's "special role" in NATO had endangered European peace.

West Rejects Soviet Demands

The U.S., Britain and France Dec. 14 issued a formal rejection of Soviet demands that they withdraw their troops from West Berlin and agree to the liquidation of the 4-power Allied occupation of Berlin. Their rejection was supported by NATO Dec. 16 at the annual meeting of the NATO Ministerial Council.

The U.S.-British-French statement was made public in Paris following a meeting Dec. 14 of U.S. State Secy. Dulles, British Foreign Secy. Selwyn Lloyd and French Foreign Min. Maurice Couve de Murville with West German Foreign Min. Heinrich von Brentano and Governing Mayor Willy Brandt of West Berlin. It "reaffirmed the determination" of the U.S., Britain and France "to maintain their position and their rights with respect to Berlin, including the right of free access" to the city through East Germany. It rejected Soviet proposals that East Germany be given control of Allied traffic and other Berlin functions currently carried out by the USSR.

The statement was considered a victory for West German Chancellor Adenauer, who had demanded unqualified rejection of the Soviet proposals for a free city of West Berlin. Adenauer, who had cancelled plans for a London meeting with British Prime Min. Macmillan Dec. 9 for health reasons, was known to be opposed to British plans to accept East-West talks on Berlin with the objective of widening the talks into a new

East-West conference on German reunification. Bonn dispatches said Dec. 9 that a personal message to Adenauer from State Secy. Dulles had pledged that the U.S. would reject any East-West talks on the basis of the USSR's Berlin proposals. (Similar disagreement between Adenauer and West Berlin Mayor Brandt over whether the West should agree to discuss the Berlin question with the USSR was ended in a Bonn meeting Dec. 12 of Adenauer and Brandt.)

Dulles had met with Pres. Eisenhower before leaving for Paris. A White House statement read by Dulles Dec. 12 with Eisenhower's approval charged that the USSR had shown "contemptuous disregard" for its own pledges on Berlin. It warned that Soviet offers of "peaceful coexistence" had been undermined by Soviet leaders' willingness "to denounce at their pleasure any agreements which they have made as soon as ... these agreements no longer serve their purposes."

The 15-nation NATO Ministerial Council met in Paris Dec. 16 and pledged its support for the maintenance of U.S., British and French troops and responsibilities in West Berlin. At their annual meeting, the NATO foreign ministers also expressed readiness to reopen East-West negotiations on Berlin, German reunification, disarmament and European security. A NATO communique issued after the initial Ministerial Council meeting said that NATO states "could not approve a solution of the Berlin question which jeopardized the right of the 3 Western powers to remain in Berlin as long as their responsibilities require it." The NATO delegates rejected as "unacceptable" the Soviet proposal for a free city of West Berlin and asserted that "the 2 million inhabitants of West Berlin have just reaffirmed in a free vote their overwhelming approval and support of that position." The communique expressed NATO willingness to reopen talks on outstanding East-West differences, but it warned that the Berlin question could be settled only within "the framework of an agreement with the USSR on Germany as a whole." The formulation of the NATO statement on Berlin came after Dulles had told the Ministerial Council Dec. 16 that the U.S., Britain and France "consider that the [USSR] will not risk war over Berlin." He declared that NATO was "strong enough not to be frightened by the threats of Soviet propaganda."

The U.S. State Department warned Dec. 20 that Russia was endangering its own occupation rights in East Germany by its continued efforts to force the U.S., Britain and France to withdraw their military forces from West Berlin. A State Department memo of Dec. 20, "Legal Aspects of the Berlin Situation," disputed Khrushchev's claims that Western violations of the 1945 Potsdam Agreement had nullified the 4-power Berlin occupation. It reminded the USSR that its rights in East Germany, together with Western rights in Berlin, were derived from "the total defeat of the 3d Reich and the subsequent [Allied] assumption of the supreme authority in Germany." It warned that if this doctrine were nullified, the U.S. "would now be free to require the Soviet Union to withdraw from that part of the Soviet zone originally occupied by the American forces and to assume control of the area." The memo made clear that Western rights "in Germany and in Berlin do not depend in any aspect on the sufferance ... of the Soviet Union." "Further," it declared, "the rights of the 3 Western powers to free access to Berlin" were "an essential corollary of their rights of occupation there." The USSR "did not bestow upon the Western powers rights of access to Berlin. It accepted its [the Soviet] zone of occupation subject to those rights of access," the memo asserted.

A final communique issued Dec. 18 by the NATO Ministerial Council at its meeting in Paris reaffirmed NATO's intention to support the U.S., Britain and France in their continued Berlin occupation role. However, the NATO Council pledged Western action in settlement of the German question, general European security and controlled disarmament. It expressed NATO's "sincere belief ... that the interests of peace require equitable settlements of the outstanding issues" dividing the Western and Soviet blocs.

Gen. Lauris Norstad, NATO supreme commander, warned the USSR Dec. 19 that it risked "total annihilation" from nuclear weapons if it launched an attack on Europe. Norstad, addressing the Western European Union Assembly in Paris, told Soviet leaders to have "no misunderstanding about the determination of this alliance to use nuclear weapons in case of aggression." NATO Secy. Gen. Paul-Henri Spaak said at the WEU meeting Dec. 20 that the USSR's Berlin demands were similar to Hitler's tactics in the 1930s but that this time the antitotalitarian nations were supported by the U.S., the "strongest force in the world."

An East German cabinet declaration Dec. 20 rejected NATO affirmations of support for the Western powers in Berlin on the ground that "NATO has no right in Berlin." It warned that NATO support for West Germany made possible NATO members' entanglement "in war adventures." The Soviet CP newspaper *Pravda* warned Dec. 20 that the USSR would deal only with those "states which have direct relations with the present Berlin situation." "NATO," it declared, "did not even exist" when "the anti-Hitler coalition struggled ... to defend the cause of independence of European countries." Maj. Gen. Matvei V. Zakharov, Soviet military commander in East Germany, warned Dec. 19 that Soviet and East German armed forces were "prepared to give a devastating answer" to any violation of East German territory by Western forces attempting to force entry to Berlin. Zakharov termed Gen. Henry I. Hodes' Nov. 30 declaration of intent to defend the U.S. garrison in Berlin a case of "sabre-rattling and trying to create a war psychosis."

Various Soviet leaders warned Dec. 25 that the West's determination to maintain troops in Berlin by force, if necessary, could lead to general war fought with nuclear missiles. Speaking at the closing session of the USSR's Supreme Soviet (parliament) in Moscow, Soviet Foreign Min. Andrei Gromyko warned that an East-West incident in Berlin could lead to a "big war" that would claim millions of lives and hit "the American continent too." Gromyko, however, denied that the USSR had presented the West with an "ultimatum" on Berlin. He said that Soviet leaders were "ready to consider any proposals that would lead to a solution of the problem." Marshal Vasily D. Sokolovsky, Soviet General Staff chief, warned that "if the Western generals unleash a conflict over Berlin, then ... [Soviet and Warsaw Pact forces] will come out in defense of Berlin." He asserted that if war came, the USSR would have "intercontinental rockets, and no oceans will save the U.S. from retaliation."

The official Western rejection of the Soviet notes of Nov. 27 came Dec. 31 when the U.S., Britain and France delivered identic diplomatic notes to Moscow. These Western notes had been coordinated and approved by the NATO Council in Paris

Dec. 29. In their notes, the Big 3 formally rejected Soviet demands for the liquidation of the postwar military occupation of Berlin and for the creation of a "free city" of West Berlin. The Western powers, instead, proposed renewed East-West efforts to settle the Berlin dispute as part of broad negotiations for a reunified Germany, a German peace treaty and a European security settlement.

The American message rejected Russia's Berlin demands on grounds:

● Allied agreements of Sept. 12, 1944 and May 1, 1945 permitted "Soviet occupation of large parts of Mecklenburg, Saxony, Thuringia and Anhalt" (captured by Western troops) in return for the occupation of "the Western sectors in Berlin" (then held by Soviet troops). "The 3 Western powers are not prepared to relinquish the rights that they acquired through victory just as they assume the Soviet Union is not willing now to restore to the occupancy of the Western powers the position which they had won in Mecklenburg, Saxony, Thuringia and Anhalt."

● The U.S. could not "accept a unilateral denunciation of the accords of 1944 and 1945" nor "relieve the Soviet Union from the obligations which it assumed in June, 1949 [terminating the Berlin airlift by assuring Western access to the city] ... since the agreements can only be terminated by mutual consent." "Insofar as the Potsdam Agreement is concerned, the status of Berlin does not depend on that agreement," and "it is the Soviet Union that bears responsibility for the fact that the Potsdam Agreement could not be implemented."

● The U.S. "cannot prevent the Soviet government from ... termination of its own authority in the quadripartite regime in the sector which it occupies in ... Berlin." However, the U.S. "will continue to hold the Soviet government directly responsible for the discharge of its obligations" in Berlin and "will not accept a unilateral repudiation" of Soviet "obligations in respect to ... freedom of access" into Berlin. "Nor will it accept the substitution of [the East] German Democratic Republic for the Soviet government in this respect."

● The USSR's "proposal for a so-called 'free city' for West Berlin" is "unacceptable." It would "have the effect of jeopardizing the freedom and security of these [West Berlin] people." The continued "rights of the 3 [Western] powers to remain in Berlin with unhindered communications by surface and air" are "essential to the discharge of that ... responsibility."

The American note asserted that the Berlin dispute was "only one aspect, and not the essential one, of the German problem in its entirety." This problem involved "[German] reunification, European security, as well as a peace treaty," the U.S. note stated. Citing a Sept. 30 U.S. statement on the German question, the new message reaffirmed that the U.S. was "ready at any time" to "discuss the question of Berlin in the wider framework of negotiations for a solution of the German problem as well as that of European security."

The West German rejection of the Soviet note of Nov. 27 was delivered to Moscow Jan. 5. The West Germans made the following points with respect to Berlin:

● They shared the Allied view that "a unilateral denunciation of the inter-allied agreements concerning Berlin" by the USSR was "not admissible."

● Nothing in the Soviet note could deprive the Allies of their rights in Berlin "or release the Soviet Union from its obligations."

● "... The Soviet government is not entitled to transfer to authorities of the so-called GDR, the powers held by it under occupation law and relating to the presence of Western armed forces in Berlin and to the freedom of access to that city."

● General fears of war over Berlin have been caused by the "Soviet government in connection with the ... unilateral denunciation of the 4-Power status" of Berlin.

● West Berlin was not a center of espionage and diversion, and such activity was not supported by the West German government. The "Communist side" engaged in "the forcible abduction of people," however.

● It was regrettable that Berlin still "has to live under an occupation statute" because "no peace treaty has yet been concluded." However, Allied troops in Berlin "have been regarded by the population ... as a protective power guaranteeing their security and freedom," as was shown by the Berlin blockade of 1948-9 and by the West Berlin elections of Dec. 7, 1958.

● The Soviet "proposal for ... a so-called 'free city' of West Berlin is indeed unacceptable." First, because this would "deprive Berlin of any effective protection ..." 2d, because the proposal would divide Germany "not only into 2 but into 3 separate states: the so-called 'free city' would be the 3d German State." 3d, past experience with "free" or "internationalized" cities had led only to "difficulties, tensions and international crises." UN participation would make little difference.

A State Department pamphlet entitled "The Soviet Note on Berlin: An Analysis," issued Jan. 7, marshalled legal and historical arguments to refute views contained in the Nov. 27 Soviet note on Berlin. Divided into 5 chapters, the pamphlet covered prewar developments, World War II and the postwar situation, postwar relations with Germany, reparations and rearmament. Diplomatic notes and communiques were reproduced in an appendix. The pamphlet blamed the USSR for encouraging the German attack that launched World War II and charged that disruptive Soviet policies were responsible for the post-1945 cold war.

1959

RELAXATION OF CRISIS

Berlin was used by the Soviets during 1959 as a lever to force East-West negotiations. Soviet Premier Nikita S. Khrushchev's method was to issue an "ultimatum" that made an East-West meeting necessary.

First, on the Russians' demand, a Geneva foreign ministers' conference opened May 11 amid indications of serious disarray among the Western Allies. U.S. State Department officials were quoted Apr. 17 as expressing "dismay" over the British attitude. Differences between Britain on the one hand and West Germany and France on the other were reported Apr. 24. Differences in negotiating position were reported between the West Germans and the rest of the alliance June 1 and between Britain and the other Allies July 26. Sharp differences reported between Britain and West Germany led to a meeting Nov. 17-19 between Chancellor Konrad Adenauer and Prime Min. Harold Macmillan in England.

Although the Geneva foreign ministers' meeting was clearly not productive, the Soviets increased their pressure for a "summit" conference; by dropping their "ultimatum" Sept. 28 they won agreement to the conference. The dropping of the ultimatum was regarded as a concession that the West had to match by agreeing to a summit conference even though the foreign ministers' meeting had shown that no real basis for agreement on the Berlin issue existed. The summit meeting was destined to fail even more dramatically. Many observers suggested that what the Soviets wanted were meetings during which policy cracks in the Western alliance could be widened into real splits, and that Berlin would be the lever to pry the entire alliance apart. Although this policy did not succeed in the short run, it was held that the Soviets were content to pursue it over the long term in the hopes of ultimate success.

Summit Proposals

New Year's messages exchanged Jan. 1 by Soviet Premier Khrushchev and Pres. Dwight D. Eisenhower expressed Soviet and American wishes for peace and reduced tensions during 1959. However, the messages contained no indication that either side would soften its position in the Berlin dispute.

The Soviet message, from Khrushchev and Pres. Kliment Y. Voroshilov, enunciated a hope for an end to the "cold war" and the arms race "with the aim of reducing dangerous tensions." Eisenhower replied that he shared the Soviet leaders' views on peace, but he asserted that the USSR's Berlin policies "were not in accord with your expressed aspirations." The President reiterated that the U.S. "would welcome discussion on the question of Berlin in the wider framework of the whole German problem" and "in an atmosphere devoid of any kind of coercion and threat."

Voroshilov, replying to Eisenhower's message Jan. 6, said that the U.S. would contribute to world peace in 1959 if it paid "due attention" to the Soviet proposals on Berlin.

Soviet First Deputy Premier Anastas I. Mikoyan suggested Jan. 5, on the 2d day of a 2-week "holiday" visit to the U.S., that a top-level conference at the proper time could deal successfully with many East-West problems. Mikoyan made his suggestion during meetings with State Secy. Dulles and at a dinner given for him by Eric Johnson, president of the Motion Picture Association of America. Mikoyan noted at the dinner that the Western powers had urged East-West talks on settling the Berlin problem as part of the question of German unity and a German peace treaty. Mikoyan asserted that the USSR would withdraw its occupation forces from Berlin within 6 months and that it was willing to discuss proposals for UN supervision of a "free Berlin."

Mikoyan conferred with Vice Pres. Richard M. Nixon Jan. 6 and then told reporters that the USSR would not change its Berlin stand because there was no reason to alter "a good policy." After a meeting between Mikoyan and a group of U.S.

labor leaders Jan. 6, James B. Carey, president of the International Union of Electrical Workers, said that Mikoyan had given the impression "that he is trying to take the heat out of the Berlin situation and find a solution."

Mikoyan was received at the White House Jan. 17 for a 1¾-hour exchange of views with Pres. Eisenhower on Berlin and other problems. White House Press Secy. James C. Hagerty told newsmen that the confidential talks had been "useful" but had contained no new proposals by either Mikoyan or Eisenhower for settling the Berlin dispute. Eisenhower Administration sources reported that Mikoyan and the President had exchanged detailed restatements of their countries' foreign policy positions. They also indicated that Mikoyan had argued strongly for an East-West meeting, probably at the foreign ministers' level, early in 1959.

In preparation for his meeting with Eisenhower, Mikoyan had held preliminary discussions with State Secy. Dulles and Vice Pres. Nixon Jan. 16 as well as with members of the Senate Foreign Relations Committee. Sen. J. William Fulbright (D., Ark.) of the committee later said that Mikoyan had expressed willingness to accept UN participation in a future Berlin agreement, while Sen. Hubert H. Humphrey (D., Minn.) indicated that Mikoyan had shown flexibility on proposals for nuclear-free zones in Europe. (The Senate was criticized by Sen. Styles Bridges [R., N.H.] Jan. 17 for its alleged "red carpet treatment" of Mikoyan.)

Appearing on NBC-TV's Meet the Press, Mikoyan indicated Jan. 18 that the USSR might be willing to ease its position on settling the Berlin dispute if the Western powers advanced "convincing" counter-proposals. Defending the Soviet demand for the creation of a "free city" of West Berlin as "solid and correct," Mikoyan asserted that there still was "sufficient time to consider and reconsider the matter." He said that the USSR wanted "West Berlin to be guaranteed not by foreign bayonets but rather by international organizations and the great powers, including guarantees of free access ... from the East and the West." (Mikoyan left Washington Jan. 20 to return to Moscow.)

Both West Berlin Governing Mayor Willy Brandt and West German Chancellor Konrad Adenauer reacted to the pressures for an East-West summit meeting by reassuring their constituencies. Brandt urged Berliners Jan. 1 to sustain their "courage and determination" during Berlin's "year of decision," while Adenauer stated Jan. 5 that in politics, "sharp tensions" always had "preceded great solutions."

Soviet Bloc Urges German Talks

The Soviet government called Jan. 10 for an urgent 28-nation conference to negotiate a World War II German peace treaty based on a reunified and demilitarized German state. Soviet notes delivered to the U.S. and 26 other countries (including Communist China) that had been at war against Nazi Germany proposed that the meeting be held in Warsaw or Prague within 2 months to discuss a draft peace treaty appended to the note. The Western powers quickly rejected the USSR's proposals on Germany.

The USSR, in its Jan. 10 notes to the U.S., Britain and France, specifically rejected the 3 Western powers' assertions of their rights to occupy Berlin. Russia turned down Western proposals for discussion of the Berlin problem within the wider framework of negotiations on German reunification and European security. Replying to the West's notes of Dec. 31, 1958, the USSR reiterated its Nov. 27, 1958 proposals for the creation of a "free city" of West Berlin, but Russia expressed willingness to modify its "free-Berlin" plan in a way acceptable to the West.

The Soviet note to the U.S. asserted that the quadripartite Allied occupation agreements on Berlin were "provisional" and "valid only for the period of Germany's occupation. But the occupation is over." The U.S., Britain, France and USSR had "announced the ending of the state of war with Germany," and U.S. claims of "rights to continue the occupation are obviously groundless," Moscow contended.

The note rejected 4-power talks on German reunification on the ground that unity had become an "internal German problem" for settlement by East and West Germany. It accused the U.S. of refusing to discuss Soviet proposals for assuring European security through (1) a NATO-Warsaw Pact nonaggression treaty and (2) Polish Foreign Min. Adam Rapacki's plan for the creation of a European zone free of atomic weapons.

The draft German peace treaty suggested by the Soviet note contained these provisions: (1) it would be binding on both East and West German states or an eventually unified Germany; (2) East and West Germany would withdraw from the Warsaw Pact and NATO, respectively, and would not be permitted to enter any military alliance not including all 4 major Allied powers; (3) Germany would accept its current borders and would renounce any future *Anschluss* (union) with Austria and all territorial claims against Poland, Czechoslovakia, France and the USSR; (4) all occupation forces would be withdrawn from Germany within one year; (5) Germany would be prohibited from producing or possessing nuclear, biological and chemical weapons, missiles, bomber aircraft and submarines, but would be permitted to retain defense forces; (6) West Berlin would become a demilitarized free city until the completion of Germany's reunification; (7) the Allied powers would waive all reparations claims against Germany and permit free development of Germany's economy and trade.

In memoranda delivered to State Secy. Dulles by Soviet First Deputy Premier Mikoyan Jan. 5 and to French Pres. Charles de Gaulle Jan. 7, the USSR was reported to have urged the Western powers to present counter-proposals on the Berlin problem in order to facilitate the possibility of a settlement.

An East German government declaration issued Jan. 9 by Deputy Foreign Min. Otto Winzer indicated that East Germany would accept the presence of Western troops in Berlin if they were there under UN auspices to guarantee the security of a "free city" of West Berlin.

East Germany, in a note to the USSR Jan. 7, requested negotiations on the transfer to East Germany of Soviet occupation functions. The East Germans formally accepted Soviet plans for the creation of a demilitarized free city in West Berlin.

Soviet First Deputy Premier Anastas I. Mikoyan indicated at a Kremlin news conference Jan. 24 that the USSR wanted high-level East-West talks on the Berlin question but was willing to be flexible about the deadline and duration of such talks as long as there was Western "goodwill."

Mikoyan, who returned to Moscow Jan. 23 from his visit to the U.S., asserted that the "main thing in our proposal [on Berlin] is not the 6-month deadline [for the withdrawal of Soviet forces] but the proposal to have the talks ... and to end the occupation status of West Berlin."

In an address delivered Jan. 27 before the 21st Soviet Communist Party Congress, Party First Secy. Khrushchev again urged the conclusion of a German peace treaty such as that proposed in the Russian notes of Jan. 10. The conclusion of such a peace treaty "would be a large step forward toward reunification of Germany" and would "bring about a peace-loving, democratic solution to the Berlin question," Khrushchev asserted. He noted that "West Berlin would become a 'free city' with the requisite guarantee against interference in its affairs. For the protection of this guarantee, the UN could be utilized," Khrushchev suggested.

Addressing 1,375 Soviet delegates and heads of 70 foreign Communist parties gathered in Moscow for the congress, Khrushchev also declared:

● The Warsaw Pact nations were ready to cooperate in the establishment of "'a zone of disengagement' of armed forces," as proposed by Polish Foreign Min. Adam Rapacki and to withdraw Soviet troops from Germany, Poland and Hungary in return for the withdrawal of NATO forces.

● The USSR would continue to press for a solution of German reunification "by the Germans themselves" in confederation talks by the East and West German governments. Khrushchev assailed West German Chancellor Adenauer for his opposition to all Soviet proposals on the German question. Russia, Khrushchev said, sought only to cope with "the growth of [West German] military danger."

● Soviet proposals for German unification would automatically solve the Berlin dispute. But in the absence of an agreement, the USSR would continue with plans for ending the Berlin occupation regime in May. Khrushchev asserted that "the [UN] should be called on to ensure the guarantee" of any Berlin settlement.

State Secy. Dulles replied to Khrushchev's party congress address Jan. 28 in testimony before the U.S. House Foreign Affairs Committee. "We have indicated our readiness to discuss the interrelated problems of Berlin, German reunification and

European security," Dulles declared. "But so far, the Soviet Union insists that we shall only talk about a change in the status of West Berlin—not East Berlin—and about a peace treaty which would be made with the 2 Germanys and perpetuate the partition of Germany."

West Rejects Soviet Proposals

The Jan. 10 Soviet proposals on Germany and Berlin had been immediately rejected by the U.S. and West German governments. Western spokesmen, however, welcomed a foreign ministers' conference.

The U.S. State Department said Jan. 10 that Russia's draft German peace treaty was similar to a Soviet text presented at a 1954 foreign ministers' conference in Berlin and rejected by the West. Officials asserted that the terms would recognize the existence of 2 sovereign German states and deprive a future reunified Germany of the right to join a defensive military alliance of its choice. State Secy. Dulles, at a news conference in Washington Jan. 13, rejected the Soviet draft German peace treaty as "stupid." In his comments, reasserted the next day in testimony before the Senate Foreign Relations Committee, Dulles said that although prior free elections had been "the agreed [Western] formula" for German reunification, he did not think it was "the only method by which reunification could be accomplished."

Adenauer denounced the Soviet draft Jan. 12 as "completely unacceptable." He rejected provisions for recognition of the East German government and renunciation of German claims to territory absorbed by Poland and the USSR after World War II. Adenauer expressed his concern in a conversation Jan. 14 with U.S. Amb.-to-West Germany David K. E. Bruce over the apparent abandonment of free elections as an absolute requirement for any agreement to reunify Germany. West Germany's ambassador to the U.S., Wilhelm Grewe, said Jan. 14 that Dulles had reaffirmed that it was American policy to seek German reunification through free elections.

West Berlin Mayor Brandt had asserted Jan. 11 that the Soviet bid for talks on Germany indicated a "softening" of the USSR's campaign against Berlin. Brandt, however, reiterated his rejection of Soviet terms for a Berlin settlement. (Brandt was reelected Jan. 12 to a new 4-year term as West Berlin governing mayor.)

Pres. Eisenhower, answering reporters' questions at a National Press Club luncheon Jan. 14, described the new Soviet proposals as "an exercise in futility" for attempting to "try to demilitarize, neutralize and completely disarm a people as strong, as important and virile as are the German people." He asserted that the U.S. was "ready to make any ... material moves that would assure Russia that there is no danger" from the German people.

In his State-of-the-Union message, delivered Jan. 9, Eisenhower had pledged to defend Berlin. He asserted that the U.S. and "other free nations ... have the solemn obligation to defend the people of free Berlin against any effort to destroy their freedom." "Not only the integrity of a single city but the hope of all free peoples is at stake," he asserted. He held that "the most recent proof" of the Communists' "disdain of international obligations, solemnly undertaken, is their announced intention to abandon their responsibilities respecting Berlin." Responding to this and other statements in Eisenhower's message, Soviet First Deputy Premier Mikoyan warned Jan. 19 that "force would be met with force" if Western nations used arms to maintain their access to West Berlin.

British Prime Min. Harold Macmillan told Parliament in London Jan. 20 that he would agree to Soviet terms for talks between the 2 Germanys rather than insist on Western demands for negotiation of the German question within the framework of European security.

Dulles said at a Washington news conference Jan. 27 that he would welcome a foreign ministers' conference on the Berlin question in the spring, but he expressed doubt that East-West talks could solve the dispute unless the USSR altered its Berlin policy. Commenting on Khrushchev's hopes for a "thaw" in U.S.-Soviet relations, Dulles said that Khrushchev "lives in the north country where the icy blasts come from, and if they are going to become balmy, we are ... delighted." Dulles said that he thought the USSR was trying to win the cold war, not end it.

Vice Pres. Nixon asserted Jan. 27 that U.S. leaders "want a thaw in the cold war because we realize that if there is none we will all be eventually frozen in the ice so hard that only a nuclear bomb will break it."

In a move that some Western observers regarded as part of a Soviet war of nerves designed to "pressure the West to the summit," a U.S. Army truck convoy was stopped by Red Army authorities for 54 hours Feb. 2-4 at the Marienborn *autobahn* checkpoint between East and West Germany. Although the Soviet Army authorities were not successful in inspecting the convoy's cargo, the incident was the longest halt in U.S. military truck traffic from Berlin since the 1948-9 Soviet blockade of Berlin.

The convoy was released by Soviet authorities without inspection after the U.S. filed a strong protest in Moscow Feb. 4 and charged that the Soviet Army action was "in clear violation of the [U.S.'] right of access to Berlin via the Berlin-Helmstedt *autobahn.*" The U.S. note demanded that the USSR prevent repetition of the "unwarranted and inadmissible" incident.

The 4-truck convoy, commanded by Cpl. Richard C. Masiero of West Stockbridge, Mass., had been cleared at the Soviet checkpoint at Babelsberg near Berlin under procedures permitting Soviet soldiers to verify cargo without entering the vehicles. But Soviet officers at Marienborn held the convoy when Masiero refused to submit his trucks and cargo of worn-out jeeps to detailed inspection.

The incident was terminated by an agreement reached in Marienborn Feb. 4 by Findley Burns and Lt. Col. M. F. Markushin, respectively, U.S. and Soviet army political advisers.

Pres. Eisenhower said at his press conference Feb. 4 that the U.S. regarded the Soviets' detention of the convoy as a violation of an "implied agreement" that all 4 Berlin occupying powers had the right of communication to and supply of their Berlin garrisons. The President said that "we have never acknowledged any right of inspection on the part of another of the participating powers with respect to cargoes and the ... equipment and supplies we are carrying."

Allies Consider East-West Talks

State Secy. Dulles left the U.S. for London Feb. 3 to begin talks with British, French and West German leaders on common Western policies on Berlin, German unity and European security to be followed at a possible East-West foreign ministers' conference in the spring.

Dulles, who met with Pres. Eisenhower Feb. 3, told newsmen before his departure that the President had agreed that his mission would "demonstrate once again our determination not to yield before [Soviet] threats." Dulles confirmed that he planned to "explore the possibility of subsequent talks about Germany among ... the 4 powers which have the responsibility for the settlement of the German question"—Britain, France, the U.S. and USSR. He expressed doubt that current Berlin tension would result in war.

(Members of the Working Group on German Unification & European Security, created by the U.S., Britain, France and West Germany after the failure of the 1955 Geneva foreign ministers' conference, met in Washington Feb. 3 to begin work on a coordinated Western reply to the Jan. 10 Soviet proposal for a 28-nation German peace treaty conference.)

Sen. J. William Fulbright (D., Ark.), recently elected Senate Foreign Relations Committee chairman, had conferred with Dulles Feb. 2. He told newsmen that Dulles was "considering very seriously" new Western proposals for settling the German question. Fulbright declined to discuss the new proposals envisaged by Dulles, but he confirmed that they had discussed a possible mutual withdrawal of Western and Soviet troops from a 500-mile-wide demilitarized zone across central Europe.

Dulles made his trip to Europe at a time when British Prime Min. Harold Macmillan was preparing to visit Moscow to sound out Soviet leaders on their terms for agreements on German and European security. Dulles conferred with Macmillan in London Feb. 4, and British officials reported that they had reached substantial accord on Macmillan's projected trip, although they remained divided on joint allied military measures necessary if the USSR should attempt to block Western traffic to Berlin.

French government officials were reported Feb. 4 to have made clear their opposition to a Moscow visit by Macmillan on the ground that it would give an impression of Western eagerness to begin talks before the expiration of the May 27 Soviet deadline for ending the Allied occupation of Berlin. France was reported Jan. 30 to have informed Britain of its unwillingness to begin East-West talks on Berlin until after May 27. Dulles met with French Pres. Charles de Gaulle in Paris Feb. 6 and West German Chancellor Adenauer in Bonn Feb. 7-8.

West German support for a foreign ministers' meeting on the German question had been affirmed Feb. 2 by Bonn press spokesman Felix von Eckardt despite past West German reluctance to agree to such talks except on specific terms.

(Mayor Brandt of West Berlin had said on CBS-TV's "Small World" program Jan. 25 that Polish Foreign Min. Adam Rapacki's revised plan for the creation of a European zone free from nuclear weapons could be "a basis for discussion" of a European settlement with the USSR. Brandt expressed agreement with Dulles' assertion that German unification might be attained by means other than free all-German elections. Brandt left West Berlin Feb. 5 on a 4-week worldwide trip. Official West Berlin sources described the trip as serving to inform the world about the Soviet threat to Berlin, to renew friendly ties with the U.S. and to seek understanding from the countries of Asia.)

Dulles, who reported to Eisenhower Feb. 9 on the results of his European trip, told newsmen on his arrival in Washington that the talks had resulted in substantial Western agreement on policies to be followed if the USSR carried out threats to turn its Berlin occupation functions over to the East German government. Dulles denied reports of a Western rift on Germany due to British reluctance to use armed force in Berlin and West German refusal to moderate terms for Germany's reunification. He said that his talks had "reaffirmed the unity and firmness of our position" by making clear these basic Western policies:

● "We do not accept any substitution of East Germans for the Soviet Union in its responsibilities toward Berlin and its obligations to us."

● "We are resolved that our position in, and access to, West Berlin shall be preserved. We are in general agreement as to the procedures we shall follow if physical means are invoked to interfere with our rights in this respect."

(Dulles had said at a closed session of the House of Foreign Affairs Committee Jan. 28 [testimony disclosed Feb. 8] that the U.S. and its Allies were in "complete agreement" on "standing firm in Berlin and, if need be, risking war rather than being taken out of Berlin." Dulles had predicted that the USSR would maintain "the war of nerves" over Berlin "to the very last to see if our nerve holds." "If it doesn't hold," he warned, "they will gain a great victory" and "will have destroyed the most effective outpost of freedom that we have.")

Direct negotiation by East and West Germany to achieve German reunification and a settlement of the Berlin and other disputes was urged Feb. 12 by Senate Democratic whip Mike Mansfield (D., Mont.). Mansfield asserted that direct talks between the 2 German governments were logical in view of the fact that "it is the Germans themselves ... who will make the decisive decisions on unification if they are to be made in peace."

In a 9-point German plan presented to the U.S. Senate, Mansfield said that "the divided Allies of World War II" no longer were "in a position to ordain a unification in peace for a revitalized Germany." Mansfield said that the wartime Allies might have been able to devise a German settlement "years ago when Germany lay devastated and prostrate" and there still was "mutual respect and tolerance" among the Allies. But, he asserted, such a course no longer was feasible in view of the Western-Soviet split and the resurgence of Germany as "the most dynamic nation in Western Europe."

Mansfield, who attacked the Eisenhower Administration for not revising policies on Germany that the U.S. had "devised years ago," warned that a new position must be constructed "on the premise that Germany ... is going to begin to unify soon." He asserted that the U.S. must recognize that "the East German regime ... exists ... even though Russians may pull the strings from behind the curtain." Expressing doubts that "the Western nations are going to wish away or subvert away that East German political authority," Mansfield urged that a new policy accept the premise that German unity, "if it is to come in peace, is likely to fall far short of the ultimate goals" of East and West—"the goal ... of a Communist totalitarian Germany and the goal ... of a freely representative democracy in all Germany."

Asserting that a successful settlement of the German problem would depend on the termination of the Berlin dispute and should lead to the limitation of armaments in central Europe, Mansfield proposed these points as "essentials of a sound Western policy on Germany":

● Maintenance of "forces representing the concept of freedom in peace" in Berlin, "at the least ... on the basis of equality with the forces of totalitarian communism." At the same time, the East and West Berlin communities should "begin serious efforts to unify the municipal government and public services."

● Use of UN Secy. Gen. Dag Hammarskjold's "conciliatory services" to reach an all-Berlin agreement that would provide for the replacement of Western and Soviet forces by a UN "police force" from neutral states, empowered to "supervise the agreement" and protect "all routes of access" to Berlin until it again became the capital of "a peaceful unified Germany."

● Maintenance of Western forces in Berlin in the event that no agreement was reached and the USSR withdrew its Berlin occupation force. But Western troops should be replaced "with German militia, fully supported by NATO guarantees."

● Negotiations by East and West Germany on the "harmonizing of the political economic and military systems of the 2 zones" to achieve German reunification. Details would best be "left to the Germans of the 2 zones," but any unity agreement should insure the rights of East and West Germans "to express themselves and their political preferences and to participate in political affairs without the threat of terror."

● Western and Soviet guarantees of "the kind of unified Germany which may emerge from discussions among the Germans" and assurances "that a unified Germany is neither subjected to military pressures from its neighbors nor ... becomes a source of military pressure to its neighbors."

● Western and Soviet agreements that would "lead to limitations of armaments throughout Germany and central Europe" and the withdrawal of "the so-called ultimate weapons and the [Western and Soviet] armed forces ... from the points of imminent contact in Germany and central Europe." The

West should not ignore "the Rapacki plan, the Eden plan for a demilitarized zone in middle Europe or other similar proposals."

Mansfield indicated a belief that the Russians would leave Berlin and turn their sector over to the East Germans. West Berlin would then become a Western enclave in the heart of Germany. If the East Germans did not want to reach an accommodation with the West, then the West might be compelled to fight its way into Berlin not against Russians but against Germans, he warned. This would have ramifications which—even if they did not lead to war—would be deep because with Germans, as with others, "blood is stronger than ideologies."

Mansfield's proposals for unity talks by the East and West German governments were assailed Feb. 13 by every West German political group except the Free Democratic Party, which termed the plans "optimistic." Christian Democratic newspapers attacked Mansfield as "dangerous and naive." Opposition Social Democrats asserted that his proposals lacked "wisdom."

East-West Exchanges on Talks

The U.S., Britain and France proposed Feb. 16 that the USSR join them in an East-West conference at the foreign ministers' level to renew efforts to "deal with the problem of Germany in all its aspects and implications." Similar Western messages, backed by a separate West German note to the USSR, carried the suggestion that "German advisers should be invited to the conference and ... consulted." The suggestion was regarded as a major Western concession to Soviet demands for direct East German-West German negotiations to end the partition of Germany.

The Western notes, approved Feb. 13 by the NATO Permanent Council, disclosed a willingness on the part of the 3 Western powers to meet with the USSR at any convenient date or place. They urged that detailed arrangements for the proposed conference be negotiated through normal diplomatic channels. They made clear the Western stand that a German agreement remained the responsibility of the major Allies of World War II and could be concluded only by them.

Replying to the USSR's Jan. 10 message on Germany, the American note rejected Soviet proposals for a 28-nation conference to draw up a German peace treaty. The U.S. said in its note: "The continued division of Germany constitutes a danger to European security and to world peace ... heightened by the persistent and flagrant denial to the East Germans of human rights and fundamental freedoms." The U.S. wished "to deal with this problem as urgently as possible through negotiations among the 4 powers responsible for Germany." The USSR's announced "intention unilaterally to abdicate certain of its ... agreed responsibilities and obligations in regard to Berlin" was "a danger to world peace." It would "encourage ... an attempt to assert control over the rights of the Western powers to be in Berlin" and their access to the city. The Western powers "have no choice but to declare again that they ... [will] uphold by all appropriate means ... communications with their sectors of Berlin."

The U.S. State Department had announced Feb. 13 that the U.S., British, French and West German foreign ministers would meet in Paris in March to prepare for a possible East-West meeting on Germany. The Western talks, to be held "if developments warrant," were arranged to facilitate a joint study of the Soviet reply to Western proposals on Germany and the results of British Prime Min. Macmillan's projected visit to the USSR.

Soviet Premier Khrushchev told the Western powers Feb. 18 that if they attempted to force their way through East Germany to Berlin, "this will mean the beginning of war." Speaking in Tula, USSR, Khrushchev warned the Western powers against attempting to evade future East German control of traffic to Berlin either by force or by an airlift from West Germany. He declared that "no encroachment against East German territory, in the center of which Berlin is situated, can be tolerated—either by land, sea or air." Commenting on Sen. Mansfield's proposals for disengagement and for a settlement of the German problem, Khrushchev asserted that "we consider his proposals worthy of attention. One could reach agreement with people who have adopted such sober attitudes."

Pres. Eisenhower declared at his press conference in Washington Feb. 18 that the U.S. was determined to "continue carrying out our responsibilities" to Berlin but that if fighting began it would be the Communists' fault. Noting Khrushchev's warning to the West, Eisenhower said that "he [Khrushchev] must be talking about shooting to stop us from doing our duty." The President asserted that the Western powers had not said "that we are going to shoot our way into Berlin." But, he warned, if shooting occurred in Berlin, it would be begun by "somebody else using force." Eisenhower refused to comment on Mansfield's suggestions for a revision of U.S. policy on Germany. He reiterated that the U.S. was ready to enter into East-West German talks in "good faith" and always had avoided building "up anything the Soviets could legitimately consider a menace on their border."

The East Germans freed 5 U.S. servicemen Feb. 5 after negotiations for their release by the American and East German Red Cross. This action was regarded by some diplomatic observers as related to the Soviet detention of the U.S. truck convoy Feb. 2-4 since it cast the East Germans in a favorable light and provided useful contacts between the U.S. and East German Red Cross. The 5 released U.S. servicemen, all Army members, were: Lt. Richard Mackin, 27, who had been arrested Dec. 3, 1958 when his liaison plane ran out of fuel and crashed in East Germany, Sp. 4/C Kenneth G. Carlson, 21, Pvt. Elwyn E. Bell, 21, Pvt. James W. Hayes, 21, and Pvt. Melvin Hampton, 19.

Macmillan Confers with Khrushchev

British Prime Min. Macmillan visited the Soviet Union Feb. 21-Mar. 3 for what he had described to the House of Commons Feb. 19 as an attempt to "break the ice and also to get some feeling of the general situation" that the West would face in an East-West conference on Germany. Macmillan and Soviet Premier Khrushchev met for informal talks Feb. 22 at a villa in Semyonovskoye near Moscow and conferred in more formal meetings Feb. 23 in the Kremlin and at a British embassy dinner. Press reports of the talks indicated that the 2 leaders had concentrated on the problem of Germany and the stalemated Geneva negotiations on a treaty to ban nuclear weapons tests.

While Macmillan was visiting Dubna, some 90 miles from Moscow, Feb. 24, Khrushchev made a Kremlin speech as a candidate for the Supreme Soviet (parliament). In his speech, Khrushchev rejected Western proposals made Feb. 16 for an East-West foreign ministers' conference on the German question. The rejection was reported to have shocked Macmillan and other members of the British delegation. Khrushchev was said to have given Macmillan no indication during their discussions that he was about to reject the proposed conference.

It was understood that Khrushchev also surprised the British by offering to negotiate a 25-year Soviet-British nonaggression pact. Expressing hope that his current talks with Macmillan would "promote the improvement of mutual understanding between us," Khrushchev said that the USSR would be willing to conclude such a pact for "50 years" or "even a longer period."

Khrushchev charged that the Western powers sought foreign ministers' talks on Germany to create "a labyrinth of diplomatic negotiations so that we bog down for several years." He rejected the Western plan as "outdated" and as based on an "absurd policy" of "threats and ultimatums" with "regard to your former partner in the job of destroying Hitler." Khrushchev said that it would be "better if the great powers were to have a meeting of heads of government, with full powers to discuss soberly and decide" on issues dividing East and West. He said that such a meeting should aim for a peace treaty with the East and West German states, which, he said, would automatically bring an end to the current Berlin dispute. Khrushchev said that a summit meeting also should discuss the "separation of military forces of both military groupings" in Europe, European security, the dissolution of foreign military bases and the banning of nuclear weapons.

Khrushchev warned that if the Western powers refused to sign a peace treaty with the 2 German states, the USSR would negotiate a separate pact with East Germany and terminate its occupation functions in Berlin. He warned that "any violation" of East German territory by Western nations' attempts to force entry to Berlin or to resurrect the Berlin airlift would be "regarded as a violation of [East German] sovereignty . . . and as the beginning of war."

Pres. Eisenhower told newsmen Feb. 25 that Khrushchev's speech had made clear his "palpably intransigent attitude" on the German and Berlin problems and that an East-West conference on these questions would be of little use in view of the USSR's advance rejection of all key Western proposals. The President asserted that whether or not East-West talks on Germany took place, the U.S. and other Western nations were "not going to give one single inch in the preservation of our rights and of discharging our responsibilities . . . especially [in] Berlin."

Macmillan returned to London Mar. 3 and told his countrymen in a TV address that his talks with Khrushchev had produced agreement that "these grave problems of Central Europe ought to be settled by negotiations and not by force."

In a joint communique, signed by Macmillan and Khrushchev before Macmillan's departure from Moscow Mar. 3, the 2 leaders had declared that they had "exchanged full explanations" of their views "on questions relating to Germany, including a peace treaty with Germany and the question of Berlin." They conceded that they "were unable to agree about the juridical and political aspects of the problems involved." In the communique they expressed agreement, however, on "the need for early negotiations . . . for the settlement of these differences."

Khrushchev and Macmillan continued their private talks Feb. 25 in what British spokesmen described as a "cool" meeting following Khrushchev's sudden rejection Feb. 24 of Western terms for a foreign ministers' conference. Macmillan reportedly warned Khrushchev that his rejection of the West's offer placed full responsibility on the USSR for actions the Western powers would be compelled to take to maintain their positions in Berlin and Germany.

East Bloc Views Talks & Peace Treaty

In a fresh reversal of policy, the Soviet government agreed Mar. 2 to the Western proposals for an East-West foreign ministers' conference on the problem of Germany. But it revived conditions that had already been rejected by the

Western powers. In similar Soviet notes to the U.S., Britain and France, the USSR expressed regret that the Western powers were "not ready to take part in a summit conference." The notes said, however, that in place of summit talks, "there could be convoked a conference of ... [foreign] ministers" on this basis:

● The Soviet side would receive parity with the 3 Western participants by the inclusion in the conference of Poland and Czechoslovakia as "states that border on Germany and were the first victims of Hitlerite aggression." East and West German representatives could be included for conference sessions on Germany and Berlin.

● The conference would give priority to the discussion of Soviet proposals for "the conclusion of a peace treaty with Germany" and the "abolition of the abnormal situation that has arisen in connection with the foreign occupation of Western Berlin." The USSR assumed that "decisions on a [German] peace treaty agreed to at this meeting would have to be submitted to a peace conference."

● The conferees "might also consider problems connected with the insuring of European security and disarmament," especially proposals for "mutual withdrawal of forces and the creation of an atom-free zone and a zone of disengagement between [NATO and Warsaw Pact] armed forces"; also the reduction of U.S., British, French and Soviet forces "on the territories of other states" and a ban on nuclear weapons and tests.

The Soviet conditions were considered an attempt to force the West to discuss Russia's past demands for a German peace treaty and an end to the Allied occupation of Berlin. Russia's Mar. 2 note stated the terms as those the USSR would propose for an East-West summit meeting. The USSR said in its note, however, that the same terms could apply for a foreign ministers' meeting, which had been urged in Western notes Feb. 16.

The USSR suggested that the foreign ministers' meeting begin in Geneva or Vienna in April and be limited to 2 or 3 months' duration. In its message, the Soviet Union reiterated demands for a summit meeting, to be followed by a foreign ministers' conference "to carry out the jointly agreed [summit] decisions."

Premier Khrushchev visited East Germany Mar. 4-11 and reiterated Soviet warnings that the USSR would sign a separate World War II peace treaty with the East German Communist regime if the Western powers refused to accept Soviet proposals for settling the current crisis over Germany and Berlin. Khrushchev, ostensibly in East Germany to visit the Leipzig industrial fair, met with East German CP First Secy. Ulbricht and Premier Grotewohl in East Berlin Mar. 7-11 to plan joint pressure on the West.

Arriving in Leipzig Mar. 4, Khrushchev had denounced Western "hotheads" for their rejection of Soviet proposals on Germany as "something impossible." "What do we propose?" he asked. "After 14 years we propose a peace treaty for Germany and the elimination of the boiling kettle of Berlin." Khrushchev, acknowledging that Western nations were refusing to sign a German treaty, warned that "if the Bonn republic does not want to sign, there will be a treaty for the [East] German Democratic Republic alone."

Khrushchev indicated Mar. 6 that the USSR might delay its May 27 deadline for turning its Berlin and German occupation functions over to the East German government. He said the USSR was "not trying to carry out an ultimatum.... If we negotiate reasonably, let it [the deadline] be May 27 or June 27 or on into July." But he warned that with "the signing of a peace treaty, it [the Berlin question] will be solved," "the control functions of the occupation will be given" to East Germany, "and it will have all the rights of a free sovereign state." (Khrushchev had assured a Leipzig fair audience earlier Mar. 6 that "there will be no war" over Germany.)

Khrushchev Mar. 9 advanced suggestions for forming a new Allied or neutral garrison in West Berlin should it become a free city. Speaking at a rally in East Berlin, he said, "We would not mind even if [U.S.], British, French and Soviet troops or some neutral countries maintained minimum forces in West Berlin." Khrushchev's free city proposals were supported by Ulbricht who urged the "formation of a permanent international commission to observe the maintenance of the [Berlin] guarantees."

Khrushchev conferred in East Berlin Mar. 9 with Erich Ollenhauer, West German Social Democratic Party leader, but he apparently failed to win SPD support for the Soviet proposals. West Berlin Mayor Willy Brandt had been invited to meet with Khrushchev but declined Mar. 9 on orders of the West Berlin parliament. Brandt Mar. 10 rejected as "unacceptable" Khrushchev's proposal for an "extension of Soviet occupation to West Berlin" under the guise of creating a new 4-power garrison in the Western sector of the city.

A Soviet-East German communique issued Mar. 11 after Khrushchev and East German leaders had conferred Mar. 10 announced a pledge of joint action to conclude a German peace treaty and liquidate the Berlin occupation "as soon as possible." In the communique, the Soviet and East German leaders charged that delays in signing a German peace treaty had been "exploited by the Western powers to widen the division of Germany" and to bring West Germany into NATO. They warned that West Germany's "remilitarization" had been. accompanied "by ... constantly increasing preparations for an atomic war." They made clear that the West would bear "the whole responsibility" if war resulted from its rejection of Soviet proposals. They renewed pledges for guaranteeing "the independence of the free city of West Berlin and nonintervention in its internal affairs," and they appealed for an East-West summit conference with East and West German participation to settle the entire German problem.

During a visit to London Mar. 18, Secy. Mikhail A. Suslov of the Soviet Communist Party's Central Committee told British Labor Party leaders that "the sole object of Soviet policy on Berlin is to deal with a danger spot." He expressed surprise that the Western powers considered the USSR's proposals "a sort of ultimatum." Suslov, however, reiterated demands for "either a peace treaty with the 2 Germanys or with a confederal Germany."

West German Social Democratic Party (SPD) leaders Carlo Schmid and Fritz Erler met with Khrushchev in Moscow Mar. 14 and were told that "no one wants Germany reunified." Schmid and Erler said at a news conference in Bonn Mar. 18 that Khrushchev had declared that even "the West does not want" German unity—for economic reasons, because a "reunified Germany would be too tough a competitor," and for military reasons, because "a divided Germany is the only way to maintain NATO." Khrushchev reportedly expressed the view that German unity was not probable "in the immediate future" even if an agreement were reached on the withdrawal of Western and Soviet forces from Germany. The West German Social Democrats Mar. 19 urged the creation of a "zone of relaxation" to restrict nuclear and conventional armaments in East and West Germany, Poland, Czechoslovakia and Hungary. They argued this would lead to the reunification of Germany through a "step-by-step rapprochement" and eventual agreement on a "freely elected [German] National Assembly." The SPD "German Plan," presented by Erler and SPD Chairman Erich Ollenhauer, rejected any revision of the 4-power status of Berlin except as part of a general East-West settlement on Germany. The SPD plan was attacked by Chancellor Konrad A. Adenauer as an invitation to the "Bolshevization" of all Germany.

West Considers Summit Strategy

Pres. Eisenhower told the American people Mar. 16 that he would be willing to meet Soviet leaders in a summit meeting on the German problem if such talks showed promise of success. But he said the U.S. would not "try to purchase peace by forsaking 2 million free people of Berlin" in a withdrawal of its forces from the city. The President, noting that Soviet diplomatic notes to the West Mar. 2 had accepted the idea of an East-West foreign ministers' conference on Germany, described the Soviet reply as "a move toward negotiation on an improved basis." He warned, however, that "we would never negotiate under a dictated time limit or agenda" as demanded by the USSR.

Speaking from the White House in a nationwide radio-TV address, Eisenhower said: "It is my hope ... [to] reach agreement with the Soviets on an early meeting at the level of foreign ministers. Assuming developments that justify a summer meeting at the summit, the United States would be ready to participate."

The President warned that Soviet efforts to force a Western withdrawal from Berlin had presented the U.S. with 3 "fundamental choices." He expressed these views on the 3 choices:

(1) *Abandonment of Berlin*—"The shirking of our responsibilities would solve no problems for us." It would "mean the end of all hopes for a Germany under a government of German choosing" and would "undermine the mutual confidence upon which our entire system of collective security is founded." This "is unacceptable to us."

(2) *The possibility of war*—"Global conflict under modern conditions could mean the destruction of civilization." But "whatever risk of armed conflict may be inherent in the ... Berlin situation ... was deliberately created by the Soviet rulers" and can be minimized only "if we stand firm." "War would become more likely if we gave way and encouraged a rule of terrorism."

(3) *Negotiations*—"We will do everything within our power to bring about serious negotiations and to make these negotiations meaningful." "We are ready to consider all proposals which ... will take into account the European peoples most concerned." "We seek no domination over others—only a just peace for the world and ... the people most involved."

Eisenhower gave this U.S. reply to Soviet pressure for the settlement of the problems of Berlin, German partition and European security:

Berlin—"We will not retreat one inch from our duty. We shall continue to exercise our right of peaceful passage to and from West Berlin. We will not be the first to breach the peace; it is the Soviets who threaten the use of force to interfere with such free passage."

Germany—"We cannot agree to any permanent and compulsory division of the German nation which would leave Central Europe a perpetual powder mill, even though we are ready to discuss with all affected nations any reasonable methods for its eventual unification."

At his Mar. 4 and Mar. 11 press conferences, Eisenhower rejected contentions of critics that a Western military mobilization or a marked increase in U.S. Army strength in Europe was needed to face Soviet threats in Germany. The President told newsmen Mar. 11 that a buildup of U.S. ground forces was unnecessary because "we are certainly not going to fight a ground war in Europe." Warning that it would be "a miscalculation" and "error" to engage superior Soviet-bloc ground forces as a result of the Berlin crisis, Eisenhower asserted that under these conditions, it would do little good "to send a few more thousands, or indeed, a few divisions of troops to Europe." Pressed by newsmen as to whether the U.S. would resort to nuclear warfare to defend its position in Berlin, Eisenhower refused to rule out the use of atomic force but expressed doubt that "you could free anything with nuclear weapons." He warned, however, that "we ... might as well all of us understand this: I didn't say that nuclear war is a complete impossibility."

British Prime Min. Macmillan and Eisenhower met Mar. 20-22 at the President's Camp David retreat near Thurmont, Md. and reportedly agreed on basic Western policies that might lead to East-West summit talks on Berlin and Germany.

Macmillan, on arriving in Washington Mar. 19, had told newsmen he would seek with Eisenhower to formulate a Western policy that would combine "firmness and reasonableness" at expected high-level talks with Soviet leaders. Macmillan and Eisenhower, accompanied by British Foreign Secy. Selwyn Lloyd, met briefly with State Secy. Dulles at Walter Reed Army Hospital Mar. 20 (Dulles was dying of cancer) and then flew to Camp David by helicopter to begin secluded talks on Macmillan's recent Moscow visit and on policy in the German crisis.

The Camp David talks showed early agreement on Western intentions to hold Berlin but revealed an apparent U.S.-British divergence on the need for a summit conference and on Western terms to be presented to the USSR if such a conference took place. The Macmillan-Eisenhower differences were made plain by conflicting reports on results of the Camp David talks by James C. Hagerty and Peter Hope, press officers for the White House and British Foreign Office, respectively.

British-inspired reports asserted Mar. 21 that Macmillan had persuaded Eisenhower that summit talks with Soviet Premier Khrushchev were necessary because Khrushchev was prepared to negotiate Soviet differences with the West and was the only Soviet leader with the power to bind the USSR to an eventual agreement on Germany. The President was said to have agreed to participate in such talks that summer regardless of the outcome of an East-West foreign ministers' conference in May.

U.S. officials, however, insisted Mar. 23 that Eisenhower had agreed to enter a proposed summit meeting with Khrushchev only on condition that the prior foreign ministers' talks showed meaningful progress on Germany and other differences dividing East and West. Eisenhower was said to have expressed interest in Macmillan's proposals of a series of brief recurrent summit conferences in which Eastern and Western heads of government would meet to settle points of difference arising from continuing lower-level negotiations. He also was said to have agreed to let Polish and Czech government heads act as observers but not participants in a summit meeting.

Other topics covered at Camp David:

Berlin —Macmillan was said to have urged the negotiation of new Soviet guarantees for West Berlin, possibly under international supervision. Eisenhower reportedly insisted that the Western position in West Berlin was not negotiable.

East Germany —Britain reportedly expressed willingness to permit East German control of communications to Berlin provided that the USSR gave firm guarantees of Allied rights of access to the city. The President was said to have rejected any move that would accord recognition to the East German regime.

Troop "freeze" —Macmillan was said to have won Eisenhower's qualified support for British proposals to "freeze" current Western and Soviet military strength in Central Europe. Eisenhower, however, was reported to have made clear the U.S.' rejection of "disengagement" proposals that would ban nuclear weapons or otherwise weaken NATO strength.

Macmillan, in a statement issued before his departure for London Mar. 24, asserted that "the next few months will be a testing period for the whole free world." He said "the free world has everything to gain from being ready to negotiate," but he warned that "we must also stand firmly on our rights and upon the positions which we have a duty to defend."

East & West Agree on Ministerial Talks

Speaking Mar. 26 at an unusual Kremlin press conference, his 2d since becoming Soviet premier, Khrushchev accepted in advance (before they were submitted formally) Western proposals for an East-West foreign ministers' meeting in Geneva May 11 on Germany and Berlin. Khrushchev told 300 Soviet and Western newsmen that he had called the press meeting "so that no one can misinterpret our proposals." He outlined the following Soviet policies on Germany and European questions:

● The Geneva Foreign ministers' talks should be restricted to the question of Germany. It should be followed by a summit conference at which the heads of government would be empowered to reach broad agreements. The USSR was ready to discuss any "reasonable proposals" by the West at these meetings.

● The USSR would not discuss East European affairs or the revision of Czech and Polish frontiers at either conference. The West must "forget about the possibility of reverting the people's democracies of East Europe to capitalism once again."

● The USSR's 6-month deadline for ending the Berlin occupation regime "was not intended as an ultimatum." But if negotiations failed, the USSR would sign a separate peace treaty with East Germany, which "then would be a sovereign state" with "West Berlin ... inside its territory."

● The USSR would accept the enforcement of a new political status for Berlin by troop contingents supplied by the wartime Allies, neutral countries or the UN. The USSR would continue to recognize Western occupation rights in Berlin until the signing of a peace treaty.

The Western Big 3 powers and the USSR agreed in an exchange of official diplomatic notes Mar. 26-30 to convene a foreign ministers' conference in Geneva May 11 to discuss the German problem and prepare the way for an East-West summit meeting. In similar but not identical notes sent Mar. 26, the Western powers replied to the Soviet message of Mar. 2 and suggested that the foreign ministers consider a broad agenda, including proposals for a German peace treaty and the future status of Berlin.

The U.S. and British messages asserted that the "purpose of the foreign ministers' meeting should be to reach positive agreements over as wide a field as possible and ... to narrow the differences between the respective points of view and to prepare constructive proposals for consideration by a conference of heads of government later in the summer." The

French note insisted that the foreign ministers' conference show "genuine progress" toward resolution of East-West differences before France "would be disposed to accept a conference at the summit at an appropriate place and date."

Rejecting Soviet demands for the inclusion of Poland and Czechoslovakia in the foreign ministers' conference, the Western powers proposed that the talks initially be limited to the "4 powers responsible for Germany." The Western powers, however, renewed their suggestion that "German advisers," presumably representing both the East and West German governments, be invited for consultation by the 4 foreign ministers. The Western powers agreed to consider "the participation of other governments at a certain stage in negotiations." (In a note to the USSR, West Germany agreed Mar. 26 to send advisers to the foreign ministers' meeting on condition that participating governments were not limited in the introduction of agenda items "directly connected with the problems dealt with.")

The USSR, in similar notes delivered to the U.S., Britain and France Mar. 30, agreed to join in a foreign ministers' meeting in Geneva May 11 and expressed "satisfaction" that the Western powers had agreed "to start solving urgent international questions at a foreign ministers' conference and a summit meeting."

The Soviet messages accepted Western agenda suggestions and agreed that the primary goal of the foreign ministers' session would be to pave the way for a summit meeting. Rejecting French contentions, the USSR asserted that if the foreign ministers' talks proved "inadequate," the proposed summit meeting would be more, not less necessary. The USSR expressed "regret" that the West had not agreed to the participation of Poland and Czechoslovakia in the talks, but it agreed to defer the question until the conference began. It specifically welcomed the West's agreement to the inclusion of advisers from East and West Germany.

Western Efforts to Coordinate Policy

Foreign Mins. Selwyn Lloyd of Britain, Maurice Couve de Murville of France and Heinrich von Brentano of West Germany and U.S. Acting State Secy. Christian Herter met in

Washington Mar. 31-Apr. 1 to discuss Western policy for the
forthcoming East-West foreign ministers' talks on Germany. A
statement issued Mar. 31 emphasized Western agreement that a
proposed East-West summit meeting that summer would
depend on results of the prior foreign ministers' talks.

Convened to discuss a report of the U.S.-British-French-
West German working group on German reunification, the 4
foreign ministers were said to have narrowed existing
differences, centered on (1) British proposals for increased
flexibility in the forthcoming negotiations with the USSR on
the German problem; (2) West German insistence that the West
reject Soviet demands for altering the Berlin occupation status,
demilitarizing central Europe, and unifying Germany through
confederation of the East and West German states.

In a final communique Apr. 1, the Western ministers
declared their "sincere desire to negotiate constructively with
the Soviet Union in the interests of world peace." But they
made clear their adherence to these terms of the 4-power
declaration on Germany of Dec. 14, 1958: maintenance of
Western rights in and access to Berlin; refusal to accept the
USSR's proposed unilateral repudiation of its Berlin
obligations or the substitution of East Germans for Soviet
representatives in the carrying out of these obligations. The
Western ministers agreed to submit remaining differences to a
renewed meeting Apr. 13 of the Western 4-power working
group on Germany and to reconsider their policies in a new
Western foreign ministers' meeting in Paris Apr. 29.

Foreign ministers of the 15 NATO nations convened in
Washington Apr. 2-4 and expressed "full agreement" Apr. 4 to
the basic policies on Germany outlined by the prior
Washington meeting of the U.S., British, French and West
German foreign ministers.

Addressing the NATO Council at its opening meeting Apr.
2, Pres. Eisenhower called on the Atlantic Alliance for
"courage," "sacrifice" and "perseverance" to maintain free
world security against Soviet threats and simultaneously to
"explore every avenue which offers reasonable hope for just
solutions to the issues between ourselves and the Soviet Union."
Recalling his service as the first NATO supreme commander,
Eisenhower said that in 10 years "NATO has grown into a
powerful security community by means of which the free

people[s] ... pursue the goal of a durable peace with justice."
The President said NATO's success was proved by the fact that
since its formation "there has been no further Communist
advance in Europe—either by political or by military means."
He warned, however, that NATO states "must prepare during
the years ahead to live in a world in which tension and
bickering between free nations and the Soviets will be daily
experiences." Freedom can be won, he asserted, only by
maintaining "the unity which is the very lifeblood of NATO."

Eisenhower's exhortation was followed the same day by
U.S. pledges to use America's full military power to defend
NATO if necessary. Speaking at the first working session of
the NATO Council, Acting State Secy. Herter made clear that
the U.S.' air- and missile-borne nuclear arsenal and
conventional forces would be available to deal with any Soviet-
provoked general or limited conflict. State Department
spokesmen said, however, that Herter had expressed hope that
U.S. and NATO deterrent power would discourage any Soviet
military moves and contribute to efforts to settle East-West
differences by negotiation.

(At a Washington news conference before the NATO
meeting, NATO Secy. Gen. Paul-Henri Spaak said Apr. 1 that
the USSR wished to extend its power in all areas but hoped to
do so without war. Spaak said he did "not believe we will have
war, but we cannot suffer a diplomatic defeat in Berlin.")

The NATO Council, ending its 3-day meeting Apr. 4 on
the 10th anniversary of the signing of the North Atlantic
Treaty, "confirmed its unanimous determination to maintain
the freedom of the people of West Berlin, and the rights and
obligations of the Allied powers" as expressed in the Dec. 16,
1958 NATO declaration on Berlin. The final communique
stressed a conviction that "the unity of action and policy which
the [NATO] alliance makes possible is the best guarantee of
successful negotiation with the Soviet government and of any
genuine resolution of differences between East and West."
(Washington sources said, however, that the NATO Council
had failed to resolve important differences on terms for
negotiating with the USSR. According to Bonn dispatches in
the *N.Y. Times* Apr. 6, the U.S., France, Belgium, the
Netherlands and Turkey had backed "tough" West German
terms while Canada, Norway, Denmark and Italy had backed

British pleas for concessions that might enhance chances for a settlement. West German Foreign Min. von Brentano was said to have reported to Chancellor Konrad Adenauer Apr. 6 that the NATO stand represented a victory for German efforts to prevent an easing of the Allied terms for Berlin and German reunification.)

At a special Gettysburg College convocation Apr. 4, Pres. Eisenhower said: The Communists had chosen to exert pressure on West Berlin because "they always pick the most awkward situation, the hard-to-defend position, as the place to test our strength and resolution. There will never be an easy place for us to make a stand, but there is a best one. The best one is where principle points." Rejecting "the unthinkable sacrifice of 2 million free Germans" in Berlin, the President said: "The course of appeasement is not only dishonorable, it is the most dangerous one we could pursue."

Dr. Konrad Adenauer announced Apr. 7 that he would resign as West German chancellor to succeed Dr. Theodor Heuss, 75, as West German president in September. Adenauer, 83, the architect of the postwar economic and political recovery, served notice Apr. 8 to all "friendly" and "nonfriendly countries abroad" that West Germany's foreign policy would "not change by one iota" when he quit the chancellorship. Adenauer asserted that recent Western consultations on Soviet demands in Germany had brought "a clear avowal of freedom" and agreement on basic means to frustrate the Soviet threats. But he conceded that Allied differences existed on "secondary questions," and he rebuked Britain for what he termed "the systematically contrived impairment of the mood of Great Britain against Germany." Adenauer denounced as "pure fantasy" suggestions that his relations with British Prime Min. Macmillan were "troubled," but he rejected Macmillan's proposals for a freeze of troop strength in Europe and backed French Pres. Charles de Gaulle's contention that "such a zone would only serve a purpose if carried out in the whole area between the Atlantic and the Urals."

Although Adenauer's resignation was not to take place until after the East-West foreign ministers' talks and a proposed summit meeting in the summer, European and British observers suggested that his resignation would help make possible the formulation of less rigid Western counterproposals on Germany. American sources expressed fears, however, that Adenauer's resignation and State Secy. Dulles' simultaneous incapacitation had removed the 2 principal opponents of flexibility toward Soviet demands on Germany. German informants ascribed the growing German political opposition to Adenauer as due, in part, to his refusal to soften his terms for negotiation of German reunification. (The Soviet Tass news agency reported Apr. 7 that Adenauer had been forced to resign due to differences with Christian Democratic Union leaders over the British proposals for a European troop freeze.)

French Premier Michel Debre and Foreign Min. Couve de Murville met with British Prime Min. Macmillan and Foreign Secy. Lloyd in London Apr. 13-14 to discuss coordinating Western policy before the forthcoming East-West negotiations. Macmillan, reportedly anxious to ease French and West German suspicions of the USSR's willingness to negotiate a settlement of the German problem, was said to have urged the French to support specific, negotiable Western proposals for presentation to the USSR in East-West foreign ministers' talks.

Macmillan and Lloyd conferred in Paris Mar. 9-10 with French Pres. de Gaulle, Premier Debre and Foreign Min. Couve de Murville. Broad agreement was reported that a unified Western approach to Soviet demands on Germany could not entail the surrender of Allied rights in Berlin or the Western position in Germany. But Macmillan was said to have failed in efforts to win French support for British proposals for a central European troop freeze despite assurances that the plan would require only a thinning out of NATO forces.

Macmillan and Lloyd flew to Bonn for meetings Mar. 12-13 with Chancellor Adenauer and Foreign Min. von Brentano. Adenauer and Macmillan professed to have reached full agreement on requirements for Western policy at the forthcoming talks on Germany, but Adenauer was said to have made clear his opposition to any agreement which would be based on a reduction of Western forces in Europe. The West German leaders reportedly told Macmillan that any plan for disengagement or limitation of forces in Europe would be acceptable only as part of a broad disarmament agreement which included substantial areas of the USSR.

Adenauer denied Mar. 15 that he had attempted to persuade Macmillan to drop British policies aimed at compromising with the USSR by agreeing to a new status for West Berlin and a freeze on NATO and Warsaw Pact forces. Adenauer said at a Hanover CDU (Christian Democratic Union) rally that he was "not so mad as to think that I can influence British policy." But he made clear that as "long as we run the [West German] government, there will be no dictated peace for the Federal Republic but only a peace treaty concluded on a voluntary basis."

Macmillan, replying Apr. 9 to Laborite leader Hugh Gaitskell's suggestion that the nuclear arming of West Germany be delayed until after forthcoming East-West talks, rejected any action which would discriminate against the equipping of NATO troops because of their nationality. Macmillan, however, conceded to Parliament that he had been shocked by the "utterly surprising" anti-British tone of Adenauer's Apr. 8 speech to the German people.

Macmillan said at a Conservative Party rally in London Apr. 18 that Britain would seek "pacification by negotiation and reasonable agreement" but would not "yield to pressure or follow the path of what used to be called appeasement" in projected East-West talks on Germany. Macmillan, apparently seeking to curb criticism of Britain's alleged willingness to compromise with Soviet demands on Germany, declared that the Western Allies "shall soon reach an agreed ... position for the difficult period of negotiation which lies ahead." Indicating a less positive belief that the East-West foreign ministers' conference would result in a heads of government meeting, Macmillan said that "we may, I hope, reach the summit conference." Macmillan said that the West should aim at a summit meeting designed "not as a single effort to solve all these problems ... but rather as the beginning of a series [of talks] which could bit by bit unravel ... some of these difficulties."

British delegates to the U.S.-British-French-West German working group on German unity were reported Apr. 21 to have urged Western acceptance of British plans for a central European troop freeze as part of a broad plan for German unification. Other Western delegates were said to have agreed to accept the plan on condition that it be limited to inspection of Eastern and Western forces currently in central Europe and not require immediate reduction of these forces or their armaments.

Berlin Flights Imperiled, Rules Disputed

U.S. Air Force transport planes flying the air corridors between Berlin and West Germany were "buzzed" by Soviet jet fighters Mar. 27 and Apr. 3 in an effort to make them conform to a Soviet-imposed ceiling of 10,000 feet on Western military flights to Berlin. The incidents, disclosed by U.S. authorities Mar. 31 and Apr. 14, were protested to the 4-power Berlin Air Safety Center as illegal Soviet harassment of Western military flights to Berlin and attempts to subject the 3 Berlin air corridors to unilateral Soviet control.

U.S. military authorities in Germany charged Mar. 31 that the agreements establishing air access routes to Berlin contained no reference to a ceiling for flights on those routes. They conceded, however, that U.S. piston-engine aircraft normally used on Berlin flights had flown at cruising altitudes of less than 10,000 feet.

The incidents brought an exchange of U.S.-Soviet notes and protests over alleged violations of Berlin air traffic rules. Soviet embassy spokesmen in East Berlin warned Apr. 1 that the 10,000-foot ceiling had the force of a "prescriptive right" and that "there may be incidents if the Americans fly above the altitude again without negotiating." The embassy declared Apr. 2 that, although the USSR had no intention of forcing down U.S. planes operating above the ceiling, "the present air safety system will not operate for American aircraft above that altitude." It noted that U.S. planes had always observed Soviet regulations limiting Berlin flights to between 2,500 and 10,000 feet to prevent collision with Soviet planes crossing the corridors at higher and lower altitudes.

A U.S. memo delivered to Soviet representatives at the Berlin Air Safety Center Apr. 4 rejected the Soviet efforts to impose a ceiling on Western military planes. The memo said that U.S. transports would fly to and from Berlin at whatever altitude was deemed necessary.

The Soviet Foreign Ministry protested formally to the U.S. Apr. 4 that the Berlin flights had been intended to "worsen conditions" for the forthcoming East-West foreign ministers' conference on Germany and to "wreck" the talks before they began. It termed the flights a "premeditated violation ... of the established order of air communication with Berlin" and insisted that the Western powers observe the 10,000-foot ceiling.

A U.S. note delivered to the Soviet Foreign Ministry Apr. 13 declared that the U.S. "never has recognized and does not recognize any limitation to the right to fly [at] any altitude in the [Berlin] corridors." It asserted that U.S. flight altitudes would continue to be determined by weather conditions and operating characteristics of the aircraft used. It charged that the Mar. 27 "buzzing" by Soviet fighters was a "serious violation of the flight regulations ... in the air corridors" and "intentionally created the very hazards to flight safety" about which the USSR was concerned.

The Soviet efforts to establish a 10,000-foot ceiling on Western military flights to Berlin were rejected Apr. 16 by U.S. Defense Secy. Neil H. McElroy. Speaking at a Washington news conference, McElroy said that the U.S. would exercise its right to fly aircraft in the 3 Berlin air corridors "at whatever altitude we choose," and that "from time to time" the U.S. would continue to send jet-prop C-130 transports to West Berlin at altitudes above the Soviet limit. He insisted that the C-130s, which "fly much more economically at a higher altitude," were being used because they carry "heavy loads." The "demonstration" of U.S. rights in the Berlin air lanes was "a by-product" of the planes' operating characteristics, he said.

American authorities in Berlin protested to the Berlin Air Safety Center Apr. 16 against Soviet jet aircraft escort of a C-130 sent to Berlin Apr. 15 at 20,000 feet. The U.S. officials charged that Soviet MiGs had made "menacing passes" close to the transport. Soviet embassy officials charged that the American flight had been intended to "poison" the atmosphere for forthcoming East-West talks on Germany.

British Foreign Secy. Selwyn Lloyd told the British Parliament Apr. 20 that Britain supported the U.S.' exercise of its right to send high-altitude flights to Berlin "from time to time as necessary." Lloyd said that British views on the flights had been transmitted to the U.S. He held that it was "the responsibility of the individual Allied governments to decide what orders should be given to ... their aircraft flying along the [Berlin] corridors." Lloyd's statement was made in answer to protests by Laborites and leading British newspapers Apr. 16-19. They charged that the Berlin high-altitude flights had been ordered by the U.S. Defense Department to force the State Department, the Eisenhower Administration and Western Allies to support strong military policies during the Berlin crisis. Laborite MP Harold Davies demanded Apr. 19 that the U.S. take action to assure "that these threats of war are repudiated and the generals are kept under control."

State Department officials Apr. 17 had expressed "dismay" at "the attitude expressed in [British] news stories of timidity toward anything we do in the maintenance of our rights in Berlin." They asserted that Pres. Eisenhower had personally approved the use of C-130 transports on the Berlin air routes. State Department spokesman Lincoln White told newsmen that "there is government-wide approval of the use of C-130s into and out of Berlin." He denied British contentions that the use of these planes at high altitudes constituted "a provocation to Russia."

White confirmed Apr. 20 that Acting State Secy. Christian Herter and British Foreign Secy. Lloyd had discussed the Berlin flights during recent NATO Council meetings in Washington. But White denied that Britain had objected to the U.S. action. British newspapers had said that Herter had assured Lloyd the flights would be stopped to avoid provocation of incidents in the Berlin air corridors.

The Soviet government Apr. 28 rejected American arguments against a ceiling on Western military flights to Berlin and warned that continuance of high-altitude flights by U.S. planes would be "dangerous." A Soviet note disputed American contentions that the Soviet-imposed ceiling of 10,000 feet on Berlin flights had no basis in Allied agreements establishing Western air corridors to Berlin.

Washington officials reported Apr. 30 that high-altitude flights in the Berlin air corridors had been suspended on orders of the State and Defense Departments to prevent any further incidents.

West Prepares for Geneva Conference

Christian Herter was named by Pres. Eisenhower Apr. 18 to succeed the ailing John Foster Dulles as U.S. State Secretary. Herter flew to Paris Apr. 28 for talks with Foreign Mins. Lloyd of Britain, Couve de Murville of France and von Brentano of West Germany on formulating the Western position at forthcoming East-West negotiations on Germany. Herter, on his first diplomatic mission as State Secretary, conceded to reporters on his arrival in Paris that the Western nations "regard the questions to be discussed with the Soviets from somewhat different points of view." But he expressed confidence that "we shall be able to agree wholeheartedly on the course we must follow in our common interest."

The 4 foreign ministers conferred privately Apr. 29 and were reported to have reached tentative agreement on a Western "package" plan that would offer the USSR a German settlement on the following basis:

● Progress toward establishing a European security system would be made dependent on parallel measures for achieving German reunification. Until agreement was reached on both questions, the 4-power occupation of Berlin would continue.

● East and West Germany would issue a series of declarations renouncing aggression or support of aggressor nations. They then would join in establishing an all-German commission to multiply contacts and prepare for free all-German elections.

● A parallel East-West commission set up by the U.S., Britain, France and the USSR would examine proposals for assuring European security. It would aim at imposing broad disarmament controls simultaneously with the initiation of measures for German unity.

The U.S.-British-French-West German working group on German unification held a series of meetings in London and ended them Apr. 24, reportedly without substantial progress toward resolving disagreement on Western terms for negotiating a German settlement with the USSR. The Western rift continued between British appeals for compromise and French-West German fears that the USSR would succeed in negotiating the dismantling of the Allied position in Berlin and Germany. The rift continued despite a British agreement to revise its proposals for a "freeze" on current NATO and Warsaw Pact forces.

London diplomatic sources reported Apr. 26 that Britain had agreed to broaden the troop-freeze plan to meet French and West German demands that any European disarmament pact extend from the Atlantic to the Urals. The revised British plan reportedly envisaged the establishment of 2 zones: (1) a smaller zone covering parts of West Germany and the Netherlands and all of East Germany, Poland and Czechoslovakia, in which arms and troop levels would be fixed and open to joint inspection and control; (2) a larger zone, extending from Paris to Moscow, that would be open to air inspection.

U.S. Amb.-to-West Germany David K. E. Bruce went to Lake Como, Italy Apr. 25 to explain the revised British proposal to vacationing Chancellor Konrad Adenauer. Bruce was reported to have said the U.S. would support the British plan if both France and West Germany agreed to do so. But Adenauer was reported Apr. 27 to have ordered Foreign Min. von Brentano to reject the British plan at the Paris foreign ministers' talks. Adenauer's opposition was said to be based on the fear that any freeze of current NATO and Warsaw Pact forces would discriminate against West Germany by ruling out Bundeswehr acquisition of nuclear weapons and missiles.

Adenauer was said Apr. 26 to have overruled von Brentano and to have ordered a West German veto of Western working-group proposals for German unity. He was said to have rejected U.S. suggestions for the creation of an all-German council on unification made up of 10 West Germans for every 6 East Germans. The basis of the representation was the formation of West Germany from 10 pre-war German states and of East Germany from 6 states. Adenauer was said to have insisted on a 3-1 preponderance of West Germans to East Germans, based on the relative populations of the 2 countries.

The foreign ministers of the U.S., Britain, France and West Germany announced Apr. 30 that they had reached "complete agreement" on Western strategy to be followed in the forthcoming East-West Geneva negotiations on Germany and Berlin. Ending 2 days of talks in Paris, State Secy. Herter and Foreign Mins. Lloyd, Couve de Murville and von Brentano reaffirmed "their willingness to enter into negotiations with the

Soviet Union with a view to establishing a just and durable peace in Europe." But they made clear that until an agreement was reached with the USSR on Germany and Europe, the West was determined "to maintain the freedom of the people of West Berlin and the rights and obligations there of the Allied powers."

The Western "package plan" on Berlin, German unity and European security was presented to the NATO Permanent Council by Couve de Murville May 2. It was approved informally by all 15 member states.

Premier Khrushchev indicated May 5 that the USSR would reject the Western "package plan" for German reunification. Khrushchev told a group of West German Social Democratic newsmen visiting Moscow that the USSR would press for the approval of its own proposals for a German peace treaty. He reiterated that if the Western powers refused to accept the Soviet proposal, the USSR "will settle these questions with East Germany and will sign a separate peace treaty." Khrushchev urged that the West agree to a summit conference even if the foreign ministers' meetings "fail to produce any remarkable progress." He said that the USSR would agree to the retention of "token forces of the Western powers ... in Berlin" even if it signed a separate East German peace treaty. He urged that the West accept a "new status" for Berlin "guaranteed by the United Nations" and free from interference by "East German authorities."

The Soviet government newspaper *Izvestia* May 3 had denounced the Western "package plan" for Germany and European security as an attempt to complicate negotiations and "hamper an agreed solution on a peace treaty."

An estimated 550,000 West Berliners, led by Mayor Willy Brandt, turned out May 1 for a "Berlin will remain free" rally said to have been the city's largest popular demonstration since World War II. Brandt had returned from a visit to Britain and the Scandinavian countries, where he had sought support for the Western position on Berlin. He had said in a speech before the London Foreign Press Association Apr. 21 that he favored closer study by the West of Polish Foreign Min. Adam Rapacki's plan for military disengagement in central Europe; Brandt urged the reconsideration of "international military dispositions from time to time" to see if "gradual changes can be made without weakening the over-all security system of the West." He told Berliners May 1: "We are only a few millions, and we have no weapons. But we have the right to live and to work in freedom. We will not allow this right to be taken from us." The West Berlin rally was also addressed by United Auto Workers Pres. Walter Reuther of the U.S. (Some 500,000 East Berliners May 1 attended Communist May Day ceremonies in which East German troops paraded before Communist Party [SED] Secy. Walter Ulbricht, Gen. Matvei V. Zakharov, Soviet commander in East Germany, and Marshal Peng Teh-huai, Communist China's defense minister.)

Pres. Eisenhower conceded May 5 that an East-West summit meeting was a "foregone conclusion" provided that "anything"—presumably the foreign ministers' talks scheduled for May 11 in Geneva—gave "enlarged hope for decreasing tensions in the world." Eisenhower had been briefed by Herter May 2 on the results of the Western foreign ministers' meeting in Paris. The President expressed the hope that there would be "some progress" at the Geneva talks, but he apparently did not rule out a summit meeting if the Geneva meetings failed to produce substantial East-West agreement. Eisenhower indicated that his heightened willingness to enter summit talks was due partially to the fact that "within the Soviet regime there is only one man who can talk authoritatively"— Khrushchev. The President had said at his Apr. 29 news conference that although "a great many different approaches" might be made toward easing tension in central Europe, the U.S. would "not desert 2 million free people" in West Berlin or abandon its "rights to discharge the responsibilities that are still ours."

Before flying to the Geneva foreign ministers' conference, newly-appointed U.S. State Secy. Herter addressed the American people May 7. Cautioning his audience against "great expectations," Herter said that Western policy, as understood in Washington, included these requirements:

● Unity "for the German people in one nation, under a government of their own choice." "We recognize, however, that the consequences of the division of Germany during the last 14 years cannot be removed overnight. Reunification will therefore have to be a gradual process assuring time ... to adjust."

● Effective "security safeguards and arms control arrangements for the nations so that they can have assurance of being able to develop in peace and prosperity."

● Guaranteed "freedom for Berlin, with no reduction of our existing rights and obligations, until Berlin can again assume its appropriate place in a united Germany."

Herter said that "the heart of our policy can be clearly and simply said to be this: A Germany reunited in freedom, a security system linked with ... arms control, and in the interim, a free and secure Berlin." He warned that the U.S. was "convinced that as long as Germany remains divided, the peace in Europe will continue to be threatened. And twice in this century we have seen that when major war comes to Europe it comes to all the world. In the meantime a precarious peace will live hand-to-mouth from month to month."

Herter flew from Washington to Bonn May 8 for pre-conference talks May 9 with West German Chancellor Adenauer before continuing to Geneva. Herter reportedly reassured Adenauer of his intention to maintain a strong American policy on Germany in negotiations with Soviet Foreign Min. Andrei Gromyko, but he was said to have won Adenauer's agreement to the separation of the Berlin question from other parts of the Western "package plan" should the plan be rejected by Gromyko in its entirety.

GENEVA CONFERENCE OF FOREIGN MINISTERS

East-West Arguments

The long-awaited conference of Big 4 foreign ministers on problems of Berlin, Germany and European security opened May 11, 1959 in Geneva, Switzerland. Welcomed to Geneva's Palais de Nations, the former seat of the League of Nations, by UN Secy. Gen. Dag Hammarskjold May 11, the foreign ministers delayed their opening statements until May 13. In the interim, the Soviets tried to expand the conference to include Polish, Czechoslovak and East German delegations.

Soviet Foreign Min. Andrei A. Gromyko proposed that the 2 German delegations be seated as full participants, but the Western powers rejected this plan as inconsistent with the pre-conference agreement, reached in an earlier exchange of diplomatic notes, that the 2 German delegations would enjoy advisory status only. A meeting between Gromyko and the 3 Western ministers (Selwyn Lloyd, Christian A. Herter and Couve de Murville) produced a compromise agreement May 11: the 2 German delegations would be seated as advisers and would be permitted to address the conference—but only with the unanimous consent of the Big 4 ministers.

Gromyko, chairman of the conference's first closed working session, held May 12, then proposed that Poland and Czechoslovakia be invited to take part in the talks in recognition of their sufferings as the first foreign victims of Nazi Germany. The Soviet proposal was rejected by Herter on the ground that the Big 4 alone held the "major responsibility" for settling the German question as a result of their leading roles in the wartime conquest of Germany. Herter declared that a 4-power conference would have a "better chance of engaging in ... serious negotiations on the problem of Germany." He noted that many countries had suffered from Nazi aggression. He suggested that other countries be invited if their participation became helpful in later stages of the talks.

Gromyko raised the question of Polish and Czechoslovak participation again May 13 but dropped the matter when Herter, conference chairman that day, refused to act on the Soviet request.

The Eastern and Western delegations seemed to agree that the root cause of their problem was the division of Germany as dramatized by divided Berlin. As to who was responsible for this problem, however, opinion clearly differed. In a series of opening statements May 13, the foreign ministers indicated these differences:

● U.S. State Secy. Herter said: "The root of the problem remains the same—the German people are being prevented from establishing a government of their own choice for all of Germany. The problem will remain until the entire German people can express their will freely." In the 1955 Geneva conference, "our heads of government ... acknowledged responsibility ... [for] German reunification. We cannot now abdicate this responsibility."

● Soviet Foreign Min. Gromyko declared: No settlement could be reached "in the heart of Europe where peace with Germany has not yet been made." "Under present conditions the reunification of Germany can be achieved only by means of negotiations between the 2 German states ... without any interference from outside into this internal affair of the German people." An agreement must be sought "to remedy the ... deeply abnormal, the dangerous situation in West Berlin, which is still under occupation of the NATO powers, although this ... status has been obsolete for a long time now and is ... intolerable in a city lying in the center" of East Germany.

● British Foreign Secy. Lloyd said: The Western powers could not accept the USSR's "conception of 2 Germanys" or its "idea that the German question and German unity was a domestic matter which should be solved by the 2 Germanys." A German settlement could only be reached among the wartime Big 4. (Lloyd rebuked Gromyko for assertions that the West had created the current tension by increasing armaments in Western Europe and particularly in West Germany.)

● French Foreign Min. Couve de Murville drew a connection between the conference and the Soviet "ultimatum" on Berlin. He said: The "present conference has been convened ... to try to dispel" the crisis caused by "measures taken by the Soviet government over the past 6 months." "The concern which the Soviet government states that it feels today in regard to Berlin merely corroborates what we have been saying ... for ... 15 years—namely, that there can be no real security and stability in Europe until there is an over-all settlement of the German problem," which remained "the responsibility of the 4 powers represented around this table."

Both Sides Present Plans

In the first major address of the conference, Herter May 14 submitted a 4-stage Western plan for a "permanent settlement in Europe" through "closely interrelated" solutions of the questions of Berlin, German unity and European security. The 4 stages would be:

Stage 1—East and West Berlin would be reunited through free elections, held under quadripartite or UN supervision, for a city council to administer all Berlin until the city became the capital of a reunified Germany. The freedom of and access to a reunited Berlin would be guaranteed by continued 4-power military occupation, pending a German peace treaty. Other provisions of Stage 1 included East-West agreements outlawing aggression, pledging loyalty to the UN, denying aid to aggressor states and discussing the exchange of information on military forces in various agreed areas of Europe.

Stage 2—A mixed German committee would be established by the Big 4 to expand contacts and prepare for elections. In this stage further arms reductions and inspections would be introduced.

Stage 3—An all-German assembly would be chosen in both East and West Germany to draft a constitution and establish a democratic government to replace the East and West German governments. Additional disengagement of foreign troops would be carried out followed by further reductions of force levels by the Big 4.

Stage 4—A "final peace settlement" would be concluded with "a government representing all Germany." It would be signed by the Big 4 and all UN members which had been at war with Germany. Thus, in Stage 4, all Germany would be reunited, East-West divisions in Europe bridged and the Berlin problem would be solved.

Gromyko outlined the East-bloc plan May 15. It called on the Western powers to join the USSR in negotiating separate peace treaties with East and West Germany, to establish West Berlin as a demilitarized free city and to turn over to the East and West German governments the responsibility for the establishment of a unified Germany. The plan was based on suggestions made in diplomatic notes issued by the USSR Jan. 10 and Mar. 2. Under the Communist plan, (a) a permanent solution of the Berlin problem would be negotiated as part of the German peace treaties, and (b) pending German reunification and a peace settlement, West Berlin would become a demilitarized free city and the 4-power occupation regime would be dissolved.

The Soviet plan also called for the signing of a peace treaty with each of the 2 German governments or with an all-German government as well as prohibitions on certain "Fascist militarist" groups and on missile and nuclear weapons, although "essential" armed forces would be permitted. A phased withdrawal program from various countries in Central Europe as well as from a reunited Germany was also proposed.

The Western and Soviet proposals for a German settlement were each rejected May 18 by Gromyko and Herter.

A joint statement issued May 18 by the U.S., British and French delegations denied as "incorrect" press reports that the West would be willing to separate the problem of Berlin from the rest of the Western "package plan" and negotiate an "interim settlement" of the city's status. The reports were traced to a U.S. delegation spokesman who had told newsmen May 17 that the West would agree to discuss Berlin as an individual subject if the USSR persisted in its refusal to negotiate on the Western plan in its entirety.

It was reported from Geneva May 19 that Gromyko, at a private meeting with Lloyd May 18, had offered to negotiate on these 3 alternatives for solving the Berlin question: (1) the withdrawal of the Western garrisons from West Berlin; (2) the addition of small Soviet forces to the 3 Western garrisons, or (3) the replacement of the Western garrisons by unspecified "neutral forces" under UN supervision. Lloyd was said to have rejected all 3 proposals.

UN Secy. Gen. Hammerskjold May 21 expressed opposition to proposals for the formation of a UN "garrison" in Berlin. He said at a UN news conference that the UN's assumption of a military role in Berlin would be "of a very serious political nature" and was "basically quite unsound." Hammerskjold currently was said to favor the stationing of UN observers in West Berlin and on access routes to Berlin to supervise any agreement reached by the Big 4 powers.

Herter May 26 presented the following plan for unifying Berlin: (1) free elections throughout "greater Berlin" for a constitutional council, which would draft a Berlin constitution and election law, both to be ratified by plebiscite; (2) the proclamation of a Berlin constitution with the 4 powers continuing "to maintain forces in Berlin"; (3) a 4-power agreement to insure "free and unrestricted access to Berlin"; (4)

4-power "military police patrols ... to deal with all incidents involving military personnel"; (5) authorization for the Berlin government to apply to Berlin proposals of the mixed German committee; (6) Berlin's designation as "the capital of reunified Germany" on the promulgation of an all-German constitution and government; (7) the settlement of the issue of 4-power occupation under German peace treaty terms.

The Geneva foreign ministers' conference was recessed May 27-28, following the death of John Foster Dulles, to permit Herter, Lloyd, Couve de Murville and Gromyko to attend the funeral of the late State Secretary in Washington. The ministers agreed to resume their talks on a secret basis May 29 after their return.

In the meantime, the 6-month Soviet deadline for the dissolution of the 4-power occupation status of Berlin set by the USSR Nov. 27, 1958 expired May 27 without any overt attempts by Soviet authorities to disrupt Western access to the city or to hand over their own prerogatives to the East German government. Lord Mayor Willy Brandt said at a news conference in West Berlin May 27 that, under Western protection, the city had prospered despite the Soviet ultimatum. He warned, however, that the city still was like a "lemon waiting to be squeezed" if the West acquiesced in Soviet demands for the creation of a free city of West Berlin.

Geneva Talks Resumed, Split Blocks Agreement

The foreign ministers' conference resumed informally aboard a U.S. Air Force plane bound for Geneva May 28. The Western ministers had agreed to an early end to the conference if the USSR accepted a final communique that (a) reaffirmed 4-power occupation rights in Berlin, (b) pledged a peaceful settlement of the German problem, (c) promised steps to reunify Germany with free elections and (d) outlined subjects to be discussed at the projected East-West summit meeting.

At the foreign ministers' meeting in Geneva May 30, Lloyd voiced the first Western offer to untie the West's "package plan" and negotiate on Berlin alone. Lloyd suggested that the ministers agree to "leave the present [Berlin] situation as it is" and try to "improve it ... from both points of view." Lloyd's proposal followed a speech in which Gromyko denounced West

Berlin as a center of anti-Soviet propaganda and espionage, largely carried out by agents of the U.S., Britain and France. Gromyko's charges were rebutted by Herter, Lloyd and Couve de Murville June 1 in a restricted meeting at which they attacked the extensive espionage and subversion network of the East German Communist Party's West Bureau.

Gromyko said at an open conference session June 2 that the USSR had not considered Western troops to be in Berlin "in some unlawful way." He said it was "incorrect" to say that the USSR sought the establishment of a free city of West Berlin in violation of the 1944-5 Allied agreements concerning Berlin. But he reiterated that the postwar Allied agreements were "outdated" and "artificial" and should be ended to avert "poisoning the relations" of the Big 4 powers. He renewed Soviet suggestions that the Western powers either accept Soviet troops in West Berlin or let Western forces in Berlin be replaced by a garrison of neutral troops.

At a secret meeting June 3, the Western ministers informed Gromyko that the U.S., Britain and France were willing to accept a freeze on the strength of their current 11,000-man garrison in West Berlin in exchange for Soviet assurances of free Western access to Berlin from West Germany. Herter, Lloyd and Couve de Murville were said to be seeking access guarantees for West German civilian and Allied military traffic to forestall any Soviet attempt to reimpose a Berlin blockade. Gromyko reiterated that the USSR was ready to guarantee access to West Berlin on condition that the city's military occupation regime be liquidated.

The West German advisory delegation June 1 expressed opposition to any temporary Berlin settlement not specifically linked to a German reunification accord. Spokesmen also warned "against a solution of the Berlin problem limited only to [the convening of] a summit conference." The West Germans urged preservation of "the *status quo* on Berlin until there is an agreement on Germany's reunification."

Pres. Eisenhower told the USSR June 3 that U.S. participation in an East-West summit meeting on Germany was dependent on the USSR's formal acceptance of Western rights in Berlin until the achievement of Germany's reunification. Speaking at his news conference in Washington, the President denied that he was setting a new "condition" for a summit meeting. But he made clear that he expected the USSR to withdraw its Berlin ultimatum in order to avoid going to a summit conference "in response to ... a threat." (The 6-month Soviet deadline for the dissolution of the 4-power occupation status of Berlin, set by the USSR Nov. 27, 1958, had expired May 27.)

The foreign ministers' conference was reported to be near a breakdown June 10 following each side's rejection of the other's proposals for a Berlin settlement. The East-West stalemate occurred over these conflicting proposals discussed in private and plenary meetings June 4-10 by Herter, Lloyd, Couve de Murville and Gromyko:

Western plan —Presented to Gromyko by the 3 Western ministers at a restricted meeting June 8, a general statement of Western views laid down these 5 requirements for a Berlin settlement: (1) Western retention of all occupation rights granted by the 4-power Berlin Occupation Statute of 1945; (2) an East-West declaration of readiness to reduce Berlin tension by formation of a commission of the Big 4 powers and East and West Berlin governments to control subversion and propaganda in Berlin; (3) a freeze of the Western powers' current Berlin garrison strengths; (4) Big 4 guarantees of freedom of military and civilian movement between West Berlin and West Germany, with a commission of Big 4 and East and West Berlin representatives to oversee rights of access; (5) maintenance of these conditions until the reunification of Germany.

Soviet plan —Presented by Gromyko June 10 as an offer to extend certain Western rights in Berlin for one year, the USSR proposed a Berlin settlement on these terms: (1) The Western powers would "temporarily" retain "certain" occupation rights in West Berlin for a one-year period; (2) an all-German commission would be composed of East German and West German representatives on a parity basis to promote contact between East and West Germany and work out measures for German reunification and a German peace treaty; (3) the all-German commission or "any other body" deemed suitable for the task would have a "definite" one-year time limit on its work; (4) if Western Berlin garrisons were reduced to "symbolic contingents," West Berlin propaganda and spy activities were suppressed and nuclear and missile weapons were barred from West Berlin, the USSR would be "prepared to agree" to guarantee Western access to the city.

The Western plan was rejected by Gromyko June 9 in an address in which he demanded that the West dismantle its occupation regime in West Berlin. Gromyko's position was backed by a statement of Soviet Premier Khrushchev, published June 8 by *Pravda,* in which Khrushchev declared that "the Soviet Union will not under any kind of pressure make an agreement which would perpetuate the occupation regime in West Berlin."

The Soviet proposals for a conditional one-year extension of Western rights in Berlin were rejected as "wholly unacceptable" by Herter June 10. Herter, who said that the Soviet plan aimed at further reduction of the 11,000-man "token" Western garrison in Berlin, warned that the U.S. would "never negotiate under deadlines, threats or duress." The British delegation termed the Soviet plan an attempt to replace the expired 6-month Soviet deadline on Berlin with a new "monstrous and impudent" ultimatum.

The Western powers warned the USSR June 11 that the Geneva conference would end in failure, without an agreement on proposed East-West summit meetings, unless the Soviet government withdrew what the Western representatives regarded as the Soviet "ultimatum" of June 10, the offer of a one-year extension of Western rights in Berlin. At a private meeting with Gromyko, Herter was said to have conveyed a joint Western warning that results of the next few sessions would "determine the fate of the conference." A joint Western statement issued after the Herter-Gromyko meeting asserted that the conference had gone "on a day-to-day basis."

In a major address at a plenary conference session, Gromyko denied June 12 that the USSR's June 10 offer of a one-year extension of Western rights in Berlin was intended as "a menace" or a *"diktat"* aimed against the current Western position in Berlin. Gromyko emphasized, however, that "the Soviet government is against the perpetuation of the occupation regime ... in West Berlin." "We cannot sign any document which in one way or another would facilitate a perpetuation of the occupation regime in West Berlin," he said, "and we believe that there should be no unclear points in the

Soviet government's position," particularly in the light of recent statements by Soviet Premier Khrushchev.

Gromyko declared that the Soviet "attitude" toward Berlin was based on the fact that "the present order in Western Berlin and the occupation regime represent a great danger to the overall situation in Germany and Europe, since Western Berlin has ... become a dangerous breeding ground of friction and conflicts between ... the great powers." Gromyko rebuked the West for its warnings that the Geneva conference's failure would cripple chances for a later East-West summit meeting. He warned that "a summit conference must not be approached from positions of bargaining or any deals." He said a heads-of-government meeting was necessary to hasten "the end of the 'cold war.'"

Gromyko met privately with the Western ministers June 15, after a 2-day recess in which Lloyd returned to London for talks with Prime Min. Harold Macmillan. French spokesmen said that the meeting, at which the Western representatives reiterated their rejection of Russia's June 10 plan for Berlin, had ended in a "total impasse."

East Rejects Western Plan; Conference Recessed

A draft of final Western terms for Berlin was handed to Gromyko June 16 at a private meeting with Herter, Lloyd and Couve de Murville. The draft reportedly did not ask for explicit Soviet acceptance of Western occupation rights in Berlin. But other terms, first outlined in the West's 5-point plan submitted at the conference June 8, were said to require the continued presence of Western troops in Berlin, with or without a formal declaration of Western rights in the city.

Gromyko, who delayed making a formal reply to the draft Western proposal, was said by U.S. delegation spokesman Andrew H. Berding to have "indicated that there was no change whatsoever" in Russia's stand against perpetuating the West's occupation rights in Berlin.

The U.S. delegation June 17 made public a summary of the Western draft. It called for the issuance, at the conclusion of the current Geneva talks, of a 4-power declaration containing these provisions:

- A general statement by the 4 foreign ministers that they (1) wanted a Berlin settlement and (2) recognized that the Berlin problem derived from the division of the city and of Germany and could be settled best by German unification.
- Western forces in Berlin would be armed only with conventional weapons. A reduction of the Western Allied garrison in Berlin (reportedly from 11,000 men to 3,000-4,000) would be considered if developments permitted.
- Pending the reunification of Germany, the 4 powers would recognize certain modifications of current Berlin agreements in line with (1) the USSR's determination to dissolve its Berlin occupation force and (2) the intentions of the Western powers to maintain their Berlin garrisons.
- A guarantee that continued unrestricted access to West Berlin would be exercised by the Western military forces and German civilians for persons, goods and communications.
- Western acceptance of East German supervision of traffic to West Berlin with the understanding that such supervision did not lessen Soviet obligations under this and other Berlin agreements.
- The reaffirmation of the right of freedom of movement between East and West Berlin.
- The formation of a 4-power commission to settle all disputes relating to access to West Berlin.
- Measures to suppress subversive and propaganda activities in both East and West Berlin.

The foreign ministers' Geneva conference on Berlin, German unification and European security was recessed June 20 until July 13. Herter, Lloyd, Couve de Murville and Gromyko had reached agreement June 19 on Western proposals for a recess after the USSR rejected the June 16 proposals of the Western powers.

The Soviet rejection, delivered by Gromyko at a restricted conference session June 19, contained a counter-offer to extend to 18 months the Soviet deadline for the liquidation of the Berlin occupation regime. Gromyko, insisting that the Western powers had misunderstood previous Soviet offers to delay action on Berlin, denied that the new plan constituted a renewed "ultimatum" on Berlin. He asserted that the USSR would pose no difficulties about "necessary time limits" if agreement were reached on the "main questions of principle" for a Berlin settlement.

The Soviet proposal stated as a "premise" that "it is impossible to delay a peace settlement with Germany and to preserve the occupation regime in West Berlin *ad infinitum.*" It proposed: (1) the establishment by the East and West German governments "on a parity basis," of an "all-German committee" to "work out concrete measures for the unification of Germany and consider questions pertaining to the preparation and conclusion of a peace treaty with Germany"; (2) a "reduction of the occupation forces of the Western powers in West Berlin to symbolic contingents"; (3) the "termination of subversive activities from West Berlin"; (4) the "non-location in West Berlin of atomic and rocket weapons."

The Western foreign ministers rejected the Soviet plan and proposed a recess until July 15. Gromyko accepted a recess but won agreement to resume July 13.

A formal statement issued June 19 by the U.S., British and French foreign ministers detailed the West's objections to Gromyko's latest (June 19) Berlin proposals. The Western ministers charged that the Soviet plan reserved to the USSR "freedom of unilateral action" on the expiration of the 18-month deadline. "Moreover," the Western statement declared, it clearly was "the Soviet intention that the Western powers ... would acquiesce in the liquidation of their rights in Berlin and the abandonment of their responsibility for maintaining the freedom of the people of Berlin." If no 4-power Berlin accord were reached during the 18-month period, the statement said, "the Western powers would enter into any negotiation at the end of that period without any rights at all so far as Berlin or ... access ... were concerned."

The Soviet and Western foreign ministers met briefly June 20 to approve the recess and prepare a joint communique, which declared their intention "to resume the work of the conference in Geneva." Herter and Gromyko met privately the same day to discuss "the issues of the conference" but reported no change from their "well-known positions." Gromyko, in a statement issued as he left Geneva for Moscow June 21, asserted that the first round of Geneva talks had provided a "good basis for agreement."

Herter told newsmen on his arrival in Washington June 21 that the USSR had "revealed clearly that its true desire is to absorb West Berlin into East Germany and to keep Germany divided until it can be brought under Soviet domination."

Herter met with Pres. Eisenhower at the White House June 22 and, at the President's request, reported on the progress of the Geneva conference in a radio-TV address June 23. Herter told the American people that "no significant progress was made" at Geneva "toward settlement of the problem of the continued division of Germany and of Berlin." He charged that Gromyko had "engaged in a good deal of propaganda and some threats" and had given "no indication of being interested in genuine negotiation." He said that the USSR had "flatly rejected the Western peace plan" and had proposed instead a Soviet plan which "could only have led to the absorption of West Berlin into the Communist empire." He warned that the ultimate aim of the Soviet proposal for a free city of West Berlin was to "free [it] of the protection of Allied forces" and "make it like East Berlin, ... a slave city."

Sparring During Geneva Recess

The Geneva conference recess lasted officially from June 20 to July 13. During and even before that period representatives of both East and West issued statements obviously intended to strengthen their positions when talks resumed.

Pres. Eisenhower told newsmen June 17 that prospects for an early East-West summit meeting appeared "no brighter" due to the USSR's "unreadiness" to negotiate realistically on the Berlin and German questions. He derided as "a step backward in diplomacy" the idea that summit meetings were necessary to solve the world's problems. He noted that foreign ministers and ambassadors provided the "mechanism through which these agreements are supposed to be obtained."

Khrushchev urged Western leaders June 19 to cooperate in a fresh attempt to reach accord in the Geneva talks and hold a summit meeting. In what was generally regarded as a conciliatory address, Khrushchev nevertheless warned: "It would be naive to think that the Soviet Union would agree at the foreign ministers' conference or at [the summit] to sign any document perpetuating the occupation regime in West Berlin and leaving Germany without a peace settlement for an indefinite time." The USSR was "not ready to pay any price" to get a summit meeting.

Khrushchev asserted that the USSR was "ready to guarantee by all possible ways and means that no one shall interfere in the life of the free city of West Berlin." "Taking into account that they [the Western powers] are not ready now to abolish ... the occupation regime in West Berlin," Khrushchev said, the USSR agreed "to the continuation, for a definite period, of the 3-power occupation rights in West Berlin." "Only someone who does not want to achieve agreement could call our proposal an ultimatum," he declared. Khrushchev asserted, however, that a time limit for a Berlin accord, while not a "basic" issue, was necessary to prevent Chancellor Adenauer from "frustrating all peaceful accommodation with Germany and the country's unification." He reiterated that if "reactionary quarters preclude the conclusion of a peace treaty with the 2 Germanys, there will be nothing else to do but sign a peace treaty" with East Germany. Khrushchev warned that a separate treaty would give East Germany "all ... sovereign rights" and would entitle it to armed support by the Warsaw Pact states against any Western effort "to restore the occupation regime by force."

In a statement issued June 28, Soviet Foreign Min. Gromyko declared that the recessed Geneva talks had forced the Western powers to give *"de facto* recognition" to the East German government. He said that the U.S. had been forced to concede that the West German government "does not and cannot represent all of the German people." He expressed hope that the West would use the recess to "evaluate more soberly the Soviet proposals" and reconsider its intention to maintain West Berlin as "a cancer in the body of Germany."

Eisenhower said at his July 1 news conference that he failed to understand "the reason for his [Gromyko's] conclusions" that the Geneva conference had produced progress toward an East-West summit meeting. He reiterated his objection to summit talks without "some kind of promise" of success at a summit meeting.

British Foreign Secy. Lloyd told Parliament June 24 that the Geneva talks had forced the USSR's leaders to declare "their willingness to West Berliners' remaining free to choose their own way of life." He reiterated British hopes that "our resumed [Geneva] conference will lead to a meeting of heads of governments."

Soviet Deputy Premier Frol R. Kozlov, in the U.S. for a 13-day tour and the opening of a Soviet science exhibition, asserted in Washington July 2 that the USSR would accept a Berlin settlement only on the basis of its proposals for the creation of a free city of West Berlin. He threatened that "force will be met with force if war is unleashed" over the Berlin dispute. In a nationally televised address at a joint Washington luncheon of the National Press Club and Overseas Writers, Kozlov warned that Russia would sign a separate peace treaty with East Germany if the West refused to accept one of 2 alternative Soviet plans: (1) an independent West Berlin or (2) an 18-month interim status for the city to let an all-German committee plan German reunification. Kozlov rejected Western assertions that the Soviets' Berlin proposals were an "ultimatum" advanced with "aggressive intentions."

W. Averell Harriman, former New York governor and wartime U.S. ambassador to the USSR, had met with Soviet Premier Khrushchev in Moscow June 23 and 24 and was told in 3 lengthy interviews that the USSR would not retreat from its stated intentions to oust the Western Allies from Berlin. Harriman's account portrayed Khrushchev as "blunt and threatening" in his assessment of the Berlin situation. Harriman quoted Khrushchev as warning the West that "if you send in tanks [to Berlin] they will burn, and make no mistake about it." "If you want war," Khrushchev warned, "you can have it, but remember, it will be your war. Our rockets will fly automatically."

Harriman conceded that it appeared that "some of his [Khrushchev's] bellicose threats were mere acting," but, he warned, it "would be a grave mistake to believe it is all bluff." Khrushchev, he said, appeared to be "profoundly ignorant" of conditions outside the USSR, particularly in the U.S., and "might well overplay his hand." Khrushchev, who was accompanied in the interview by Foreign Min. Gromyko, told Harriman that Gromyko could say nothing but "what we tell him to" and had been instructed to tell the West that "these days of the [Berlin] occupation are gone forever."

In a CBS-TV interview July 12, Harriman expressed the view that the current Berlin situation was largely a diversion from the key issue of nuclear weapons control. He asserted that a possible solution of the German problem might be found if the West gave "the East German regime ... *de facto* acceptance, not recognition in the diplomatic sense," to encourage "a development in East Germany along the lines of Poland."

Eisenhower rebuked Khrushchev July 8 for indulging in "ultimatums" and "threats" of war over the Berlin situation. Commenting on Harriman's account of his interview with Khrushchev, the President asserted that such statements by "responsible people" were "not the way to reach peaceful solutions." Eisenhower warned that American determination to uphold Western rights in Berlin was like an "unmovable stone." However, the President said, "we are ready to talk ... because we ... want to find ... a solution that will not keep the whole world on edge."

Eisenhower said at a news conference July 15 that State Secy. Herter had been given "the authority to make any kind of a plan" for East-West summit talks, "subject, of course, to [the President's] final approval." Eisenhower made clear, however, that his participation in a summit meeting would remain contingent on (1) reasonable progress at the Geneva foreign ministers' conference and (2) unqualified Soviet recognition of Western occupation rights in Berlin.

Geneva Talks Reconvened

The Geneva conference of Big 4 foreign ministers was reconvened July 13 after a 3-week recess. London dispatches said July 10 that the British embassy in Moscow had been given strong assurances that Western occupation rights in Berlin would be retained intact during the period of the USSR's proposed interim agreement on West Berlin.

In a statement issued when he arrived in Geneva July 12, Herter had expressed the view that "our earlier discussion here had revealed possible elements of agreement concerning specific arrangements for Berlin." He conceded, however, that "I do not come here with high hopes." Herter's view that a limited

Berlin agreement might be achieved was echoed in Geneva statements by Lloyd and Couve de Murville the same day.

Herter in his opening statement July 13 expressed belief that "a satisfactory long-range solution to the German and Berlin problems can be found if we realistically face the dangers created by the artificial division of this great country and ... eliminate them by ... reunification within the framework of a general agreement on [European] security."

Statements issued July 14 by the U.S. and British delegations rejected as unsatisfactory Gromyko's assurances that Western rights in Berlin would be safeguarded by Soviet proposals for an interim Berlin agreement. Andrew H. Berding, U.S. Assistant State Secretary for public affairs, told newsmen that the West would require "a much more categorical statement" of its Berlin rights and "in writing."

An initial disagreement over the status of the East German representatives hardened into deadlock July 15 after Gromyko announced that the USSR considered a Berlin settlement conditional on Western agreement to Soviet proposals for an all-German committee to study reunification and a German peace treaty. Gromyko's demand was considered an effort to reopen the German question as a whole, abandoned for detailed consideration of Berlin when the issue proved intractible in conference discussion. Couve de Murville charged that Gromyko's tactic had "placed the whole negotiation in jeopardy." "We are in complete confusion" and "neither side knows what the other is talking about," he said.

Gromyko agreed July 16 to resume secret conference sessions from which the East and West German advisory delegations would be barred. Speaking at a plenary meeting of the Big 4 and German delegates, Gromyko asserted that the conference had reached the stage for specific negotiation of a Berlin settlement and that the USSR was willing to proceed with bargaining either publicly or privately. He did not revive demands for East German inclusion in the private conference sessions.

Analyzing the Western and Soviet proposals made thus far for a Berlin settlement, Herter indicated July 16, for the first time, that the West would agree to the stationing of UN personnel in Berlin to assure compliance with any agreement barring propaganda and subversive activities in the Western and Soviet sectors of the city. Herter reiterated Western offers to control West Berlin propaganda and maintain Western garrisons in Berlin at their current "token" levels, but he made clear that the West would insist on (1) guaranteed access to the city and (2) a Berlin settlement lasting until the reunification of East and West Germany.

Gromyko met privately with the Western ministers July 17 to press Soviet demands for the formation of an all-German committee to study German reunification. Western conference sources reported that Gromyko had insisted on the establishment of the committee as a precondition for fruitful talks on the Berlin question. Western delegates reportedly conceded that the problems of Berlin and German unity were linked, but they rejected Gromyko's demands on these grounds: (1) the all-German committee proposed by the USSR would grant East Germany parity with West Germany and would imply recognition of East Germany, (2) the USSR had offered no guarantees of Western rights in Berlin if no agreement were produced by the committee in its 18-month working period.

Herter proposed July 20 that the ministers' conference be transformed into a permanent body to continue the search for a settlement of "the German problem as a whole."

Gromyko in his "preliminary" reply rejected the Herter proposal the same day and indicated that the USSR would accept an interim agreement only if it provided for direct unity talks between "the 2 Germanies" on a basis of equality. Gromyko, warned by Herter July 20 that the USSR's position on the Berlin question threatened a "very rapid termination" of the conference, again refused in the plenary session and in a private session July 21 to say whether the USSR would insist on the acceptance of its all-German committee proposal as a prerequisite to an agreement on Berlin.

Gromyko, in an address at a plenary conference session July 22, said, however, that the USSR would agree to the "simultaneous" discussion of an interim Berlin accord and of the formation of the all-German committee on unification. He also declared formally that "no unilateral action will be taken [in Berlin] by the Soviet Union" while "an interim agreement on West Berlin is in force" or further negotiations on Berlin were held by the "participants in this Geneva conference." Gromyko attacked the West's plan for permanent Big-4 discussion of German unity as a renewed effort by "foreign powers to foist their decisions upon the Germans" from "atop a sort of pyramid."

Gromyko's assurances on the Berlin negotiations and Western rights in the city during the talks were rejected as inadequate July 22 by the 3 Western ministers.

East-West Comment on Berlin

Comment by East and West spokesmen continued outside the framework of the Geneva Big 4 talks. Pres. Eisenhower indicated to Washington newsmen at an off-the-record dinner July 21 that he had virtually abandoned hope for a summit meeting with Premier Khrushchev. Eisenhower reportedly said he was certain that Soviet leaders did not want war but that he feared a Soviet miscalculation in Berlin could result in armed conflict. The possibility of war over Berlin had forced him to consider in advance whether the U.S. and its allies would use nuclear weapons to defend their position in the city.

Eisenhower also reportedly was convinced that Khrushchev wanted a summit conference only on terms that would permit the eventual absorption of West Berlin by the Soviet bloc and that would prevent German unification. The West would accept summit talks only if guaranteed continued Western access to and occupation rights in Berlin and German unity through free elections, Eisenhower said.

Eisenhower reiterated at his regular news conference July 22 that "the real measure of ... probability" of a summit meeting was progress at the Geneva foreign ministerial talks. The Western ministers would decide whether to accept Soviet calls for a summit meeting, Eisenhower indicated.

A communique issued in Warsaw July 22 by Khrushchev, Polish Premier Jozef Cyrankiewicz and Polish United Workers' (Communist) Party First Secy. Wladyslaw Gomulka pledged that Poland and the USSR would support East German attempts to "liquidate the abnormal situation in West Berlin" if the Geneva conference produced no settlement. The joint declaration said that the West had not advanced acceptable terms for a Berlin accord and German peace treaty. It warned that failure of the Geneva talks would "lead to a new aggravation of the situation, pregnant with danger to the cause of peace in Europe."

Khrushchev and the Polish leaders made clear in their statement that their governments could "no longer agree to ... the continuation of the occupation regime in West Berlin for an indefinite time." They warned that if the Western powers torpedoed efforts to conclude a peace treaty "with the 2 existing German states," the USSR and Poland would "sign a peace treaty" with the East German government that would "also be signed by other states."

Vice Pres. Richard M. Nixon, in Moscow to open a U.S. trade exhibit, met with Khrushchev July 25 at a private dinner in the residence of U.S. Amb.-to-USSR Llewellyn E. Thompson Jr. Accompanied by Mrs. Nixon and the President's brother, Dr. Milton Eisenhower, Nixon met at Khrushchev's villa outside Moscow with Khrushchev and his wife and First Deputy Premiers Kozlov and Mikoyan and their wives. Khrushchev and Nixon reviewed U.S.-Soviet relations for 5½ hours in what U.S. spokesmen termed "a full and complete discussion ... of major issues."

Nixon cabled reports on the talks to Eisenhower and Herter July 26. He told newsmen in Leningrad the next day that he had made "no substantial progress" with Khrushchev on resolving U.S.-Soviet differences over Berlin. Khrushchev was said to have opposed Western terms for a Berlin settlement and German unification as efforts to change the "Socialist borders" of Eastern Europe. But Nixon did not rule out hope that Khrushchev would change the Soviet position at Geneva.

East & West Exchange Drafts, Recess Talks

Western and Soviet foreign ministers exchanged new draft documents in Geneva July 28. The drafts outlined their positions on an interim Berlin settlement and steps toward the reunification of Germany. An agreement to set forth the conflicting Western and Soviet views in writing had been reached July 27 at a private meeting of the Big 4 ministers at which Gromyko reportedly presented Soviet demands that Western garrisons in Berlin be cut to a maximum of 3,500 men.

The Western draft proposal submitted July 28 called for a 5-year interim agreement on Berlin that would safeguard Western occupation rights in the city without requiring an explicit statement or public Soviet acceptance of those rights. The Western plan, an elaboration of Berlin proposals made at the conference June 16, would provide for (1) a UN presence in Berlin to supervise the elimination of propaganda and subversion in the East and West sectors of the city; (2) the maintenance of the current 11,000-man Western garrison in West Berlin without missiles or nuclear weapons; (3) "free and unrestricted access" to West Berlin for Western civil and military traffic under East German control; (4) a Big 4 commission to settle disputes arising under the Berlin agreement. The Soviet draft was known to have demanded a reduction of the Allied Berlin garrison to 3,000-4,000 men, a level the West previously had rejected.

Herter, Lloyd, Couve de Murville and Gromyko had resumed private talks on a Berlin settlement July 24 after Gromyko had dropped Soviet demands for prior agreement on an all-German committee on German reunification. U.S. delegation spokesmen had warned July 23 that "so long as this condition hangs over our heads, the utility even of talks on Berlin must remain in question."

Some evidence of a difference in assessment between the British and other Western delegations in Geneva was indicated July 26 when Lloyd was reported to have told the other Western foreign ministers that enough progress had been made in Geneva to draft a "standstill" Berlin agreement and to convene a summit meeting. Prime Min. Macmillan had told the British Parliament July 23 that he opposed Western imposition of a time limit on the Geneva negotiations and had expressed renewed hopes that the talks would lead to a summit meeting. U.S. delegation spokesmen made clear July 25 that the U.S. opposed summoning a summit conference on the basis of the Geneva talks' limited progress.

The Big 4 foreign ministers recessed their conference indefinitely Aug. 5 after failing to reach agreement on terms for settling the Berlin and German problems. Agreement on the recess was reached by Herter and Gromyko at a private meeting July 29 after both sides July 28 had exchanged drafts of their proposals of minimal conditions for settling the

German problem. Herter had pressed for the recess and reportedly had warned Gromyko that he would leave Geneva whether or not the USSR agreed to suspend the talks.

In final addresses, Lloyd and Gromyko stressed that the forthcoming Eisenhower-Khrushchev talks could prepare the way for a German settlement. Couve de Murville reiterated the Western view that "the German people must have the last word" on any agreement to unify Germany.

A committee of experts set up by the 4 foreign ministers began July 30 a study of 6 points deemed necessary for an East-West accord but adjourned July 31 after failing to agree on a definition of nuclear and missile weapons to be banned from Berlin. The 6 points were discussed by the foreign ministers at a private meeting July 31 without resolving the differences.

Herter met with Gromyko privately Aug. 1 in an unsuccessful attempt to win Soviet assurances of Allied rights in West Berlin without the specific 5-year guarantee previously demanded by the West. A similar effort, also unsuccessful, was made by Lloyd at a private meeting with Gromyko Aug. 3. A private meeting of all 4 ministers Aug. 4 failed to bring progress on the Berlin question, but newsmen reported that it had produced tentative agreement to permit a resumption of disarmament negotiations by a revised UN Disarmament Commission. A last private session of the Geneva conference was held Aug. 5 to prepare the final communique.

EISENHOWER-KHRUSHCHEV VISITS

Eisenhower Announces Fall Visits

Pres. Eisenhower announced Aug. 3 that he and Premier Khrushchev would exchange visits in the fall. The President emphasized at a specially-summoned Washington news conference that the visits had "no direct connection with any ... later summit meeting." Eisenhower did disclose, however, that he planned to visit Europe in August—prior to the Khrushchev exchange—for talks with Prime Min. Macmillan, Pres. de Gaulle and Chancellor Adenauer on "problems of mutual interest and the exchange of visits."

Khrushchev pledged Aug. 5 that there would be "no sabre-rattling" during his trip to the U.S. At an extraordinary Kremlin press conference, Khrushchev told newsmen that the "principal and most important question" for discussion with Eisenhower would be "liquidating the consequences of the 2d World War." Paramount among these were a German peace treaty and cutting the "Gordian knot" of Berlin. Khrushchev called anew for (1) a peace treaty by the "2 German states" and (2) the transformation of West Berlin into "a free city with guarantees of non-interference in its internal affairs or in its communications with the rest of the world."

A renewed warning that German reunification and the settlement of the Berlin problem were possible only on Soviet terms was transmitted by Khrushchev to Adenauer Aug. 17. The Khrushchev note, published by the Soviet news agency Tass Aug. 27, asserted that the USSR would never accept Adenauer's demands for German "reunification through the efforts of others" and for "the liquidation of the Socialist system" in East Germany. Western proposals for accomplishing these aims by Big 4 agreement were, Khrushchev said, "insolvent." He also warned Adenauer that German unification could be achieved only by West German recognition of the East German government and by negotiations between the 2 German states. Khrushchev again warned that if Adenauer did not follow this road, the USSR would sign the threatened peace treaty with East Germany; he spoke of "thermonuclear weapons [that] would be exploded on the territory of Western Germany" "in case of war," and he urged Bonn not to equip its army with missiles and nuclear weapons.

Prior to his planned trip to the USSR, Eisenhower visited Bonn, London and Paris. In a talk at Wahn airport near Bonn, the President assured West Germans that "the American people stand by your side" in "the determination of the German people to remain strong and free." He pledged American support "in insuring that the loyal free people of free Berlin will ... continue always to enjoy that great privilege."

The President and British Prime Min. Macmillan held a televised conversation from 10 Downing St. Aug. 31. Macmillan said he had visited Moscow in February because he felt that "the Russian ultimatum in November about Berlin" posed "a danger that we might drift into something [war] by mistake." In response to Macmillan's remark that "I always have wanted a summit meeting," Eisenhower said that if Khrushchev "does things that show that he recognizes" the necessity of maintaining peace, "a summit would be profitable."

Eisenhower and Pres. de Gaulle conferred for 2 days in Paris Sept. 2-3. The 2 leaders then announced a full policy accord "on the question of Berlin" and "on a summit conference," which they described as "useful in principle" but which they said "should take place only when there is some possibility of definite accomplishment."

Eisenhower returned to the U.S. Sept. 7 and declared Sept. 10 in a radio-TV report on his talks with Western European leaders, that in his discussion with Khrushchev of possible terms for settling East-West differences, "no principle or fundamental interest will be placed upon any auction block." He particularly stressed his intention of maintaining the Western legal and defensive position in Berlin.

Khrushchev in the U.S.

Khrushchev was welcomed by Eisenhower Sept. 15 as he arrived at Andrews Air Force Base near Washington for an unprecedented 2-week visit to the U. S. The President and premier met privately at Camp David Sept. 26 with interpreters to discuss the Berlin and German problems. A joint communique issued Sept. 27 said Khrushchev and Eisenhower had agreed to reopen negotiations to seek peaceful settlement of world problems. It disclosed these agreements:

● "All outstanding international questions should be settled not by the application of force but by peaceful means through negotiation."

● Berlin "negotiations would be reopened with a view to achieving a solution which would be in accordance with the interests of all concerned and in the interest of the maintenance of peace."

● Mr. Eisenhower's reciprocal visit to the USSR, originally planned for the fall, would take place "next spring" at a time to be set later.

Berlin Ultimatum Dropped

An announcement of the 2 leaders' agreement to cancel the Soviet ultimatum on Berlin as a prelude to a possible summit meeting was made by Eisenhower Sept. 28 and confirmed by Khrushchev the next day.

Reporting at his press conference on the results of his talks with Khrushchev, Eisenhower said Khrushchev had "stated emphatically that never had he any intention" to apply "duress or compulsion" to the Berlin situation. He asserted that "no one is under any kind of threat" with respect to Berlin. The President said he and Khrushchev had agreed to seek "a [Berlin] solution that will protect the legitimate interests of the Soviets, the East Germans, the West Germans and ... the Western people." "And, over and above this, we agreed ... that these negotiations should not be prolonged indefinitely...."

Eisenhower indicated that he had retreated from his previous insistence that any Berlin settlement must guarantee Allied occupation rights in West Berlin. "I can't guarantee anything of this kind," he said, "for the simple reason [that] I don't know what kind of a solution may finally prove acceptable." In an apparent concession to Soviet views, the President admitted that the Berlin "situation is abnormal." "It was brought about by ... a military truce after the end of the war ..., and it put, strangely, ... a number of free people in a very awkward position."

A clarifying statement issued later Sept. 28 by White House Press Secy. James C. Hagerty said the President "did not mean that the freedom of the people of West Berlin is going to be abandoned or that Allied rights are going to be surrendered by any unilateral action. What he was referring to was that he could not now give in detail the ultimate solution to the Berlin question."

During his press conference the President asserted that his talks with Khrushchev had "removed many of the objections that I have heretofore held" against an East-West summit meeting. A positive decision to go the summit was, he said, "a matter for negotiating and consultation with our allies." Eisenhower described Khrushchev as "a dynamic and arresting personality" and said he had shown willingness to modify past Marxist dogma if experience showed this necessary or justified.

Khrushchev, in a statement issued in Moscow Sept. 29 before his departure for a visit to Communist China, confirmed that "Pres. Eisenhower has given a correct account of the [Berlin] agreement we reached." "We have indeed agreed," he said, "that negotiations on the Berlin question must be resumed; that no time limit should be set for them, but that they must not be delayed indefinitely." He expressed Soviet "confidence that all the parties concerned will strive for the settlement of the Berlin problem without procrastination."

It was reported from Bonn Sept. 29 that, in a personal message, Eisenhower had reassured Chancellor Adenauer that in his talks with Khrushchev he had spoken out in defense of a free West Berlin. The President's message was reported to have backed formal assurances given West German Amb.-to-U.S. Wilhelm Grewe by Deputy State Undersecy. Livingston T. Merchant Sept. 28 that there had been no change in fundamental U.S. policy on Berlin.

West German and Berlin political leaders had expressed fears of a softening of the U.S. position on Berlin, allegedly indicated in Eisenhower's Sept. 28 statement and a Sept. 22 remark by Herter that the U.S. would "have no objections" if the USSR carried out its threat to sign a separate peace treaty with East Germany. The U.S. embassy in Bonn had reassured the West German Foreign Ministry Sept. 25 that Herter's remark made to the UN Correspondents Association in New York, was meant to convey the idea that the U.S. could not prevent the signing of a Soviet-East German peace treaty but that it would "object strenuously" to any effort to abrogate Allied rights in Berlin.

West German press spokesman Felix von Eckardt indicated to newsmen Sept. 30 that Bonn would accept a negotiated change in the status of Berlin. He refused to restate West German opposition to a Berlin accord that would provide for the withdrawal of Western troops from the city.

Berlin & the Summit

British Labor Party leader Hugh Gaitskell told newsmen Sept. 9 that Khrushchev had agreed to discuss a Laborite plan for ending the Berlin crisis at an East-West summit. Khrushchev "might well be prepared" to accept the Laborite formula for ending the crisis, Gaitskell reported. The plan would be a basis for a "temporary agreement" on Berlin. The Laborite plan for Berlin, originally proposed by Aneuran Bevan, Labor's foreign policy spokesman, had been presented at the recent Geneva conference by British Foreign Secy. Selwyn Lloyd but was not accepted by Gromyko. The plan suggested the creation of a mixed commission to negotiate a Berlin settlement under a strict time limit. Western occupation rights in Berlin would be maintained if the commission failed to reach a settlement within the time limit.

Prime Min. Macmillan told the British people Oct. 3 that "everybody is agreed" on a summit meeting and that it was only "a matter of ... the date and the place and the people."

White House Press Secy. James Hagerty denied at a news conference Oct. 4 that a final agreement to hold a summit meeting had been made by Eisenhower with Khrushchev or with any Western leaders.

U.S. State Secy. Herter told newsmen Oct. 6 that he could give no "assurance" that a summit meeting would have more success in dealing with the Berlin dispute than the recent unsuccessful Geneva foreign ministers' conference. Herter conceded that Khrushchev's talks with Eisenhower had lessened "existing tensions" and had "eased the question of any threat in connection with further negotiations" on Berlin. But he made clear that their meeting had not succeeded in removing Soviet determination to sign a separate peace treaty with East Germany and give it control of access to Berlin—actions that still were opposed by the U.S. Herter reiterated that the contradiction between these Soviet policies and the West's determination to maintain troops in Berlin until the unification of Germany remained unresolved by Khrushchev and Eisenhower.

In a cabinet statement said to have been written by Pres. de Gaulle, the French government called Oct. 21 for the postponement of the projected East-West summit conference until the spring of 1960. The French proposal to delay a summit meeting was attributed (a) to de Gaulle's wish to meet Khrushchev and arrange an Algerian settlement before a summit meeting and (b) to French hopes to attend a summit conference after nuclear weapons tests had made France a full nuclear power. Eisenhower indicated Oct. 21 his disappointment at the French attempt to postpone a summit meeting. The British Foreign Office also declared that Britain hoped the conference would take place "rather earlier" than the spring of 1960. A Soviet statement issued by the news agency Tass declared Oct. 23 that "the sooner" a summit conference was held "the better for the cause of peace."

Eisenhower disclosed Oct. 28 that Allied leaders including Pres. de Gaulle had reached a tentative agreement to convene a Western summit meeting in mid-December. He declared that any progress on disarmament at an East-West sumit meeting would entail "some mention" of the problem of Germany.

In a major foreign policy address at a CDU meeting in Baden-Baden, Adenauer had called Oct. 25 for the exclusion of the problems of Berlin and Germany from an East-West summit conference. Adenauer backed a delayed East-West meeting to permit careful Western preparation. He called for an East-West agenda limited to a study of controlled nuclear and conventional disarmament. "If a decisive step forward could be made on this question," he said, "then the German problem could be solved much more easily than at present." Adenauer said West Germany would renounce participation in an East-West meeting to avoid counter-demands for the inclusion of other nations (presumably East Germany).

State Secy. Herter said Nov. 16 that he believed the U.S. and USSR would find a "common language" to settle their differences because the threat of nuclear war had given them "a common interest" in the "will to survive." Herter said there was evidence "the Soviet leadership is reaching a conclusion similar to our own—that unless the course of events is changed and changed soon, both sides face unacceptable risks of general nuclear war, which would approximate mutual suicide." He asserted that "The main task for the negotiations that lie in the months and years ahead" was the creation of "ground rules" so that "the great rivalry between political systems can work itself out without exploding into thermonuclear war." He concluded that "such an explosion has been uncomfortably close"—"lately over Berlin."

A statement distributed by Tass Nov. 18 declared that the Soviet goverment was confident of a summit agreement to "liquidate the remnants of World War II" by the signing of peace treaties with the 2 German governments "or with the one

which desires to sign a treaty." The statement reiterated
Russia's acceptance of the Western thesis that "the rights and
duties possessed by the U.S., Britain and France in Berlin result
from the unconditional surrender ... of Hitlerite Germany." It
denied that the USSR sought to deprive "anyone of these rights
and duties," but it urged "an agreed solution of the [Berlin]
question" by the wartime Big 4. The statement was in reply to
remarks attributed to Chancellor Adenauer during his visit to
Britain.

In notes to the U.S., Britain and France Nov. 11 and to
West Germany Nov. 13, the USSR protested that West
German plans for the construction of a new radio station in
West Berlin would violate "the existing statute on West
Berlin," which was "not part of the state territory" of West
Germany and not subject to West German law. The creation of
the new station, proposed in the West German Bundestag
(lower house) Sept. 30, was rejected Nov. 13 by the Bundesrat
(upper house) on the ground that it violated the exclusive
control of broadcasting by West Germany's *Laender* (states).

In what some observers argued was an effort to reduce
British-West German differences over questions to be discussed
at the proposed East-West summit talks, Adenauer and British
Prime Min. Macmillan conferred Nov. 17-19 in London and at
Chequers, the prime minister's country retreat. These talks were
paralleled by discussions between West German Foreign Min.
Heinrich von Brentano and British Foreign Secy. Selwyn
Lloyd. The West Germans finally conceded Nov. 17 that the
question of West Berlin's political future should be included on
the summit agenda. Adenauer, who had opposed any
negotiation of the West Berlin problem on the ground that it
might weaken the Western position in the city, was said to have
agreed to summit consideration of Berlin on condition that it be
discussed as an integral part of the entire German question.

West German press spokesman Felix von Eckardt
disclosed Dec. 1 that Adenauer had won de Gaulle's promise to
oppose any summit conference attempts to deal with Berlin as
an issue separate from the "whole German problem." In talks in
Paris with de Gaulle Dec. 1-2, Adenauer also won concessions
from de Gaulle on integration within NATO. Adenauer also
reportedly feared that a separate settlement would entail
Western concessions on Berlin without commensurate Soviet

concessions on German reunification. Adenauer and West Berlin Mayor Willy Brandt had said after a Nov. 30 Bonn meeting that "the present 4-power status of Berlin is still the best means of protecting the freedom of West Berlin."

At a 3-day Western summit meeting held in Paris Dec. 19-21, Eisenhower, Macmillan, de Gaulle and Adenauer agreed that an East-West Big 4 summit conference (with Germany excluded) should be held in Paris beginning Apr. 27, 1960.

A Western summit communique issued Dec. 21 reaffirmed the determination of Eisenhower, Macmillan, de Gaulle and Adenauer to accept no diminution of Allied occupation rights in Berlin as part of an East-West agreement on new status for the city. The communique reiterated Western adherence to "principles ... on Berlin" set forth in the U.S.-British-French-West German declaration of Dec. 14, 1958 and the NATO Council statement of Dec. 16, 1958. The Western summit statement apparently nullified an offer of concessions on Berlin made by the West at the Big 4 foreign ministers' May-Aug. Geneva conference on the German question.

The decision to return to earlier and harder terms on Berlin was made at a meeting of the 4 Western leaders Dec. 20 at de Gaulle's presidential estate in Rambouillet. It reportedly marked the success of Adenauer's efforts to prevent Western leaders from entering East-West summit talks committed to the interim concessions on Berlin offered the USSR at the Geneva meetings. The new Western position, opposed at first by Macmillan, was hailed by Adenauer Dec. 20 as "extraordinarily" strengthening the West's negotiating stance on Berlin during East-West Big 4 talks from which he would be excluded.

The Western communique indicated that Eisenhower, de Gaulle and Macmillan were prepared to begin their meetings with Khrushchev without an agreed agenda but hoped to discuss disarmament and East-West relations in addition to the Berlin question. Previous East-West meetings had often been broken off due to deadlock on the agenda question.

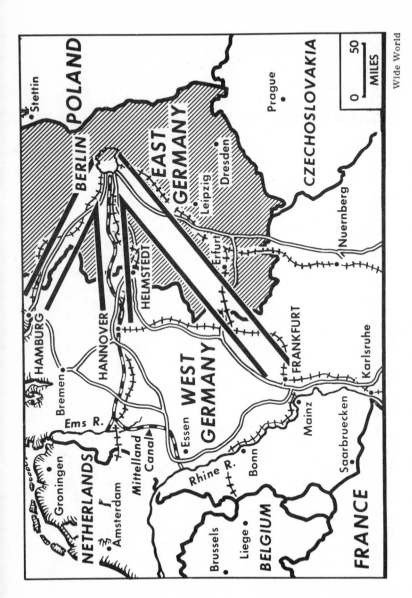

Air corridors and rail access routes to West Berlin.

1960

THE ABORTIVE PARIS SUMMIT CONFERENCE

During 1960 Soviet Communist Party chief Nikita Khrushchev continued to use the threat that World War III could follow a Western refusal to turn Berlin into a free city. He indicated Jan. 28 that the USSR would sign a peace treaty with East Germany unless the free-city proposal were accepted. The Soviets then let it be known that the Western powers could avoid these disasters by agreeing to a summit meeting. This led to additional evidence of division within the Western alliance. West German Chancellor Konrad Adenauer, in particular, opposed any summit conference on Berlin. His attitude was that the only possible result would be concessions that would weaken the Western position in the city. At a Mar. 15 meeting with Pres. Dwight D. Eisenhower, however, Adenauer agreed to a summit meeting. Eisenhower suggested Apr. 27 that an East-West summit meeting had been accepted as a result of Soviet policy; he did so by conceding that it did not seem "feasible" or "possible" that the planned Paris summit conference could settle the Berlin dispute.

The Paris summit meeting collapsed May 16, before it had really begun, with Khrushchev charging that Eisenhower had deliberately tried to wreck the conference by permitting a U-2 spy-plane flight over the USSR. Such flights, however, had taken place for many years, were well known to Soviet authorities and had never before been cited as a reason for disrupting a meeting that the Soviets wanted to take place.

Khrushchev again threatened July 8 to sign a peace treaty with East Germany. Meanwhile, however, various trade agreements seemed to promise some relaxation of the East-West tension.

East-West Disputes Over Berlin Accord

West German Chancellor Konrad Adenauer told Pope John XXIII Jan. 22 that the German nation had a special mission to defend the West against communism. Answering the pope's blessing for "the noble German nation," Adenauer said: "I believe that in these calamitous times we are traversing, God has entrusted a special task to the German people—that of being a dike for the West against the powerful influence that militates against us from the East."

Adenauer had told West Berlin leaders Jan. 11 that interim Berlin concessions offered to the USSR at the 1958 Geneva foreign ministers' conference on Germany were "finished." Alluding to forthcoming summit talks on Germany, Adenauer declared that "nothing could be worse or more mistaken than to begin again where one left off at Geneva. All the Western proposals on Berlin are no longer existent since the USSR rejected them." He reiterated West Germany's contention that "the legal status of Berlin must not be touched upon because that would be ... a capitulation."

In a message to Adenauer Jan. 28, Soviet Premier Khrushchev again raised the possibility that the East bloc would negotiate a separate peace treaty with East Germany if the West did not respond favorably to Soviet proposals for making West Berlin a free city. Khrushchev asserted that, although the question of German unification could be settled only by East and West Germany, Berlin was a matter for the 4 powers occupying the city. He warned that failure to change the current Berlin situation would force the USSR to sign a separate peace with East Germany and to "regulate" the question of Germany's frontiers with Poland and Czechoslovakia. Once Germany's "existing borders" were fixed by treaty, he warned, any effort to alter them would "bring the case to a war."

Communist leaders from 8 Warsaw-Pact states meeting in Moscow Feb. 4 issued a declaration calling on the West to accept their terms for the settlement of the Berlin crisis and to match announced Soviet troop cuts. The declaration, issued in the name of the Warsaw Treaty organization's Political Consultative Committee, warned that all Soviet-bloc states were prepared to sign a separate peace treaty with East Germany unless the West agreed to make West Berlin a free city. *The declaration said:*

● "It is the common concern of all these states that German militarism should never again imperil the security of Germany's neighbors and world peace, and this makes them determined ... for the signing of a peace treaty with Germany.... An abnormal ... situation has emerged when ... a peace treaty is refused by a ... successor state] of the defeated side." The Soviet bloc favored "a peace treaty which in the obtaining conditions can only be signed by both German states."

● "If these efforts toward the conclusion of a peace treaty with both German states do not meet with support and if the solution of this question comes up against attempts at procrastination, the [Warsaw-Pact] states ... will have no alternative but to conclude a peace treaty with the German Democratic Republic, together with the states ready for this, and to solve on this basis the question of West Berlin."

The assertion that Warsaw-Pact members sought only a peaceful resolution of the Berlin and German problems was rejected by U.S. State Department press officer Lincoln White Feb. 5 and by State Secy. Christian A. Herter Feb. 8. White asserted that the USSR's professions of peace were contradicted by its bellicose stand on Germany. "We would be gratified," he said, "by any move of the Soviet bloc which would provide practical confirmation of the frequently repeated [Soviet] denials ... of aggressive intent. We find such disavowals, however, difficult to reconcile with the ... repetition of the Soviet threat to take unilateral action with respect to Germany." Herter said at a Washington news conference Feb. 8 that the Warsaw Treaty declaration indicated a hardening of the Soviet position on Berlin but that, "as far as we know, ... Khrushchev's agreement [with Eisenhower] that there was no time limit in terms of an ultimatum still stands."

Conflicting positions on Berlin and Germany were indicated by official Soviet spokesmen Feb. 19 and 20. A memo given to West German Socialist leaders Erich Ollenhauer and

Herbert Wehner by Soviet Amb.-to-West Germany Andrei A. Smirnov and published Feb. 19 reiterated threats that East Germany would be given control of Berlin access routes unless the West accepted Soviet conditions for a Berlin and German settlement. Yet spokesmen for the Soviet embassy in East Berlin told the West German DPA news agency Feb. 20 that the USSR would accept a Berlin settlement that did not require East German participation. (These spokesmen also dismissed a military travel pass issue as minor; the issue was resolved Mar. 14 when Soviet authorities rescinded the passes.)

At the end of a 12-day tour of France, Khrushchev defended his views at a press conference and farewell broadcast. Both were carried Apr. 2 over the Eurovision TV network, covering Western Europe and temporarily extended to selected stations in Eastern Europe. Khrushchev stressed that the USSR felt the Berlin dispute should be ended by the creation of a free city of West Berlin with "serious [Soviet] guarantees of its status."

After his return to Moscow, Khrushchev Apr. 4 renewed charges that Adenauer was behind efforts to prevent Western-Soviet agreement on Germany and Berlin and was following a "dangerous policy which can bring the world to the brink of war." He declared that "we can guarantee peace in Europe by a solution of the disarmament question and by concluding a peace treaty with both German states."

Khrushchev's contentions Apr. 2 in his farewell Paris press conference that a Soviet-East German peace treaty would void "all the rights of the occupying powers" in Berlin were rejected by the U.S. State Department the same day as of "no substance whatsoever." The U.S. statement noted that "such an action would have no legal basis since the agreements under which the present status of Berlin was established can be terminated only by mutual consent of all the signatories." It said that the U.S. regarded "these agreements as valid and binding upon all the signatories, including the Soviet Union." The U.S. statement added that the fulfillment of Western rights in the city required "the 3 Western powers to remain in Berlin with unhindered communications by surface and air between that city and ... [West] Germany."

Contesting what it termed East German efforts "to implant through ... propaganda means the notion that Berlin is 'part of' or 'on' the territory ... [of the Soviet occupation zone and] of the regime in East Germany," the State Department Mar. 24 had made public the wartime U.S.-British-Soviet agreement setting up separate occupation zones in Germany and designating Berlin as "a separate area to be jointly occupied." The State Department said that the agreement, signed in London Sept. 12, 1944, made it clear that there was "no basis for suggesting that Berlin has somehow been mysteriously merged with or placed on the territory of one of the occupying powers."

Addressing the annual convention of the National Association of Broadcasters in Chicago Apr. 4, State Secy. Herter warned that the West "can hardly move forward confidently in negotiating new arms-control agreements with the Soviet Union if our existing agreements with them about Berlin are ... violated or threatened with violations. There is a clear relation between these 2 crucial issues."

Pre-Summit Stances on Berlin

A warning that a Western surrender to Soviet demands for a Berlin settlement could bring the loss of West Germany as well as Berlin had been voiced by Adenauer Feb. 15. Speaking at a Cologne student meeting, Adenauer reiterated West German demands that the East-West summit conference deal with Berlin as an integral part of the German problem. Adenauer, who had failed in efforts to persuade the West against summit discussion of Berlin, warned that if the West compromised on Berlin, it risked losing the "confidence that keeps both us and the zone [East Germany] upright." Adenauer had told the West German Bundestag Feb. 10 that suggestions by Italian Pres. Giovanni Gronchi that West Berliners be permitted to vote on Soviet proposals for a free city had been rejected by Khrushchev during a Kremlin meeting.

Pres. Eisenhower said at his news conference Feb. 17 that the Western terms on Berlin and Germany presented at the summit would encompass the "common convictions" of the U.S., Britain, France and West Germany. But he refused to comment on the West's current Berlin views.

Ex-State Secy. Dean G. Acheson, in an article written for North American Newspaper Alliance (NANA) on the basis of extensive talks with West German leaders, expressed support Feb. 28 for Bonn's refusal to compromise on Berlin or to accept neutralization as the price of German reunification. He urged Western leaders to seek summit agreement to limited disarmament based on the reduction of military forces between the Atlantic and the Urals.

British Foreign Secy. Selwyn Lloyd told Parliament Feb. 11 that a summit conference settlement on Berlin and Germany was "possible and desirable" but that an accord would have to respect "fundamental" allied and German rights in the city. Lloyd, however, rejected Bonn's claims that West Berlin was an integral part of West Germany.

The U.S., Britain and France refused Feb. 19 to use new travel passes issued to Western military missions at Soviet occupation headquarters in Potsdam, East Germany. The Western powers contended that the wording of the passes demonstrated an attempt by the Soviets to secure implied recognition of East German authority by the Western powers. The Soviet passes, issued Feb. 3, were made valid for travel in the "German Democratic Republic" rather than the "Soviet zone of Germany" and bore notice that they had been registered with the East German Interior Ministry. The U.S. mission suspended all travel between Berlin and Potsdam rather than use the new passes; the British and French missions permitted travel for administrative reasons only. The rejection of the passes was made in notes from the 3 allied military commanders in West Germany to Maj. Gen. Matvei V. Zakharov, Soviet commander in East Germany.

Soviet military missions in the former U.S. and British zones of West Germany were restricted Mar. 11 to headquarters areas in Frankfurt and Buende by order of Gen. Clyde D. Eddleman and Gen. Sir James Cassel, commanders, respectively, of the U.S. and British armies in Germany. The retaliatory restrictions were imposed in the Baden-Baden headquarters area of the former French occupation zone Feb. 24.

The new Soviet travel passes were rescinded Mar. 14. Lt. Gen. G. F. Vorontsov, Soviet Army chief-of-staff in East Germany, informed the Western military missions that the passes had been cancelled in order "not to worsen ... the relations between the great powers, especially prior to the summit conference." The old Berlin military passes, in use since the end of World War II, were restored.

Washington sources reported Feb. 29 that the U.S., Britain and France had agreed to inform Soviet occupation authorities of their intent to resume military transport flights in the air corridors from West Germany to Berlin at altitudes above the 10,000-foot ceiling demanded by the USSR. The Western powers had defied Soviet efforts to impose the ceiling in 1959 but had limited their high-altitude transports (primarily the U.S.' C-130 turboprop) to less than 10,000 feet on Berlin flights. State Department spokesman Lincoln White reaffirmed the West's refusal to accept the flight restrictions Mar. 1.

First Secy. Yuri Beburov of the Soviet embassy in East Berlin warned Mar. 1 that any attempt to send Western planes to Berlin above the 10,000-foot ceiling would be a "a unilateral violation of East German air sovereignty" unless preceded by agreements with the USSR and East Germany.

A delay in the West's reported plan to reassert its right to high-altitude flights to Berlin was disclosed Mar. 9 by Herter. He said Pres. Eisenhower had decided not to order such flights to Berlin because study had shown there was no current "operational necessity" to use the higher altitudes. He said the U.S., Britain and France were in agreement that, "should that operational necessity arise, ... we have the absolute right to fly [to Berlin] at whatever altitudes we see fit."

Adenauer met with Eisenhower at the White House Mar. 15 and won from him a joint pledge that "any future agreement" on Berlin would preserve "the freedom of the people of West Berlin and their right of self-determination." Their joint statement, issued after the meeting, contained, in addition to the Berlin pledge, a reaffirmation of their "efforts to achieve the reunification of Germany in peace and freedom." The statement's reference to a "future" agreement on Berlin made it clear that Adenauer had failed in efforts to prevent summit discussion of Berlin and thus avert the danger that an East-West accord might alter the city's occupation status.

In an address to the National Press Club in Washington, Adenauer called Mar. 16 for a West Berlin plebiscite "before the East-West summit meeting, putting the very simple question to the Berliners whether they want the present [occupation] status to remain or ... to be changed." Adenauer held that West Berliners would overwhelmingly reject any alteration of the city's status and that "the Western powers could go to the summit" backed by "the fact that ... the Berliners absolutely reject that demand of Khrushchev" to change their status. Adenauer reiterated his warning that any concession to Khrushchev's plans for Berlin would bring "a terrible decrease in the prestige of the free peoples all over the world" and "an immense increase in the prestige of the Soviet Russian[s]." Asked what he would do if the USSR closed access to West Berlin or turned control of access over to East Germany, Adenauer declared: "I believe the Western Allies would be strong enough to do away with ... those obstacles. And I don't think ... the Soviet Union would start a war ... because Mr. Khrushchev needs peace."

Adenauer, in a taped interview broadcast Mar. 20 on NBC-TV's "Meet the Press," said Eisenhower had assured him "that the flag of the United States will continue to fly over Berlin."

Adenauer told the German Press Club in Bonn Apr. 12 that he had proposed holding a Berlin plebiscite on rival Western and Soviet plans for the city's future in order to warn Western leaders against any summit agreement altering Berlin's status at the expense of West Germany. Reiterating his "concern that Berlin will finally become the only object of negotiation at the summit conference," Adenauer termed a potential summit agreement on the city "worse for Berlin than the present status." He said a Berlin plebiscite would have permitted Western leaders to tell Khrushchev: "Against our will the Berliners have freely cast their vote. We must respect it."

Adenauer criticized West Berlin "authorities" for their failure to hold the plebiscite before the summit meeting. West Berlin Mayor Willy Brandt had opposed carrying out the plebiscite without the encouragement of the Western occupation powers. Adenauer and Brandt had met in Bonn Apr. 5 and had announced agreement that a plebiscite was up to the city's government.

A bill to authorize the plebiscite was introduced in the West Berlin city parliament Apr. 12, but it did not specify a date for the vote. The city's Senate Apr. 6 had announced that

it would support a plebiscite only if it were "desired by the ...
[Bonn] Government in conjunction with the Western Allies."

Plans for a massive West Berlin "Freedom Rally" May 1
"to make sure that world opinion will be unable to overlook our
appeal for liberty" were announced by Brandt in Bonn Apr. 17.

A U.S. pledge not to permit the people of West Berlin to be
"sold into slavery" at the summit conference was issued Apr. 20
by State Undersecy. C. Douglas Dillon in an address at an
AFL-CIO Conference on World Affairs held in New York Apr.
19-20. The Dillon speech was characterized as a "major
statement of pre-summit policy" by an official State
Department spokesman. In his address, Dillon refuted Soviet
claims that Western rights in Berlin would be voided and the
city made a part of East Germany by unilateral Soviet action
in signing an East German peace treaty. Summarizing U.S.
policy, he said:

"The problem of Germany and Berlin can only be solved
through German reunification. This the Soviets have so far
rejected, fearing to put their rule in East Germany to the test of
a free vote.... Meanwhile, we are willing to consider interim
arrangements to reduce tensions in Berlin.... But we are
determined to maintain our presence in Berlin and to preserve
its ties with the Federal Republic. We will not accept any
arrangement which might become a first step toward the
abandonment of West Berlin or the extinguishing of freedom"
in West Germany.

Pre-Summit Activity

The foreign ministers of 6 Western nations—the U.S.,
Britain, France, West Germany, Italy and Canada—met in
Washington Apr. 12-14 in an attempt to unify the Western
positions on problems to be discussed at the East-West summit
meeting scheduled to open in Paris May 11. It was reported
from Washington Apr. 12 that the U.S., Britain and France
had agreed on this summit agenda: (1) disarmament and A-test
ban; (2) Germany and Berlin; (3) other East-West relations.

Western plans for the creation of a unified Berlin through
free elections were drafted and approved Apr. 13 by U.S. State
Secy. Christian Herter, British Foreign Secy. Selwyn Lloyd,
French Foreign Min. Maurice Couve de Murville and West

German Foreign Min. Heinrich von Brentano. No communique on Berlin was issued, but newsmen reported that agreement had been reached on a plan for the phased reunification of Berlin and then of East and West Germany. Pending Berlin's restoration as the capital of a reunified Germany, its freedom and Western access to the city's Western sector would be guaranteed under this agreement, by the U.S., Britain, France and the USSR as the 4 postwar occupation powers.

An "Open Letter" from the Central Committee of the East German Socialist Unity (Communist) Party was published in the party organ Apr. 17. The Open Letter, addressed to the workers of West Germany, discussed 3 basic policy "alternatives" with the first allegedly leading to war and the 2d to a deepening of Germany's territorial division. The "3rd alternative," leading to "understanding and peace," would require the signing of a peace treaty between both German states; it would "finally liquidate" problems left over from World War II, bar the door to a 3rd world war and effectively exclude "West German militarism."

The Open Letter also proposed a "German Plan of the People," the realization of which could be "decisively furthered" by the scheduled Paris summit conference. As part of this "German Plan," an "interim settlement" of the Berlin problem by the Paris summit conferees was suggested. Proposed by the party's First Secy. Walter Ulbricht and other members of the Central Committee and published in East Berlin's *Neues Deutschland,* the party organ, the "interim settlement" called for (1) guarantees of "all ways of access from East and West" and temporary maintenance of the city's occupation status; (2) the elimination of the use of the city as "a base for sabotage, subversion and other forms of hostile activities" against Eastern countries; (3) a ban on the stationing of nuclear forces in the city; (4) "a gradual reduction of military forces and the step-by-step abolition of the occupation status."

Warnings were renewed by Khrushchev Apr. 25 that the U.S., Britain and France would "lose the right of entry into West Berlin by air, water or land" if the USSR were forced to sign a separate peace treaty with East Germany. Speaking at a Baku rally on the 40th anniversary of the Azerbaijan Communist Party, Khrushchev made this declaration: "The

Soviet government will do its best to convince its [summit] partners of the necessity of signing a peace treaty with Germany and the establishment of a free city in West Berlin"; "if ... the Western powers refuse to sign such a treaty ..., we will go ahead and sign a peace treaty with [East Germany]"; "the Western powers [then] will lose all rights attendant to the capitulation of Germany, including the right to maintainance of an occupation regime in West Berlin."

Khrushchev said certain Western leaders had pledged to defend their rights by force. "I must warn such hotheads," he declared, "that this force will be opposed by force from the other side." Khrushchev stressed that Berlin was an enclave within the territory of East Germany and asserted: "It is quite natural that ... [East Germany] after signing of the peace treaty will carry out all soverign rights on its territory."

Eisenhower Apr. 27 rejected Khrushchev's contentions that the Western powers' occupation rights in West Berlin would be voided if the USSR signed a peace treaty with East Germany. The President said at his press conference that Khrushchev's statement was "just a reiteration of ... the same old story" and that "we are not going to give up the juridical position that we have" in Berlin. He warned that if Khrushchev meant his statement "as an ultimatum ..., then I would have to reply ... [that] I shall never go to any meeting under threat of force, the use of force, or an ultimatum of any kind." He expressed doubt that the statement amounted to a new ultimatum. Eisenhower conceded that it did not seem "feasible or possible" that the Paris summit conference would succeed in settling the Berlin dispute.

A final communique issued May 4 by the ·NATO Council after its May 2-4 meeting in Istanbul, Turkey stated: "The Council reaffirms the view that the solution of the problem of Germany can only be found in reunification on the basis of self-determination. It recalls its [Berlin] declaration of Dec. 16, 1958 and ... expresses its determination to protect the freedom of ... West Berlin."

An estimated 800,000 West Berliners—one out of every 3 of the city's residents—turned out May 1 to hear Mayor Brandt proclaim again the city's determination to remain free of Communist rule. Speaking at what was said to be Berlin's largest rally since World War II, Brandt read these 2 "messages": the first, to "our friends in America and Britain, in France and everywhere," declared that they "can rely on the Berliners"; the 2d, to "those in power beyond the Brandenburg Gate" in East Germany, said that "Berliners know what freedom means" and "are determined to remain masters in our own house." (East Berlin celebrated May Day with a 5-hour military review held within a mile of the West Berlin rally.)

Paris Summit Conference Collapses

The East-West summit conference collapsed at its opening session in Paris May 16 when Soviet Premier Khrushchev refused to begin talks unless Pres. Eisenhower formally apologized for the sending of U.S. aircraft on military intelligence missions across the USSR. Khrushchev acted after a U.S. U-2 high-altitude jet, piloted by ex-U.S. Air Force First Lt. Francis Gary Powers, 30, on behalf of the U.S. CIA, was shot down near Sverdlovsk, USSR May 1 while on a spying mission.

Western leaders and Khrushchev in Paris May 16-17 traded accusations of responsibility for the destruction of the summit conference. 2 major charges and rebuttals were given by Khrushchev in an unusual Paris press conference held May 18 and by Eisenhower in a radio-TV report broadcast to the American people May 25. Chancellor Adenauer also expressed his views. Adenauer had arrived in Paris May 14 for talks with de Gaulle, and he left May 15. In talks with the 3 Western leaders, Adenauer had emphasized West German opposition to unilateral concessions to Soviet demands on Germany and Berlin.

At a tumultuous 2½-hour news conference held in Paris May 18 before his departure for East Berlin, Khrushchev said that the USSR intended to sign "a peace treaty with [East Germany] ... to put an end finally to World War II. In that case the Western powers will be deprived of their occupation rights ... in West Berlin." The "necessary drafts have already been prepared," and they would be signed "when we consider the time to be right," Khrushchev asserted. The USSR intended to do what the U.S. "did with regard to Japan," he added.

The 3 Western heads of state met May 18 with their foreign ministers for a final discussion of the summit meeting's collapse before Eisenhower and British Prime Min. Harold Macmillan left Paris.

The West's position in the summit meeting was supported unanimously by the 15-member NATO Permanent Council in Paris May 19 after French Foreign Min. Couve de Murville, British Foreign Secy. Lloyd and State Secy. Herter presented their report on the conference. A Council communique reaffirmed "complete solidarity" with the Western Big 3 leaders and "paid tribute to ... the calm and dignity they showed."

After leaving Paris following the collapse of the summit conference, Khrushchev flew May 19 to East Berlin, where he pledged to maintain the *status quo* in Berlin and Germany so as to permit negotiation of these problems at a new summit conference. Speaking to a welcoming crowd at East Berlin's Schoenfeld Airport, Khrushchev renewed his charges that the U.S. had wrecked the summit meeting because it had "no proposals that could lead to the solution of present international problems." He was hopeful, however, that a summit conference would be possible in 6 or 8 months, Khrushchev said.

Speaking at an East Berlin rally May 20, Khrushchev promised that "we will not do anything that might aggravate the international situation and bring it back to the worst time of the cold war." He said the USSR would preserve "the existing situation" in Germany and Berlin for a reasonable period until a new summit meeting. Urging East Germans to wait for the situation to "mature," Khrushchev declared that "it is worthwhile to wait a little while longer and try to find by joint efforts of all 4 victorious powers a solution of the ... question of signing a peace treaty with the 2 German states." He made the Soviet pledge of restraint conditional on Western avoidance of "unilateral action" in Berlin.

Eisenhower denounced Khrushchev June 4-5 for his personal attacks on Western leaders and said Khrushchev's abusive remarks had served only to unite the West against Soviet intransigence.

In a televised address to the French people, de Gaulle May 31 reviewed the summit meeting events and outlined proposals to recreate conditions for an East-West accommodation.

Conceding that the American U-2 flight May 1 over the USSR had been "ill-timed," de Gaulle nevertheless argued that "this was not sufficient reason for refusing to open the discussion of the affairs of the world at the summit." France "shall remain an integral part of the Atlantic alliance" but "must acquire a nuclear armament" and "must be sole mistress of her resources and her territory," de Gaulle said. Nevertheless, France would work "to build Western Europe," he asserted. De Gaulle said he foresaw a European entente stretching "from the Atlantic to the Urals."

Adenauer indicated to the West German parliament May 24 that the collapse of the summit conference had vindicated his earlier view that nothing had been gained by submitting the Berlin and German problems to East-West negotiation. Adenauer charged that Khrushchev had arrived in Paris with the "preconceived intention to sabotage the conference" and that there was ample "cause ... to doubt the credibility" of Khrushchev's professed desire for new summit talks in 6 to 8 months.

A June 5 report from Bonn indicated that the West German Social Democratic Party had abandoned its demands for German reunification negotiations with the USSR and had approached Christian Democratic leaders on the formulation of a bipartisan West German foreign policy along lines set down by Adenauer. The vice chairman of the Social Democrats, Herbert Wehner, pledged June 30 that his party would support NATO as the only hope for eventual reunification. West German Foreign Min. Heinrich von Brentano, however, rejected the Social Democrats' demands for a bipartisan West German foreign policy unless the Social Democrats accepted Adenauer's political aims and concepts.

In notes to the U.S., Britain and France July 29, the USSR protested against West German plans to establish a radio network headquarters in West Berlin. The USSR charged that the West German plan was an "open encroachment" on postwar Allied agreements that "Berlin is not a part of West Germany and cannot be governed by West German agencies." The U.S. State Department replied July 29 that Western replies to a similar Soviet protest in Nov. 1959 had held that the Bonn radio project was not "incompatible with the special status of Berlin."

The *N.Y. Times* reported July 31 that the 3 Western allies had barred the enforcement in West Berlin of a West German law against the distribution of Communist propaganda. The action, reportedly taken to avoid provocation of new Soviet pressure in Berlin, made clear continued Western Big 3 refusal to recognize a West German Constitutional Court ruling that West Berlin was an integral part of West Germany and subject to its laws.

Khrushchev visited Austria June 30-July 8. In a farewell TV address to the Austrian people July 7 and at a final Vienna news conference July 8, Khrushchev said that the USSR would consider signing a peace treaty with East Germany if West German leaders carried out plans for "a meeting of the German Bundestag in West Berlin next September." (The West German parliament held one session in West Berlin each September to emphasize the city's ties with West Germany). Khrushchev warned that he would discuss with East German leaders "whether it would be possible that we also sign a peace treaty ... at the same time in September." The West German Bundestag members might then have to obtain East German visas to return to Bonn, Khrushchev declared. (West Berlin Mayor Willy Brandt charged July 20 that Adenauer was considering the cancellation of the West German parliament's annual Berlin session. Bonn spokesman Felix von Eckardt denied the allegation and accused Brandt of using the Berlin problem for political advantage.)

Khrushchev told British Prime Min. Macmillan Aug. 5 that he would be willing to attend a new East-West summit meeting on the problems of Germany, Berlin and disarmament after the Nov. 1960 U.S. Presidential election. In reply to a letter sent by Macmillan July 19, Khrushchev warned that the USSR would (1) retaliate against further Western spy flights and (2) sign a peace treaty with East Germany to remove "the prime factor that produces the cold war ..., the German question." Khrushchev's letter listed many allegedly hostile acts against the USSR: Western support of Adenauer's policy of German "chauvinism," the Western violation of the Potsdam treaty "obligation to prevent the rearmament and remilitarization of Germany," and the West's military encirclement of the USSR. The message warned against "dangerous accidents" that might "trigger off a 3d world war."

An East German-West German trade agreement signed in Berlin Aug. 16 contained assurances of continued freedom of traffic between West Berlin and West Germany. The trade pact, the first long-term agreement to be signed by the 2 German governments, specifically provided for the cessation of all West German trade with and deliveries to East Germany if Communist authorities interfered in any way with traffic on the *autobahn* system linking the city with West Germany. Other provisions of the agreement, which replaced all earlier trade accords between the 2 states and was made self-renewing: an annual exchange of $130 million worth of coal, steel and heavy machinery; unrestricted trade in food, chemicals, textiles, instruments and leather goods.

New East-West Disputes over Berlin

In protest against scheduled meetings in Berlin of POW (prisoner-of-war) and expellees' associations from areas of Germany under Polish administration, the East German government limited travel from West Germany to Berlin Aug. 31-Sept. 4. The travel curbs, announced Aug. 30, barred all West Germans without East German travel permits from air and road travel to Berlin and barred all Germans not Berlin residents from entering East Berlin (normally open to all Berliners, East and West Germans and foreigners). East Germany warned the Western Allies against permitting their military aircraft to be used to bring "militarists" to the "agitation meetings in West Berlin."

The travel regulations were enforced Aug. 31 at checkpoints on the access routes to Berlin through East Germany and on the border between East and West Berlin. About 1,000 West Germans were turned back on the highways and rail lines to West Berlin, but 685 of them flew to Berlin at the city's expense to take part in the veterans' meetings Sept. 2 and the refugees' Homeland Day rally Sept. 3. At least 12 West Germans were arrested in East Berlin before the travel curbs were lifted Sept. 4.

A Western protest against the travel curbs, attacking them as "a flagrant violation of the right of free circulation in Berlin," was transmitted Aug. 31 to Maj. Gen. Nikolai F. Zakharov, Soviet commandant in Berlin, by Maj. Gens. Ralph

Osborne, Rohan Delacombe and Jean Lacomme, respectively the U.S., British and French commandants in Berlin.

West Berlin Mayor Brandt called Sept. 4 for a "moral boycott" of the East German regime if it again limited access to Berlin from West Germany. Brandt suggested "certain economic measures" to be taken against further East German curbs. He said West German Economy Min. Ludwig Erhard would visit Berlin to plan joint action to defend the city against East German encroachment.

23 West German barges bound for Berlin were detained at the East German checkpoint in Schnackenburg on the Elbe River Sept. 5 because they were alleged to be overloaded.

An East German decree made public Sept. 8 by the ADN news agency imposed permanent restrictions on entry into East Berlin by West German citizens. West Germans were told they would have to get special passes for East Berlin from the "[East] German People's Police." The restrictions were not applied to Western military personnel, non-Germans or residents of West Berlin. The decree was signed by East German Interior Min. Karl Maron.

A new Allied protest delivered to Zakharov Sept. 9 denounced the restriction as a violation of the 4-power agreements on Berlin and warned that they could "endanger peace" in the city. In his reply to the Western protests, Zakharov said Sept. 13 that a Soviet-East German treaty of Sept. 20, 1955 had given East Germany "full legal sovereignty over territory under its control." Zakharov said that the treaty, which reaffirmed Soviet control over Western military traffic to Berlin, had given East Germany sovereignty over "all questions connected with German travel on [East German] ... territory" to Berlin.

East German People's Police were reported Sept. 9 to be issuing the special permits to all West Germans applying for them.

West German Economy Min. Erhard met with Mayor Brandt in West Berlin Sept. 10 and called on West German businessmen to begin a voluntary boycott of East Germany by refusing to apply for the travel permits. West German industrial leaders met with Erhard in Bonn and promised to observe the boycott. The West German cabinet said Sept. 14 that it would act to "prevent" West Germans from attending the semi-annual Leipzig Fair, East Germany's major industrial exhibition.

Allied officials in Berlin announced Sept. 11 that they would not issue special travel documents needed by East Germans travelling to countries that did not recognize East Germany or its passports. They said the curb would be imposed on East German Communists but not on ordinary East German citizens travelling for personal reasons.

The West German government Sept. 30 canceled the 1961 renewal of its trade agreement with East Germany and warned that all West German trade with East Germany would be suspended by Jan. 1, 1961 unless the East German government ended its restrictions on West German access to Berlin. Bonn press spokesman Felix von Eckardt told newsmen Sept. 30 that the trade accord had been nullified in reprisal for East German restrictions on Berlin but that West Germany was willing to negotiate a new 1961 trade pact with East Germany if the restrictions were dropped. Von Eckardt conceded that East German officials had granted passes valid for East Berlin to all West Germans applying for them, but he made it clear that West Germany was challenging East Germany's right to impose any pass system for Berlin travel. Von Eckardt added that any new trade pact with East Germany "must nullify any threat to cut West Berlin from its links with the West." (West German goods worth $256.8 million had been shipped to East Germany during 1959 in return for minor East German exports and the supply of certain essential fuels and foods to West Berlin. The renewed trade agreement had provided for the expansion of inter-German trade to $500 million in 1961.)

Notice of the cancellation of the 1961 trade pact was transmitted to the East German Trade Ministry Sept. 30 by Kurt Leopold, director of West Germany's Interzonal Trade Office in Berlin. The West German decision to cut off trade with East Germany was reached in Bonn Sept. 28-30 at meetings of the Adenauer cabinet and of the U.S., British and French ambassadors. The Bonn government announced Oct. 1 that West Berlin Mayor Brandt and Chairman Erich Ollenhauer and Vice Chairman Herbert Wehner of the Social Democratic Party had taken part in the cabinet discussion of the measure at Adenauer's invitation.

The East German Foreign Trade Ministry confirmed Oct. 12 that it had halted the delivery to West Berlin of certain goods shipped from Poland and other Soviet-bloc countries. It said transit permits for Soviet-bloc shipments to West Berlin via East Germany would be refused for such goods as West Berlin had refused to accept from East Germany. West Berlin officials charged that the cutoff affected Polish deliveries of building materials unobtainable in East Germany. (Shipments to Berlin from Soviet-bloc countries were required to have East German transit permits for the journey across East Germany; shipments to the city from the West were unrestricted and guaranteed by the postwar Big-4 agreements on access to Berlin. West German shipments to Berlin had not been subjected recently to East German interference. West Berlin was said to have a one-year food-and-fuel reserve.)

East German Pres. Walter Ulbricht called Oct. 4 for new negotiations to assure both East Germany's sovereignty and Western access to Berlin. Ulbricht, addressing the East German parliament, proposed 2 sets of negotiations: (1) talks between West Berlin and East Germany on guaranteeing Berlin's right of traffic and trade with "other countries" and East Germany's right to deny West German "militarists" access to the city; (2) talks between East and West Germany on a new inter-German trade pact and assurances for the transport of West German supplies to West Berlin.

In notes delivered Sept. 26 to the U.S., Britain and France, the USSR protested against the use of Allied air corridors to Berlin for the transport to the city of German war veterans and refugees refused land access to the city by East Germany. The Soviet notes asserted that Allied rights in air corridors applied only to supply of the Western military garrisons in Berlin. Letters from the 3 Western military commanders to the Soviet commander in Berlin said Sept. 27 that "the 3 Allied powers do not recognize any restriction on the use of these [Berlin] corridors by their aircraft."

In other apparent efforts to demonstrate control over Berlin, East Germany had (1) barred Archbishop Corrado Bafile, apostolic nuncio in Germany, from entering East Berlin Sept. 17; (2) announced Sept. 21 that diplomats accredited to West Germany would need East German Foreign Ministry permission to cross East Germany or enter East Berlin; (3)

unsuccessfully attempted to bar U.S. Amb.-to-West Germany Walter C. Dowling from entering East Berlin Sept. 22 in an apparent test of East Germany's intention to apply the ruling; (4) barred Berliners' access Oct. 1 to the U.S. sector enclave of Steinstuecken, ¼ mile from Berlin in East German territory, without East German travel permits.

Pres. Eisenhower, in a message marking the 10th anniversary of the gift of the Freedom Bell to West Berlin by the U.S.' Crusade for Freedom movement, asserted Oct. 24 that Americans "stand with Berlin in its great task of maintaining and extending human freedom." U.S. Amb.-to-West Germany Dowling told the West Berlin parliament the same day that the U.S. would "continue to discharge our responsibility until the Berlin question is finally solved within a framework of a reunified Germany."

The 3 Western Allies warned the USSR Oct. 26 that they would hold it "fully responsible" for the consequences of any attempt to restrict the use of the air corridors linking Berlin with West Germany. In identical notes made public Oct. 27, the U.S., Britain and France asserted that their rights in the Berlin air corridors had been delineated in the Nov. 30, 1945 Allied Control Council agreement setting up the air lanes and that there had been "no subsequent change in the status of the 3 air corridors."

The *N.Y. Times* had reported Oct. 23 that Soviet Premier Khrushchev, at a meeting Oct. 18 with West German Amb.-to-USSR Hans Kroll, had given assurances that the USSR would refrain from further political attacks on West Germany if the Western Allies agreed to a summit conference on Berlin and Germany by Apr. 1961.

East German authorities confiscated 2 West Berlin trucks Oct. 29 as they sought to leave Berlin for West Germany with what the East Germans charged was a cargo of radio sets for military use. East and West German officials met in Berlin Oct. 13 to begin talks on the revocation or extension of the 2 nations' trade agreement recently cancelled by West Germany.

New East-West Trade Agreements

An agreement was reached in Berlin Dec. 29 on

implementing the accord governing East German-West German trade during 1961. The Berlin talks, begun Dec. 6 by delegations headed by Kurt Leopold of West Germany and Heinz Behrend of East Germany, produced a compromise in which (1) West Germany agreed to withdraw its demands for public retraction of East German restrictions on West Germans' travel in East Berlin and to end its boycott of East German trade fairs and other commercial activities; (2) East Germany agreed not to enforce the restrictions on West German entry into East Berlin and to permit continued unhampered West German and Allied train and truck traffic to Berlin under annexes to the trade accord.

The 1961 trade accord provided for the exchange of $500 million worth of goods by the 2 countries. West German steel and industrial equipment was to be traded for East German coal and synthetic fuels.

Several developments had preceded the agreement. East Germany had warned Nov. 27 that it would demand separate agreements to cover its trade with West Germany and West Berlin. West Germany had announced Nov. 20 that it was willing to resume talks on implementing the trade pact. East Germany then warned Dec. 19 that agreements ending the 1948 Soviet blockage of Berlin and assuring rail and truck traffic between West Germany and West Berlin were regulated by trade accord annexes and would become inoperable if the trade accord lapsed.

A new 3-year Soviet-West German trade agreement was signed in Bonn Dec. 31 without written guarantees concerning Berlin originally demanded by West Germany as a condition. The trade accord, signed by West German State Secy. Hilger van Scherpenberg and Soviet Amb. Andrei A. Smirnov, was accompanied by a West German letter to Smirnov stating the assumption that the pact's "area of application" was the same as that of the expiring agreement, which included West Berlin. The new pact provided for a 20% increase in the value of Soviet-West German trade, to approximately $200 million annually each way. West German metals, machinery and consumer products were to be traded for Soviet oil, grains, coal and other raw materials.

The Soviet-West German trade negotiations had broken down Dec. 12 over West German insistence that the agreement be drawn to specify that it applied to West Berlin. Soviet negotiators, led by Deputy Foreign Trade Min. Sergei A. Borisov, had rejected the so-called "Berlin clause" on the ground that it was a political issue unconnected with the trade talks. The deadlock was ended Dec. 28, when Smirnov met with Chancellor Adenauer and apparently won his assent to basing the new agreement's territorial provisions on those contained in the old accord.

New Summit Sought

Against a background of a an effort by 5 neutral states to bring about a U.S.-Soviet summit meeting, British Prime Min. Macmillan and Soviet Premier Khrushchev met Sept. 29 at the Soviet UN mission in New York. A statement issued by British spokesmen after their 2½-hour talk said the 2 leaders had discussed "the main problems which should have been tackled at the [Paris] summit meeting, had it taken place." The British statement indicated the 2 leaders had agreed to reconsider their views on disarmament and Berlin and to meet again.

Khrushchev said Oct. 7 that he had been assured by Macmillan that a Big 4 summit conference would be held soon after Pres. Eisenhower's successor took office. Khrushchev declared in an interview with the UN Correspondents' Association that Soviet leaders would "keep our word" to maintain the *status quo* in Berlin and Germany if the promised summit meeting were held. He also said, however, that if there were "no desire" to hold a conference or to reach an agreement on Germany, "a peace treaty will be signed [with East Germany], and that will mean the end of the occupation regime in West Berlin." He told newsmen that he had suggested to Macmillan that, rather than hold a summit meeting on the German problem, "it might be better to convene a conference of all the competent countries ... to sign a [German] peace treaty. But ... Macmillan assured me that a summit conference would take place."

In a pledge to Americans at the end of a 2¼-hour interview on the David Susskind "Open End" TV program Oct. 9, Khrushchev declared "categorically" that "we shall never start a war, so you can sleep in peace." He also declared that the USSR would not "advance any threats of any kind" over Berlin, but "I cannot believe the ... U.S. will start a war because of the signing of a [German] peace treaty."

During a national TV debate held Oct. 13, U.S. presidential candidates Richard M. Nixon and John F. Kennedy agreed that the U.S. would honor its commitments to keep West Berlin free.

Prime Min. Macmillan Oct. 15 urged a renewed effort to hold a 4-power summit meeting. In an address at the annual Conservative Party conference in Scarborough, Macmillan suggested that the summit conference particularly concern itself with Berlin and Germany.

A call for talks among all "interested nations" on a World War II peace treaty with East and West Germany was reiterated by Khrushchev Nov. 12. In a message to an international students' meeting in East Berlin, Khrushchev said: "The Soviet Union demands a solution of the German question that is in accordance with the interests of all nations who have suffered under the aggression of Hitler, that takes into account the interests of the German people and that does no harm to any interested party." Khrushchev said the treaty must be signed by "the 2 German states" and must provide for a free city status for Berlin.

Chancellor Adenauer suggested Nov. 10 that Khrushchev and John F. Kennedy, who had won the 1960 U.S. Presidential election, should meet to "clarify their viewpoints" before further attempts to renew Big 4 summit negotiations. Adenauer, however, made it clear that he hoped Kennedy would take "a major step forward in the sphere of disarmament," rather than reopen negotiations on the German question. (Adenauer told the *Neue Ruhr Zeitung* of Essen Nov. 12 that Khrushchev, "a different man from Stalin," was "a man with whom one can talk.")

In a New Year's Eve speech in East Berlin, East German Pres. Walter Ulbricht called Dec. 31 for "10 years of peace in Germany" as "a kind of 'truce of God'" between the East and West German governments. Ulbricht, who had originally made the suggestion in an address (reported Dec. 17) to the East German Socialist Unity (Communist) Party Central Committee, asserted that "during this period discord may lessen and understanding begin between the 2 German states ... so that finally a start may be made at overcoming the split" in Germany.

In a New Year's Eve radio address to West Germans, Pres. Heinrich Luebke warned that if "we cherish our freedom and our material well-being, we must be ready to assume a greater financial burden to strengthen our defenses and to assist ... young nations."

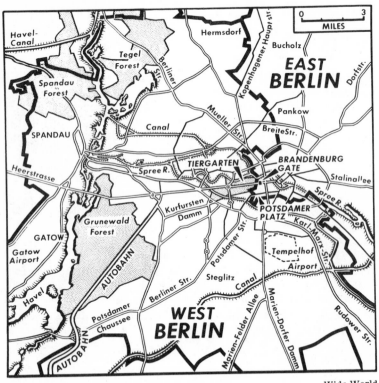

Wide World

Surface access routes to and main roads and railways in West Berlin.

1961

YEAR OF THE WALL

Hardened positions were indicated by both sides during early 1961. Talks between Nikita S. Khrushchev and John F. Kennedy in Vienna June 3-4 did nothing to soften either Eastern or Western positions on Berlin. This was indicated by a grim report made by Pres. Kennedy to the U.S. public June 6 and by an 8-point Soviet memo on Berlin handed to American representatives in Vienna. U.S. Senate majority whip Mike Mansfield proposed June 14, however, that Berlin be transformed into an "internationally guaranteed and protected free city."

Khrushchev added heat to the Berlin issue June 15 with a statement indicating that the USSR would not postpone its peace treaty with East Germany much longer. Kennedy replied with 2 tough statements June 28 and an address July 25; he suggested that "the 'crisis' over Berlin is Soviet-manufactured," and he added: "There is peace in Berlin today.... If war begins, it will have begun in Moscow, not Berlin." The Warsaw Treaty countries announced their support of the Soviet Union Aug. 5 while the Western Allies indicated a unified position on Berlin Aug. 8. Meanwhile the Westward flow of East Germans continued to make inroads on East Germany's technically and professionally educated population.

In mid-August the Communists ended the exodus from the East by building a wall between East and West Berlin. Some analysts suggest that the Berlin Wall—attacked and derided by Western spokesmen as a symbol of the imprisonment in which Communist states allegedly held their citizens—actually helped avert war by blocking the unsupportable drain of manpower from the East. The border closing apparently surprised the Kennedy Administration despite reports printed Aug. 23 that the West had known since 1958 of plans for a Berlin wall.

Despite the Wall, conciliatory proposals still came from Western sources. Canada's Prime Min. John G. Diefenbaker suggested Sept. 11 that Berlin be internationalized under the UN if 4-power agreement could be reached. The N.Y. Times reported Oct. 5 that the U.S. had urged West Germany to reconsider its past refusal to negotiate directly with East Germany. A planned London meeting of senior Western foreign service officials was cancelled Oct. 15, however, apparently because of inter-Allied differences over projected German talks with the USSR.

East & West Renew 'Hard' Berlin Positions

U.S. State Secy. Christian Herter presented what was described as a gloomy review of the current world situation Jan. 6 in an appearance before the Senate Foreign Relations Committee. He suggested that the USSR could be expected to press for new negotiations over Berlin and to renew its pressure on the city to force an agreement on Soviet terms.

At his first official Washington press conference, newly appointed State Secy. Dean Rusk asserted Feb. 6 that there had been "no change" in the Berlin views of the U.S. or Pres. Kennedy in the sense that "We are [still] deeply concerned about the security and the safety of the people of that city."

The virtual elimination of restrictions on the travel of West Germans to East Berlin, however, was announced Feb. 15 by the East German police. Officials said that West Germans no longer would be forced to obtain police passes to cross from West to East Berlin.   The pass controls, imposed Sept. 8, 1960, remained in effect despite the nonenforcement of their provisions. The East German action was attributed partially to West German and Allied threats of retaliation for the barring from West Germany Feb. 12 of Evangelical Church leaders who sought to attend an All-German Church Synod service in East Berlin's Marienkirche. The churchmen included Bishops Hanns Lilje of Hanover, Julius Bender of Karlruhe, Gerhart Jacoby of Oldenburg, Wilhelm Halfmann of Kiel and Karl

Haug of Stuttgart. The U.S., Britain and France protested the incident to Soviet Army headquarters in East Berlin Feb. 13.

In a series of notes and statements issued in February and March, both the Western and Soviet blocs withdrew the concessions each had offered at the 1959 Geneva foreign ministers' conference on Germany and stressed the differences in their approaches to a Berlin settlement.

The initial move was made by Soviet Premier Khrushchev in a personal message and a memo delivered to West German Chancellor Adenauer in Bonn Feb. 17 by Soviet Amb. Andrei A. Smirnov. It was reported from Bonn Feb. 23 that Khrushchev had retreated from the Soviet position taken at Geneva in 1959 and had demanded that any solution—even temporary—of the Berlin problem provide for the ultimate transformation of Berlin into a demilitarized free city as first proposed by the USSR in Nov. 1958. The Khrushchev note was said to suggest that direct Soviet-West German negotiations be opened both on the Berlin question and on a separate Soviet-German peace treaty formally ending World War II. It made clear that such a treaty would have to sanction "contractually" the existence of 2 German states. It offered in return to reopen the question of repatriation of German nationals held in the USSR since World War II.

A U.S. State Department statement issued Mar. 10 declared that the Kennedy Administration considered the U.S. to be "no longer bound" by the concessions it had offered at the 1959 Geneva conference. The withdrawal of the U.S.' Geneva proposals was linked specifically to the question of the U.S.' position "with respect to any future negotiations with the Soviet Union on Berlin." State Department spokesman Lincoln White said the U.S. assumed that Britain and France took the same position. Referring to the U.S.' Geneva offer to accept a reduction in the number of Western troops stationed in Berlin (to a total of 11,000, including 6,000 U.S. soldiers), White said "unequivocally that the United States has no intention of reducing its garrison in Western Berlin." The U.S. statement was issued after State Secy. Rusk, at a Washington news conference Mar. 9, had indicated that the Kennedy Administration would maintain the *status quo* in Berlin despite the U.S.' final proposals at Geneva.

Adenauer replied to Khrushchev's note Apr. 14 in a message cabled from Washington, where he was meeting with Pres. Kennedy. Adenauer welcomed Khrushchev's indication of willingness to resume the repatriation of German nationals from the USSR, but he did not accept the suggestion that West Germany bypass Western Big 3 responsibility for the German and Berlin questions and begin direct negotiations with the USSR on these problems. Adenauer reportedly deferred a detailed response to Khrushchev's message on the ground that most of the Soviet proposals would involve consultation with other Western nations. This formal West German response to Khrushchev's note was not made until July 12. It rejected any German-Soviet negotiations on a peace treaty unless they were carried out by a freely-elected government representing all of Germany.

Leaders of the USSR and of the 7 other East European Soviet-bloc nations had met in Moscow Mar. 27-28 for the regular annual session of the Warsaw Pact's Political Consultative Committee. In a communique issued Mar. 31 they proclaimed their belief that West Germany was "the major hotbed of war danger in Europe" and their major potential enemy. They announced that their meeting had produced agreement on the "consolidation of their defense potential and [on] strengthening peace" in line with recommendations made in Nov. 1960 at a Moscow conference of 81 Communist parties. They renewed pledges of peaceful coexistence with the West but demanded that the West agree "to eliminate the vestiges of World War II by concluding a peace treaty with both German states" and agreeing to turn Berlin into a free city.

The Warsaw Treaty meeting was attended by the governmental heads of all Warsaw Pact states except Albania, which was represented by Deputy Premier Beqir Balluku. East German Socialist Unity (Communist) Party First Secy. Walter Ulbricht served as chairman. Khrushchev was said to have opened the meeting and to have held parallel talks with the other leaders.

(Reporting in the *N.Y. Herald Tribune* Apr. 19 on an exclusive interview granted by Khrushchev, Walter Lippmann said the Soviet leader had stressed his determination to force a rapid settlement of the German problem. Khrushchev reportedly told Lippmann that the USSR could not accept an indefinite prolongation of the *status quo* in Germany because of the probability that West Germany's 12 divisions would be given nuclear arms. Before this happened, he reportedly said, the USSR must win a peace treaty with West Germany recognizing the existence of the East German state and the current frontiers of East Germany, Poland and Czechoslovakia. He implied that Soviet pressure against the West in Berlin was directed to this end.)

In further moves presumably intended to coordinate a harder Western line on Berlin, West Berlin Mayor Willy Brandt and Chancellor Adenauer made separate visits to the U.S. in March and April for their first meetings with Pres. Kennedy since his inauguration.

Brandt, visiting the U.S. Mar. 11-19, made clear that current West German policy toward the USSR and the West would be maintained if the Social Democrats won West Germany's fall election and he succeeded Adenauer as chancellor. Brandt met with Kennedy at the White House Mar. 13 and afterwards expressed to reporters his confidence that the new U.S. administration would maintain the uncompromising support given West Berlin by the U.S. in the past. At a Roosevelt Day dinner in Washington sponsored by Americans for Democratic Action, Brandt declared Mar. 13 that it was in "the vital interest" of the U.S. to prevent the replacement of West Berliners' freedom with "the false flag of a free city."

Adenauer arrived in Washington Apr. 11. In 2 days of White House talks with Kennedy, Adenauer won reassurance of the U.S.' determination to maintain the freedom of West Berlin and to reject any East-West accommodation at the expense of Germany's future. Adenauer met with U.S. State Secy. Rusk at the State Department Apr. 12 and was given a clear U.S. pledge to maintain Western occupation rights in Berlin and to oppose with force any Soviet military pressure on the city. A joint communique issued Apr. 13 by Adenauer and Kennedy reaffirmed past pledges to seek a just settlement of the German problem on the basis of self-determination and to "preserve the freedom of ... West Berlin pending ... the restoration of Berlin as the capital of a reunified country."

Speaking at the annual spring meeting of the NATO Council in Oslo May 8, U.S. State Secy. Rusk restated the determination of the U.S. to act with its allies to prevent any

Soviet or East German encroachment on Western rights of access to and occupation in Berlin. Rusk warned that the USSR might act in the summer to carry out its threat to sign a separate peace treaty with East Germany and end its occupation regime in Berlin. Rusk made it clear, however, that no Soviet treaty or threat of force would be permitted to abrogate the West's postwar rights in Berlin.

French Pres. de Gaulle flew to Bonn May 20 for a one-day meeting with Adenauer. The results of the de Gaulle-Adenauer talks were reported at a Bonn news conference held later May 20 by State Secy. Karl Carstens of the West German Foreign Ministry. Carstens said de Gaulle and Adenauer had reached "particularly complete agreement" on the West's continued position in Berlin. This comment was taken as a reiteration of de Gaulle's belief that the current Berlin situation was preferable to any revision of the city's status acceptable to the USSR.

Pres. and Mrs. Kennedy arrived in Paris May 31 on a 3-day state visit to France. A report on the personal talks between Kennedy and de Gaulle stated that the 2 leaders had discussed Berlin and expressed a "complete identity of view" on the readiness of France and the U.S. to meet with force any Soviet threat to Berlin. (U.S. newsmen reported from Paris May 31 that the 2 leaders' swift accord on Berlin implied Kennedy's acceptance of de Gaulle's belief that the West should be prepared for open military action—apparently including limited nuclear war—to counter any Soviet move deemed a major threat to the city. The *N.Y. Herald Tribune* had reported from Paris May 29 that U.S.-British-French military staffs had prepared a 3-stage "contingency plan" providing for this non-nuclear riposte to a new Soviet blockade of Berlin: [1] a "war alert" that would send all NATO troops to battle stations; [2] the creation of a special U.S.-British-French military force opposite Helmstedt, the East German entry point on the *autobahn* to Berlin; [3] the seizure of Helmstedt and a limited penetration of East German territory, using only non-nuclear weapons unless Soviet forces responded with such weapons.)

The Soviet embassy in East Berlin had announced May 9 that Col. I. Solovyev had succeeded Maj. Gen. Nikolai F. Zakharov as commander of Soviet occupation forces in Berlin.

Soviet-West German negotiations on cultural exchanges were broken off in Bonn May 23 after the Soviet delegation insisted that West Berlin artists and scientists be excluded from the projected exchanges. West Germany made it clear May 24 that it would not sign any cultural pact that did not include West Berliners.

Kennedy-Khrushchev Talks in Vienna

Pres. Kennedy and Premier Khrushchev met in Vienna June 3-4 after Kennedy's visit to Paris. This was the first private contact between the Soviet and U.S. leaders; although Kennedy had attended a Capitol reception for Khrushchev in Washington in Sept. 1959, he did not talk with him. (Ex-Pres. Eisenhower had met with Khrushchev 3 times: in Geneva in 1955, in the U.S. during the Soviet leader's 1959 visit, and in Paris at the abortive May 1960 summit conference.)

The agreement to hold the meeting had been announced in simultaneous statements issued in Washington and Moscow May 19. The announcements indicated that the Vienna meeting was not considered a "summit" conference or an attempt to negotiate U.S.-Soviet political differences. The U.S. version stated: "The President and the chairman .... understand that this meeting is not for the purpose of negotiating or reaching an agreement on the major international problems that involve the interest of many other countries. The meeting will, however, afford ... opportunity for the first personal contact between them and a general exchange of views on the major issues which affect the relationships between the two countries."

Washington sources differed on whether Kennedy or Khrushchev had taken the initiative in arranging the Vienna meeting. Following the collapse of the 1960 Paris summit meeting, Khrushchev had repeatedly voiced a desire to meet with whoever succeeded Eisenhower as President of the U.S. The first formal suggestion of a Kennedy-Khrushchev meeting, however, was believed to have been made in a personal message from the President to Khrushchev. It was carried by U.S. Amb.-to-USSR Llewellyn E. Thompson Jr. when he left Washington for Moscow Feb. 22 after participating in policy talks held by the incoming Kennedy Administration. Thompson arrived in Moscow Feb. 27 but was unable to deliver the message to Khrushchev, who left Moscow the next day for an extended tour of the Urals and Siberia. After repeated efforts to see Khrushchev, Thompson was summoned to Novosibirsk, Siberia, where he delivered the note during a 4-hour meeting Mar. 9. The Kennedy proposal, reportedly discussed at a White House meeting Mar. 27 between Kennedy and Soviet Foreign Min. Andrei A. Gromyko, remained dormant until May 3-4, when Gromyko was said to have asked Thompson if Pres. Kennedy still wished a meeting. Khrushchev's formal assent to the Vienna talks was delivered to Kennedy at the White House May 16 by Soviet Amb.-to-U.S. Mikhail A. Menshikov.

The Kennedy-Khrushchev meeting produced no substantive agreement on any of the problems discussed. The 2 leaders June 4, however, issued a joint communique affirming their support for a neutral Laos and their willingness to maintain contact on all differences between their governments. The communique said in part: "Pres. Kennedy and Premier Khrushchev have concluded 2 days of useful meetings, during which they have reviewed the relationships between the U.S. and the USSR, as well as other questions that are of interest to the 2 states ... The President and the chairman have agreed to maintain contact on all questions of interest to the 2 countries and for the whole world."

The 2 leaders had arrived in Vienna separately: Khrushchev from Bratislava, where he had rested and held talks with Czechoslovak Pres. Antonin Novotny, and Kennedy from Paris, where he had met with French Pres. de Gaulle.

Khrushchev arrived in Vienna by train June 2, accompanied by his wife, Nina Petrovna Khrushchev, and an official party that included Foreign Min. Gromyko and Amb.-to-U.S. Menshikov. He was welcomed by Austrian Pres. Adolf Schaerf and by a crowd of Austrian and foreign officials, among them Vyacheslav M. Molotov, former Soviet premier and foreign minister who had led the 1957 "anti-party" plot to depose Khrushchev. (Molotov currently was serving as Soviet representative to the International Atomic Energy Agency.)

Pres. and Mrs. Kennedy landed at Vienna's Schwechat Airport June 3 and were greeted by Pres. Schaerf and other Austrian and diplomatic officials. Then they drove into Vienna to pay a formal call on Schaerf at the presidential Hofburg

Palace. The Kennedy motorcade then went directly to the U.S. embassy residence.

Khrushchev, accompanied by Gromyko and Menshikov, arrived at the U.S. embassy residence shortly thereafter to begin the first discussions.

The 2 leaders conferred with their advisers for $1\frac{1}{4}$ hours before stopping for an informal lunch. They then resumed their conversations, with interpreters but without the advisers, for nearly $3\frac{1}{2}$ hours. The advisers present during the initial discussion: Gromyko, Menshikov, Anatoly F. Dobrynin, chief of the Soviet Foreign Ministry's American Section; State Secy. Rusk, U.S. Amb.-to-USSR Thompson, Assistant State Secy. Foy D. Kohler, Charles E. Bohlen, Rusk's chief adviser on Soviet affairs.

A joint statement read at a Vienna news conference by White House Press Secy. Salinger described the first day's talks as "frank, courteous and wide-ranging" and devoted in large part to "a lengthy and specific discussion of the problems of Laos."

Khrushchev and Kennedy met at the Soviet embassy for nearly 6 hours June 4. Their 2d meeting, held almost entirely in the presence of their advisers, was interrupted only for lunch. The discussion, described as amiable but indicative of wide disagreement, centered on the problems of Germany and Berlin and the stalemated negotiations on disarmament and a treaty to ban nuclear tests. Western newsmen reported that Kennedy emphasized to Khrushchev the West's refusal to accept Soviet proposals for Berlin's future and its determination to defend the city's freedom. (James Reston reported in the *N. Y. Times* June 5 that Kennedy had reminded Khrushchev that the U.S. had gone to war twice to defend Western Europe and that it considered the freedom of West Germany essential to the preservation of European freedom.)

A joint communique issued by the 2 leaders was read at a news conference held by Salinger and Soviet Foreign Ministry press chief Mikhail A. Kharlamov after the conclusion of the talks.

(State Secy. Rusk and Asst. State Secy. Kohler left Vienna June 4 to report to European leaders on Kennedy's impression of his talks with Khrushchev. Rusk flew to Paris to meet June 5 with de Gaulle and with the NATO Permanent Council; Kohler flew to Dusseldorf, where he briefed West German Chancellor Adenauer. Adenauer, who had written Kennedy May 22 to express his confidence that West German interests would not be sacrificed to an accord with Khrushchev, said June 5 that Kohler had described the Vienna meeting as "A tough exchange of views.")

Kennedy returned to Washington June 6 and reported to the American people in a radio-TV address from the White House later the same day on the results of his trip and talks. Kennedy made these major points in his TV report:

● "Mr. Khrushchev and I had a very full and frank exchange of views on the issues that now divide our 2 countries ... It was a very sober 2 days. There was no discourtesy, no loss of tempers, no threats or ultimatums by either side. No advantage or concession was either gained or given. No major decision was either planned or taken. No spectacular progress was ... achieved...." "I ... thought it was of immense importance that I know Mr. Khrushchev, that I gain as much insight and understanding as I could on his present and future policies.... I wanted to make certain that Mr. Khrushchev knew this country and its policies; that he understood our strength and our determination...." "No new aims were stated in private that have not been stated in public.... The gap between us was not ... materially reduced, but at least the channels of communication were opened more fully."

● "At least the chances of a dangerous misjudgment on either side should now be less, and at least the men on whose decisions the peace, in part, depends have agreed to remain in contact." "Neither of us was there to dictate a settlement or to convert the other to a cause or to concede our basic interests. But both of us were there, I think, because we realized that each nation has the power to inflict enormous damage upon the other, that such a war could and should be avoided ... since it would settle no dispute and prove no doctrine, and that care should thus be taken to prevent our conflicting interests from so directly confronting each other that war necessarily ensued." "We believe in a system of national freedom and independence. He believes in an expanding and dynamic concept of world communism. And the question was whether these 2 systems can ever hope to live in peace without permitting any loss of security or any denial of the freedom of our friends."

• "But our most somber talks were on the subject of Germany and Berlin. I made it clear ... that the security of Western Europe and therefore our own security are deeply involved in our presence and our access rights to West Berlin, and that those rights are based on law not on sufferance, and that we are determined to maintain those rights at any risk and thus our obligation to the people of West Berlin and their right to choose their own future.... But we are not seeking to change the present situation. A binding German peace treaty is a matter for all who were at war with Germany...."

Pres. and Mrs. Kennedy flew from Vienna to London June 4 for an informal 28-hour visit to Britain. Mr. Kennedy and British Prime Min. Macmillan met June 5 in London's Admiralty House to review Western policy in the wake of the Khrushchev meeting. London sources said that they had reached agreement that Khrushchev's attitude toward the West would be measured by Soviet readiness to reach an agreement on Laos. A communique issued later that day by the 2 leaders cited their governments' "common purposes" and agreement to maintain the Western position in Berlin.

(British informants said Macmillan had expressed support for a Western statement of principles on Berlin but had opposed publicly committing the West to any specific military action in the event of a new Berlin crisis. British leaders were said to believe that any Western military counter-action to a Soviet move in Berlin must be shaped to meet the specific circumstances involved. Defense Min. Harold Watkinson had told the Western European Union Assembly in London June 1 that no potential aggressor should assume that the West would limit itself to conventional weapons if attacked. His warning was linked to a reported British fear that the USSR could trigger a nuclear war by moving against Berlin in the mistaken belief that the West would not reply with atomic arms.)

Aftermath of Kennedy-Khrushchev Talks

A memo on Soviet terms for settling problems relating to Berlin and a German peace treaty was made public by Tass June 10, and the text was published in the U.S. June 12. The memo was one of 2 handed to American representatives by

Soviet officials after the Kennedy-Khrushchev meeting. The other memo dealt with disarmament.

The Soviet memo restated the major precepts of Russian policy on Germany: the signing of a World War II peace treaty with both German states and the transformation of West Berlin into a demilitarized free city within the territory of East Germany. But if the Western powers were not prepared to join the USSR in an immediate conference on a German peace treaty and reunification, the Soviets proposed in their memo that the USSR, U.S., Britain and France together call on East and West Germany to begin direct negotiations on these matters. The USSR suggested in the memo that under this "interim solution," the 2 German states be given 6 months to reach agreement on a peace treaty, which would be accepted in advance by the Big 4 powers.

The 6-month time limit on proposed negotiations between the 2 German states was not regarded as a new Soviet ultimatum despite the memo's repetition of threats that the USSR would sign a separate peace treaty with East Germany and end the Soviet occupation administration in Berlin. In the memo the Soviet Union offered to guarantee the status of a free city of West Berlin and to accept the continued presence in the city of "symbolic" Western troop contingents and of neutral troops under UN auspices. It warned, however, that if the USSR were forced to seek the creation of a free city of West Berlin through a separate peace treaty with East Germany, the Western powers would have to renegotiate with East Germany their current rights of access to Berlin across East German territory.

Excerpts from the 8-point Soviet Vienna memo dealing with Berlin:

1. "The peace settlement with Germany, dragged out for many years, has largely predetermined the dangerous development of events in Europe in the postwar period. Highly important Allied decisions on rooting out militarism in Germany, which the governments of the United States and the USSR at the time regarded as ... [a hope] of enduring peace, were implemented only in part and are now virtually not observed on the greater part of German territory.

"Of the governments of the 2 German states that took shape after the war, only the ... [East] German Democratic Republic recognizes these agreements and adheres to them. The ... Federal Republic of [West] Germany openly expresses its negative attitude to them, fosters saber-rattling militarism and comes out for a revision of the German frontiers, a revision of the results of World War II...."

2. "The Soviet government sincerely strives for the elimination of the causes engendering tension between the USSR and the United States and for a change-over to constructive friendly cooperation. Conclusion of a German peace treaty would bring both countries much closer to this aim. . . ."

3. "Proceeding from a realistic assessment of the situation, the Soviet government advocates the immediate conclusion of a peace treaty with Germany. The question of a peace treaty is the question of the national security of the USSR and many other states. It is no longer possible to leave the situation in Germany without changes. All conditions for the conclusion of a peace treaty have long since matured and such a treaty must be concluded. The essence of the matter is by whom and how it will be concluded. . . ."

4. "The Soviet government does not aim at prejudicing the interests of the United States or other powers in Europe. It does not propose any changes in Germany or in West Berlin which would benefit only one state or one group of states. The USSR deems it necessary for the sake of consolidating peace to record the situation that took shape in Europe after the war, *de jure* to formulate and consolidate the immutability of the existing German frontiers, to normalize the situation in West Berlin on the basis of reasonable consideration for the interests of all sides.

"For the sake of reaching agreement on a peace treaty, the Soviet Union does not insist on the immediate withdrawal of the Federal Republic of Germany from NATO. Both German states could for a certain period remain after the conclusion of a peace treaty members of those military alignments to which they now belong.

"The Soviet proposal does not link the conclusion of the peace treaty with the recognition of the German Democratic Republic or the Federal Republic of Germany by all parties to this treaty. To recognize or not to recognize one or another state is a matter for each government.

"If the United States is not ready to sign a single peace treaty with both German states, a peace settlement could be effected on the basis of 2 treaties. In this case the states, members of the anti-Nazi coalition, would sign a peace treaty with both or with one German state at their discretion. These treaties must not have identical texts but they must contain the same provisions on the major questions of a peace settlement."

5. "The conclusion of a German peace treaty would also solve the problem of normalizing the situation in West Berlin. West Berlin, deprived of a firm international status, is now a place where Bonn's revenge-seeking elements constantly maintain extreme tension and stage all kind of provocations very dangerous to the cause of peace. . . ."

"At present the Soviet government sees no better solution of the problem of West Berlin than its conversion into a demilitarized free city. . . . The occupation regime preserved there has long since outlived itself, it has lost any connection with the aims for the sake of which it was created and with the Allied agreements on Germany on the basis of which it existed.

"The occupation rights, of course, would discontinue with the conclusion of a German peace treaty. . . ."

"The Soviet government advocates that the free city of West Berlin should freely effect its communications with the outside world and that its domestic order should be determined by the free expression of the will of its population. Of course, the United States, like all other countries, would have every opportunity to maintain and develop their relations with the free city. In general, West Berlin, as the Soviet government sees it, must be strictly neutral...."

"The USSR proposes that the most reliable guarantees should be established against intervention in the affairs of the free city by any state.

"As a guarantor of the free city, token contingents of troops of the United States, the United Kingdom, France and the Soviet Union could be stationed in West Berlin, nor would the USSR object to the stationing in West Berlin of troops of neutral countries under United Nations auspices for the same purpose. The status of the free city could be appropriately registered at the United Nations and sealed with ... [its] authority...."

6. "The Soviet government proposes that a peace conference should be called ... [to meet] without any delay, a German treaty be concluded and the question of West Berlin as a free city settled on this basis. If for one reason or another the governments of the United States and other Western powers are at present not yet ready for this, an interim solution could be adopted for a definite period.

"The 4 powers will urge the German states to agree in any way acceptable to them on the questions pertaining to a peace settlement with Germany and reunification. The 4 powers will declare in advance that they recognize any agreement which the Germans would reach.

"In case of a positive outcome of the talks between the German Democratic Republic and the Federal Republic of Germany, a single peace treaty would then be agreed to and signed...."

"In order not to drag out the peace settlement it is necessary to establish deadlines within which the Germans must explore the possibilities of agreements on questions falling into their internal competence. The Soviet government regards a period not exceeding six months adequate for such talks...."

7. "... If the United States does not show an understanding of the necessity of concluding a peace treaty, we shall regret this, since we would have to sign ... [an East German] peace treaty, which it would be impossible and dangerous to delay further...."

"The peace treaty will specifically record the status of West Berlin as a free city and the Soviet Union, like the other parties to the treaty, will, of course, strictly observe it, and measures will also be taken to see to it that this status is also respected by the other countries.

"At the same time this will also mean the liquidation of the occupation regime in West Berlin with all consequences arising therefrom. Specifically, the questions of using land, water and air communications across the territory of the German Democratic Republic will have to be settled not otherwise than through appropriate agreements with the German Democratic Republic. This is but natural since control over such communications is an inalienable right of any sovereign state."

8. "The conclusion of the German treaty will be a major step toward a final post-war settlement in Europe the Soviet Union has invariably been striving for."

The *N.Y. Times* reported June 12 that State Secy. Rusk, in his June 5 report to the NATO Council on the Khrushchev-Kennedy meeting, had rejected the Soviet memo as a basis for reopening East-West negotiations on Germany. Rusk reportedly told the council that Soviet publication of the Vienna memos would prove they had been prepared for propaganda purposes. But the *Times* reported June 14 that the Western powers were consulting on a reply to the Soviet document that would open the way to a resumption of negotiations on the German problem.

West German Chancellor Adenauer rejected the Soviet proposals June 11. Speaking at a Hanover rally of German expellees from Silesia (incorporated into postwar Poland), Adenauer said: "We demand self-determination and freedom for all of Germany"; "we will never accept these Russian demands." Speaking in Bamberg later the same day, Adenauer asserted that "Pres. Kennedy told Khrushchev at Vienna that the security of the United States begins at Berlin."

West Berlin Mayor Willy Brandt told a Berlin radio audience June 11: The Soviet proposals "cannot be accepted by the German people"; if the West failed to halt all Soviet threats to Berlin's current occupation status, it could lead to repetition of the "disastrous Munich agreement of 1938."

The USSR protested to the U.S., Britain, France and West Germany June 8 against what it said were plans to hold a meeting of the West German Bundesrat (upper house of parliament) in Berlin June 16. Tass said the USSR had warned that the projected Berlin sessions of the Bundesrat and of several Bonn parliamentary committees were "international provocations endangering peace." The Soviet note to West Germany warned against "unlawful interference in the affairs of West Berlin, which neither has been nor is a part of the Federal Republic of Germany."

Bundesrat Pres. Franz Meyers said June 9 that a June 16 Berlin session had been considered by the Bundesrat but had been canceled before the Soviet protest because it might have been misconstrued as commemorating the June 17, 1953 East Berlin uprising against Communist rule.

The Soviet protest was rejected in statements issued June 9 by U.S. State Department spokesman Lincoln White, West German Foreign Min. Heinrich von Brentano, the French Foreign Ministry and the British Foreign Office.

Proposals for military and political measures to demonstrate the U.S.' willingness to defend its position in West Berlin were reviewed by Kennedy and other U.S. officials at a series of strategy meetings begun June 13. These major strategy meetings were known to have taken place: a National Security Council meeting June 13 at which the President reported on his Vienna meeting with Khrushchev; 6 meetings at the White House and State Department June 14, attended by Kennedy, State Secy. Rusk and British Foreign Secy. Lord Home; a White House meeting June 23 attended by Kennedy, Rusk, Defense Secy. Robert S. McNamara, Amb.-to-USSR Thompson, Senate majority leader Mike Mansfield (D., Mont.), Chairman J. W. Fulbright (D., Ark.) of the Senate Foreign Relations Committee and Chairman Richard B. Russell (D., Ga.) of the Senate Armed Services Committee; a National Security Council meeting held June 29, after Kennedy had said in a June 28 news conference statement that he was studying measures to "make meaningful" the U.S.' commitment in Berlin.

The June 29 session of the National Security Council was said to have been devoted to a report prepared by ex-State Secy. Dean G. Acheson on policy recommendations for dealing with Berlin. Washington sources had reported previously that these recommendations would include a partial mobilization of U.S. conventional forces and a limited strengthening of the 5 U.S. divisions currently stationed in Western Europe. No official statement was made on the NSC's deliberations. Defense Secy. McNamara had told newsmen, however, after the June 23 White House meeting, that no decision had been made to increase domestic or overseas U.S. military strength because of the Berlin situation.

Kennedy had made 2 key appointments relating to the U.S.-Soviet crisis over Germany. He had (a) named ex-State Secy. Acheson June 16 to head a policy task force charged with preparing a report on recommendations for countering Soviet pressures in Berlin, and (b) recalled to active service June 26 (effective July 1) retired Gen. Maxwell D. Taylor, former

Army chief of staff, to serve as Presidential military representative for foreign and military policy and intelligence operations.

An FBI investigation reportedly had been ordered by Kennedy on an alleged Pentagon "leak" of JCS (Joint Chiefs of Staff) recommendations on Berlin. The July 3 issue of *Newsweek* magazine had reported that JCS proposals prepared for Kennedy included: the evacuation of U.S. military dependents from France and West Germany; the transfer of at least one additional U.S. division to West Europe; a declaration of limited national emergency, partial mobilization of National Guard and reserve units, increased draft quotas; the commandeering of civil airliners to move troops to Germany; a demonstration of the intent to use nuclear weapons, possibly by the resumption of nuclear tests; combat deployment of NATO forces in Western Europe. The July 10 issue of *Newsweek* reported that these recommendations had been presented to the President at the June 29 National Security Council meeting.

(Deputy Defense Secy. Roswell L. Gilpatric had said at a Washington news conference June 6 that U.S. forces serving with NATO would use their nuclear weapons if Western Europe were in danger of being conquered by conventional Soviet forces. Gilpatric said: "The current doctrine is that if NATO forces were about to be overwhelmed by non-nuclear attacks from the [Communist] bloc countries, NATO would make use of nuclear arms." Gilpatric added that he had "never believed in a so-called limited nuclear war" because he didn't know "how you build a limit into it once you start using any kind of a nuclear bang." A similar statement of NATO's readiness to use nuclear weapons to defend the West's position in Berlin was made in a speech June 1 by British Defense Min. Harold Watkinson.)

State Secy. Rusk charged June 22 that Khrushchev's recent demands on Berlin and West Germany had been responsible for the current increase in world tension. Rusk said at a Washington news conference: "The Soviets talk constantly of peace but threaten the real peace which exists in West Berlin"; "the Soviet position ... is predicated on the belief that the division of Germany is normal, that the division of Berlin is normal and that the sole abnormality that persists is West Berlin; this is not a formulation of the problem which is acceptable to the United States"; the U.S. was eager "to end the tensions over Germany and Berlin which the Soviets have created"; "but such solutions cannot be at the expense of our obligations and of the basic principles of freedom and self-determination."

Vice Pres. Lyndon B. Johnson, speaking June 25 at the dedication of the Los Angeles International Airport, warned Khrushchev that he would be making a "tragic mistake if he assumes that these principles and obligations [in Berlin] count for little ... with the American people." He said at the 53d annual Governors' Conference in Honolulu June 27 that "we are not ready to run away from Berlin under Russian threats."

A proposal that the entire city of Berlin be made an internationally guaranteed and protected free city was made June 14 by Senate majority leader Mike Mansfield (D., Mont.). Addressing the Senate, Mansfield warned that "sooner or later, the Western nations and the Soviet Union must seek a new way, a 3d way, to a solution of the Berlin problem." "Unless this search is pursued with energy ... sooner or later Berlin is likely to become the pivot of a new disaster for mankind," he declared. Mansfield made it clear that he spoke "on my own responsibility" in an effort to generate public discussion on the Berlin question.

Mansfield's proposal contained the following suggestions: (a) transformation of the entire city of Berlin, including both the Western and Soviet (eastern) sectors, into a free city to be "held in trust and in peace by some international authority until such time as it is again the capital of Germany"; (b) assurance of the city's future status by agreements among the NATO and Warsaw Treaty powers and East and West Germany; (c) "international peace teams" to safeguard the West's current access routes to the city.

Mansfield's plan was criticized by Sens. Jacob K. Javits (R., N.Y.) and Hugh Scott (R., Pa.) June 14 for its possible effect on Western policy and on forthcoming West German elections. It was rejected by the West German Foreign Ministry June 15 on the ground that it would deepen the current division of Germany. (U.S. Senate Foreign Relations Committee Chairman J. W. Fulbright warned in a Senate speech June 29 that the U.S.' foreign policies were basically "correct and unassailable" and should not be abandoned in favor of "costly commitments ... to peripheral struggles in which the principal Communist powers are not ... directly involved" or for the "double standard" morality employed by the Communist world in its policies. Fulbright said: "Cuba, Laos, the Soviet cosmonaut—none of these by itself is a threat to our national security, or to the long-term success of our policies. But by exaggerating their significance and reacting to them injudiciously, we disfigure our national style and undermine our policies.")

Khrushchev reported to the Russian people June 15 on his meeting with Kennedy. His report, broadcast from Moscow by radio and TV, contained a new ultimatum on Berlin and Germany. Reviewing the USSR's proposals for a "free city" of West Berlin and for a World War II German peace treaty, Khrushchev said: "The conclusion of a peace treaty with Germany cannot be postponed any longer. A peaceful settlement in Europe must be attained this year."

All U.S.-Soviet policy differences taken up at Geneva were discussed by Khrushchev in his 75-minute address. The Vienna meeting was described by Khrushchev as not only worthwhile but necessary. He conceded that "it emerged from our talks with Pres. Kennedy that we understand the peaceful coexistence of states differently. The President's idea is to build up something like a dam against the peoples' movement to establish in their countries social systems which the ruling circles of the Western powers deem unsuitable."

Among Khrushchev's statements:

● "There can be no question of any new changes of borders. We proceed from the premise that the peace treaty with Germany will put a seal on what has already been established by the Potsdam Agreement." East Germany "has repeatedly stated that it recognizes as final the eastern border of Germany along the Oder-Neisse line."

● "When we suggest signing a peace treaty with Germany and turning West Berlin into a free city we are accused of wanting to deprive the Western powers of access to this city. But that is ... wrong.... All countries of the world wishing to maintain ... ties with this city would have the right."

● "Of course, agreement would have to be reached with the country across whose territory pass the communications that link West Berlin with the outside world. This is normal. Otherwise the sovereignty of the state within which West Berlin is situated would be jeopardized." The Western powers claim to be bound to defend West Berlin's freedom, but "in the 4-power agreements on Berlin ... nothing is said of these obligations."

● "The Soviet Union and our friends do not want war and we will not start it. But we will defend our sovereignty, will fulfill our sacred duty to defend our freedom and independence. If any country violates peace and crosses the borders—ground, air or water—of another it will assume full responsibility for the consequences of the aggression and will receive a proper rebuff."

Berlin Pressures Increase Again

The USSR's warning that it would sign a separate World War II peace treaty with East Germany unless the West agreed to negotiate on Germany was repeated by Premier Khrushchev June 21 in a speech at a Kremlin meeting marking the 20th anniversary of Hitler's invasion of Russia.

The new Soviet deadline for settling the Berlin question was reiterated by Khrushchev in his June 21 address. He said that if the West refused to negotiate, "at the end of this year, we, together with other peace-loving states, will sign a treaty with ... [East Germany]." Khrushchev declared that the USSR was forced to contemplate this step because "West Germany has now become an influential member of the aggressive military NATO bloc" and its "militarists ... have already got hold of rocket weapons and are insistently demanding atomic weapons...."

Khrushchev charged that Western leaders "would like to turn the German question into a touchstone for a test of strength." Addressing himself to Chancellor Adenauer, he said: "I warn that the Soviet Union stands firm. If you forget the lessons of history ... it will be suicide for you and your people."

Defending the Soviet plan for a Berlin and German settlement, Khrushchev said: "Contrary to the noisy allegations of those who would like to keep up international tension, we do not threaten West Berlin at all when we urge ... a peace treaty. We propose a free-city status for West Berlin. We have no intention of changing the social and political system in West Berlin.... Neither the Soviet Union nor ... [East Germany] intends to restrict the links between West Berlin and all the countries of the world. As regards those who try to threaten us with war if we sign a peace treaty with ... [East Germany], they will bear the entire responsibility for their actions." "This is not 1941—this is 1961, and we have all means to defend ourselves...."

In a telegram transmitted to East German Socialist Unity Party First Secy. Walter Ulbricht and made public June 26 by the ADN news agency, Khrushchev said: "The interests of peace and European security make a German peace treaty and the normalization of conditions in West Berlin ... a compulsive necessity." "The time for conclusion of a peace treaty is long overdue and the Soviet Union ... [and other nations] will do their utmost to sign one by the end of this year."

In his 3d major speech on the German and Berlin questions since his meeting with Kennedy, Khrushchev said at a Kremlin reception in honor of North Vietnamese Premier Pham Van Dong June 28 that free-city status would be imposed on West Berlin peacefully and without a renewal of the 1948-9 blockade. Khrushchev reiterated: "We are threatening nobody by proposing to conclude a German peace treaty and to solve ... the question of West Berlin.... We move to establish reliable international guarantees of non-interference in the affairs of West Berlin: let the 4 great powers be the guarantors and keep some contingent of their armed forces in the free city, or such guarantees could be provided by the armed forces of neutral nations [or the UN].... There will be no blockade of West Berlin and no obstacles will be put up on the routes of access to this city. West Berlin will be able to maintain free contacts with all states at its discretion. Since the communication lanes to West Berlin pass through ... [East Germany], agreement with the government of this state should be reached ... on their use."

  •   The USSR was "ready for talks" that would aim "honestly and frankly" at an East-West accord on Germany, Khrushchev continued. He said: "We propose ... to legalize what has taken shape as a result of war—to recognize the actual state of affairs in Europe." The USSR was prepared to let West Germany remain in NATO and East Germany in the Warsaw Treaty alliance. "Let the situation remain as it is until the sides reach agreement on the liquidation of the military blocs." "The unification of ... Germany into a single state can be achieved only through talks and cooperation between ... these [German] states themselves. The other nations must not interfere in this internal [German] affair."

Khrushchev warned Western leaders against attempting to deter the USSR from its aims with economic or diplomatic sanctions or with military mobilization. He said: "If the enemies of ... peaceful coexistence call a mobilization ..., we shall not allow them to catch us unawares. We ..., if need be, shall take additional steps to strengthen our security."

In a statement read at his news conference in Washington June 28, Kennedy rejected the USSR's terms for a German and Berlin settlement. (This was Kennedy's first news conference since meeting Khrushchev in Vienna.) Kennedy's statement indicated that the U.S. would resist all Soviet efforts to make permanent the partition of Germany and to deprive West Berlin of the protection afforded by Western military occupation. The President, charging that recent speeches by Soviet leaders had been "designed to heighten tension" over Germany, said that it was "of the greatest importance that the American people understand ... the threat to the peace and security of Europe and of ourselves posed by the Soviet announcement that they intend to change unilaterally the existing arrangements of Berlin." "The quote crisis unquote over Berlin is Soviet-manufactured," he declared.

Kennedy's summary of the Soviet position and the U.S. response to it:

● "In Nov. 1958, the Soviets began a new campaign to force the Allied powers out of Berlin.... Now they have revived that drive. They call upon us to sign what they call a peace treaty ... with the regime that they have created in East Germany. If we refuse, they say that they themselves will sign such a peace treaty. The obvious purpose here is not to have peace but to make permanent the partition of Germany."

● "The Soviets also say that their unilateral action in signing a ... peace treaty ... with East Germany would bring an end to Allied rights in West Berlin and to free access to that city. It is clear that such unilateral action cannot affect these rights, which stem from the surrender of Nazi Germany.... If the Soviets ... withdraw from their own obligations, ... the other 3 Allies ... must decide how they will ... meet their responsibilities."

● The USSR had said that when it signs the treaty "we will be subject to the designs of the East German regime and that these designs will be backed by force." The "free city" sought by East Germany "is one in which the rights of the citizens of West Berlin are gradually but relentlessly extinguished." "No one can fail to appreciate the gravity of this threat.... It involves the peace and the security of the peoples of West Berlin ... [and] of the Western world."

● The Western alliances were "wholly defensive." "But the Soviets would make a grave mistake if they suppose that Allied unity and determination can be undermined by threat or aggressive acts. There is peace in Germany and in Berlin. If it is disturbed, it will be a direct Soviet responsibility."

● "We would agree that there is unfinished business to be settled as concerns Germany.... We shall always be ready to discuss any proposal which would give increased protection to the right of the people of Berlin to exercise their independent choice as free men.... Discussions will be profitable if the Soviets will accept in Berlin, and indeed in Europe, self-determination ... and if they will work sincerely for peace rather than an extension of power."

In answer to reporters' questions, Kennedy denied that he had received from his advisers any proposals for a partial U.S. mobilization to make clear Western determination to defend Berlin. He said, however, that his advisers were studying "a whole variety of measures" that would "make studying our commitment" in West Berlin.

Decrees published June 28 in the East German government's official gazette made mandatory the registration with East German authorities of all air traffic to and from Berlin after Aug. 1. All foreign planes were ordered to register with an East German air safety center on entering or leaving East German airspace. Foreign planes equipped with radios were ordered to obtain permission to enter East German airspace. But foreign aircraft would be exempted if their countries signed a civil flight agreement with East Germany.

U.S. spokesmen in West Berlin said June 29 that Western civil and military aircraft would ignore the East German decrees. The U.S. State Department rejected them June 29 on the ground that the 4-power agreements governing the Berlin air lanes provided for their use "without prior notice."

East German Socialist Unity (Communist) Party First Secy. Walter Ulbricht had warned June 15 that the Western allies would have to negotiate agreements on access to Berlin "if they do not want traffic to be interrupted." Ulbricht, at a press conference in East Berlin, said that East Germany wanted "full control of all traffic on land, on water and in the air," and would assume it immediately after the signing of a Soviet-East German peace treaty. He warned that "air safety would have to be assured" and that any planes entering East Germany without permission after the signing of a treaty would be "invited to land."

Pres. Kennedy and Soviet Premier Khrushchev used an exchange of messages marking the U.S.' 185th Independence Day to imply their readiness to deal with current U.S.-Soviet tension over the future of Berlin and Germany. The Soviet message, signed by Khrushchev and Soviet Pres. Leonid I. Brezhnev, was delivered to Kennedy July 3. It expressed "the hope that the recent Vienna meeting and the exchange of opinions which took place there" would further the "urgent solution of problems ... which the last war left to us after the defeat of the aggressors." Kennedy's reply, made public July 4, declared that "on our 185th anniversary, the United States is still committed to ... revolutionary principles of individual liberty and national freedom for all peoples." The President expressed confidence that "given a sincere desire to achieve a peaceful settlement," the U.S. and USSR could end their differences.

Berlin Generates New East-West Crisis

Premier Khrushchev announced July 8 that the USSR had suspended planned troop reductions and had ordered a 25% increase in defense expenditures for 1961. He declared that the Soviet government had been "compelled" to take this decision by a Western military buildup resulting from the East-West dispute over the future of Berlin and Germany. Speaking at a

Kremlin meeting of military academy graduates, Khrushchev said:

"Comrades, the ... Soviet Union follows attentively the military measures taken of late by the United States ... and its NATO allies. We cannot disregard such facts as the building up of armed forces in the Western countries, the steps to increase considerably the number of strategic A-bombers which are constantly kept in the air. The forces of West Germany are being equipped with the latest weapons and increased numerically.... Mr. Kennedy proclaimed in his recent messages to Congress the so-called 'new course.' It provides for stepping up the program of developing rocket-missile strategic weapons, the raising of the military readiness of all services. For this purpose, Pres. Kennedy has proposed to increase military allocations ... by more than $3.5 billion. This means that the [U.S.'] military spending in the fiscal year of 1961-1962 will exceed $53 billion."

"Taking into account the obtaining situation, the Soviet government was compelled to instruct the Defense Ministry to suspend, temporarily, pending special orders, the reduction of the armed forces planned for 1961. In view of the growing military budgets in the NATO countries, the Soviet government has passed a decision to increase defense spending in the current year by 3.144 billion rubles ... raising the total ... in 1961 to 12.399 billion rubles." (The figures cited by Khrushchev were, at official rates, equivalent to an increase of $3.493 billion to a total of $13.776 billion in planned 1961 defense expenditures. They were not believed to include vast additional outlays for rocket research, defense industries and other military-connected matters. The USSR had announced plans in 1960 for a reduction of its military manpower from 3,623,000 to 2,423,000 by 1967. It was not known how many men already had been demobilized under the program.)

In his address Khrushchev summarized the history of Soviet-bloc proposals for the demilitarization of central Europe and for the settlement of the Berlin and German questions. He declared, however, that "replying to our ... most natural proposals for the conclusion of a peace treaty [with Germany], the West begins to count divisions" and "Chancellor Adenauer is shouting himself hoarse for nuclear weapons." Khrushchev reiterated: "We propose the convocation of a peace conference, and we shall go there with our draft treaty. Let the Western powers make their proposals, submit their draft for a peace settlement." The USSR had proposed a free-city status for West Berlin that would be guaranteed by the Big 4 powers, neutrals, or the UN; "if the Western powers have a better version of guarantees, let them propose it."

Khrushchev warned that the USSR would not permit the solution of the Berlin and German questions "being dragged out for many more years." He repeated that if the West failed to respond to his call for an international German peace conference, the USSR would proceed to sign a separate peace treaty with East Germany and would relinquish to that country all Soviet rights and obligations relating to Berlin and access to that city. He declared that Soviet forces were prepared "to rebuff the aggressive forces if they decided to frustrate peaceful settlement by force of arms." "They [the Soviet forces] possess the necessary quantities of thermonuclear weapons, the ... means of delivering them—close combat, intermediate and intercontinental missiles," Khrushchev warned. "If the imperialists unleash a war it will end with imperialism's complete debacle and ruin."

A general review of U.S. military strength and planned defense expenditures was ordered by Kennedy July 8 at a Hyannis Port, Mass. meeting with his 3 principal advisers on military and foreign policy. The study was ordered to determine whether current U.S. defense forces and expenditures were adequate in view of the continued crisis over Berlin and Khrushchev's announcement, earlier that day, of the USSR's plans to reinforce its armed services. The decision was made by Kennedy while he cruised off Hyannis Port with State Secy. Rusk, Defense Secy. McNamara and Gen. Maxwell D. Taylor, Presidential military representative. It was disclosed by Deputy Defense Secy. Roswell L. Gilpatric in testimony before the Senate Defense Appropriations Subcommittee July 10 and made the subject of a formal statement issued later the same day by McNamara.

McNamara's statement said: "The simplest precaution calls for still another examination of our defense posture." "Currently we are strong—if not stronger—than any potential aggressor. But in the face of the inescapable realities that confront us, such as threats to dispossess us of our rightful presence in Berlin, we can do no less than re-examine our needs. This we are doing." The USSR's decision to increase its defense budget and to cancel scheduled troop cuts was not justified by prior Western military moves; "nothing that has developed in the United States or the free world calls for increased militarism." The U.S.' recent decisions to increase its defense spending and strength were "inescapable in the face of the aggressive atmosphere in the East and nearer at home."

Gilpatric disclosed at a Washington news conference July 11 that, under the arms review order, the Defense Department had begun the study of a possible mobilization of some National Guard and Army reserve units. Gilpatric said that the manpower buildup was being considered in order to compensate for past increases in the strength of U.S. nuclear forces. He expressed doubt that the Administration would call for an increase in manned bomber production within the context of the Berlin situation.

(It was reported in AP dispatches from Washington July 6 that the FBI had ended its investigation of an alleged "leak" to *Newsweek* magazine of Pentagon military plans on Berlin. The *N. Y. Herald Tribune* reported the same day that the probe had been ordered not to trace the leak but to emphasize the credibility of the *Newsweek* report that the U.S. was studying major military moves to deal with the Berlin crisis.)

The U.S., Britain and France informed the Soviet government July 17 that Khrushchev's terms for settling the Berlin and German questions were unacceptable to the West and could not be the basis for any negotiations on these problems. The Western position was set forth in 3 separate but similar notes delivered in Moscow July 17 and made public July 18. The notes were in answer to the Soviet *aide-memoire* handed to U.S. officials at the end of Kennedy's and Khrushchev's meeting in Vienna.

In their messages, the 3 Western powers categorically rejected the Soviet threat to sign a separate peace treaty with East Germany and to impose the status of a free city on West Berlin. They made it clear that they would defend their rights in Berlin, with force if necessary. The Western powers expressed agreement with the USSR that a German settlement would enhance world peace. They declared, however, that such a settlement would be possible only on the basis of self-determination and free elections in all parts of Germany and Berlin.

Excerpts from the U.S. note, which was accompanied by a copy of the Sept. 12, 1944 Allied protocol on the division and occupation of Germany:

"The United States government fully concurs with the Soviet government that a peace settlement is long overdue. It is clear from the public record of efforts on the part of the Western powers to reach agreement with the Soviet Union on the terms of such a peace settlement that it is the Soviet Union which has blocked all progress. . . .

"With regard to Berlin, the United States is not insisting upon the maintenance of its legal rights because of any desire merely to perpetuate its presence there. It is insisting on, and will defend, its legal rights against attempts at unilateral abrogation because the freedom of the people of West Berlin depends upon the maintenance of those rights. The support and approval of the people of West Berlin for the system under which they live has been made amply clear over the years. . . .

"The United States government continues to believe that there will be no real solution of the German problem, nor any real tranquility in central Europe, until the German people are reunified in peace and freedom on the basis of the universally recognized principle of self-determination. . . .

"To justify the action it wishes to take, the . . . USSR alleges that without a peace treaty there is danger of conflagration in Europe. The United States government does not consider that this argument has any merit. Minor incidents which occur from time to time in the present situation are settled through exercise of those quadripartite responsibilities which, in themselves, constitute the most effective protection against any local aggravation . . . growing into a real threat to the peace.

"Contrary to the unfounded assertion in the Soviet *aide-memoire,* the Western powers vigorously carried out the programs to eradicate Nazi militarism, to eliminate vestiges of the 3d Reich, to prevent the rebirth of aggressive forces, and to chart a course by which Germany could recover its respect and play a constructive role in international affairs. The Federal Republic of Germany is the proof of the successful achievement of these aims by the West. The Federal Republic's foreign and military policies accept significant restraints. It has undertaken not to manufacture atomic, chemical and biological weapons, and has accepted international control to insure that this undertaking is honored. All of the Federal Republic's combat forces are completely integrated into NATO, which has only defensive—not aggressive—aims. The Federal Republic does not seek, or intend to develop, an independent nuclear capability or the transfer of nuclear weapons to its [control]. . . .

"The counterpart of the Soviet position is that unless the Western powers accept its German solution, the Soviet government will try to obtain what it wants by unilateral action. . . .

"At the end of World War II, the victorious powers entered into a number of agreements to settle the German problem, based on the principle that questions concerning Germany as a whole were a matter of joint action by the victorious powers. A peace settlement with Germany is foremost among those questions.... Under international law, the Soviet government cannot ignore these agreements in order to conclude unilateral arrangements with a part of Germany; nor would such action invalidate the rights of the United States government and the other governments responsible for the settlement of the German question, since these rights derive absolutely from the unconditional surrender of Nazi Germany, and were not granted by, nor negotiated with, the Soviet Union. This has repeatedly been acknowledged by the Soviet government....

"What the Soviet Union proposes, unless the 3 powers formally abandon their efforts to reunify Germany, is to determine by itself the fate of Germany through an agreement with the authorities of the so-called 'German Democratic Republic' which is not freely chosen, but has been created by the Soviet Union as an instrument of Soviet foreign policy."

"The Soviet Union further asserts that a 'peace treaty,' whether signed by all the interested parties or not, would bring about the establishment of West Berlin as a 'demilitarized free city.'...

"The United States considers entirely unfounded the Soviet claims that this unilateral act could deprive the other 3 participants in the joint occupation of Berlin of their basic rights in the city—rights derived from the Nazi surrender, as indicated, and expressed in binding and valid agreements, to which the Soviet Union is a party....

"The United States wishes particularly to reiterate, in discussing the legal aspects of Berlin's status, that Soviet references to Berlin as being situated on the territory of the so-called 'German Democratic Republic' are entirely without foundation. This can be readily and clearly established by reference to the attached copy of the protocol of Sept. 12, 1944. The protocol makes clear that Berlin was not a part of, or located on, the territory to be occupied as a zone by any one of the powers under the agreement....

"It is evident that the present status of the city, which the Soviet Union chooses to characterize as an 'occupation regime' which 'has already outlived itself,' is actually an arrangement that—under the existing abnormal division of Germany—does not constitute any threat to peace. Attempts by the Soviet Union to destroy that arrangement, in pursuit of its political goals, are certain to jeopardize gravely the very peace in the name of which the Soviet Union action is taken....

"The immediate cause of this threat to peace arises from the announced intention of the Soviet government to present the 3 Western powers with a *de facto* situation based on the false assertion that they would no longer be entitled to remain in Berlin, or to have free access thereto. Such a move could lead to highly dangerous developments, and would be totally devoid of legal effect. The United States considers the exercise of its rights together with its British and French allies, in order to maintain the freedom of over 2,000,000 people in West Berlin, a fundamental political and moral obligation."

"As in the past, the United States government is always prepared to consider in agreement with its allies a freely negotiated settlement of the unresolved problems of Germany. Such a settlement must be in conformity with the principle of self-determination and with the interests of all concerned. The United States government for its part has never contemplated confronting the Soviet Union with a *fait accompli*. It hopes that for its part the Soviet government will renounce any idea of taking such action, which as noted, would have unforeseeable consequences. It thinks it necessary to warn the Soviet government in all seriousness of the grave degree of such a course....

"There is no reason for a crisis over Berlin. If one develops it is because the Soviet Union is attempting to invade the basic rights of others. All the world will plainly see that the misuse of such words as 'peace' and 'freedom' cannot conceal a threat to raise tension to the point of danger and suppress the freedom of those who now enjoy it."

The Western notes had been coordinated in discussions among the U.S., British and French governments and in parallel talks with West Germany and the West European representatives to the NATO Permanent Council.

In the initial Soviet reaction to the notes, Moscow radio charged July 17 that the Western powers were "abetting the sinister forces that seek to start another war."

A long-range U.S. response to the Berlin crisis was presented by Kennedy to the American people July 25. In a nationwide radio-TV address from the White House, Kennedy again pledged the U.S. to defend West Berlin and its postwar occupation rights in the city, by force if necessary. The President disclosed that the U.S. was beginning a long-term strengthening of its armed forces to meet military commitments in Germany and elsewhere. He said he had ordered these measures for a military buildup:

(1) A request to Congress to provide "for the current fiscal year an additional $3.247 billion of appropriations for the military forces."

(2) A request to Congress for "an increase in the Army's total authorized strength from 875,000 to approximately 1,000,000 men" "to fill out our present Army divisions and to make more men available for prompt deployment."

(3) A similar request for "an increase of 29,000 and 63,000 men, respectively, in the active duty strength of the Navy and the Air Force."

(4) Doubling and tripling of draft calls; requests for authority to recall to service "certain reserve units," to "extend tours of duty" and to activate "a number of Air Transport squadrons and Air National Guard tactical air squadrons."

(5) Retention or reactivation of ships and planes, including B-47 bombers, to increase "tactical air power and ... sea lift, air lift, and anti-submarine warfare capability."

(6) The use of $1.8 billion of the $3.247 billion request "for the procurement of non-nuclear weapons, ammunition and equipment."

Kennedy said he would seek an additional $207 million in appropriations for civil defense projects; this, he said, would bring his new defense fund requests to $3.44 billion and raise military appropriations to "a total of $47.5 billion for the year." The President estimated that, added to his earlier requests for increased defense funds, the new appropriations sought would raise the U.S.' budget by $6 billion and would result in a deficit of more than $5 billion.

With respect to Berlin and the Soviet threat to sign an East German peace treaty abrogating the city's occupation statute, Kennedy said:

● "We are there as a result of our victory over Nazi Germany—and our basic rights deriving from that victory include both our presence in Berlin and the enjoyment of access across East Germany." "Thus, our presence in West Berlin, and our access thereto, cannot be ended by any act of the Soviet government. The NATO shield was long ago extended to cover West Berlin—and we have given our word that an attack in that city will be regarded as an attack upon us all."

● "For West Berlin—lying exposed 110 miles inside of East Germany— ... has many roles. It is more than a showcase of liberty, a symbol, an isle of freedom in a Communist sea." "... It has now become—as never before—the great testing place of Western courage and will, a focal point where our solemn commitments and Soviet ambitions now meet in basic confrontation."

● "It would be a mistake for others to look upon Berlin ... as a tempting target." "I hear it said that West Berlin is militarily untenable. So was Bastogne. So, in fact, was Stalingrad. Any dangerous spot is tenable if brave men will make it so." "We do not want to fight—but we have fought before. And others in earlier times have made the same dangerous mistake that the West was too selfish and too soft and too divided to resist invasions of freedom in other lands."

● "We cannot and will not permit the Communists to drive us out of Berlin, either gradually or by force. For the fulfillment of our pledge to that city is essential to the morale and the security of Western Germany, to the unity of Western Europe, and to the faith of the whole free world."

● "But I must emphasize again that the choice is not merely between resistance and retreat, between atomic holocaust and surrender." "We have previously indicated our readiness to remove any actual irritants in West Berlin." "We are willing to consider any arrangement or treaty in Germany consistent with ... peace and freedom...." "We recognize the Soviet Union's historical concerns about their security in central and eastern Europe—after a series of ravaging invasions—and we believe arrangements can be worked out [to help] ... meet those concerns...."

● The U.S. was prepared to submit to 2 tests of its position in Berlin and Germany: "If anyone doubts the legality of our rights in Berlin, we are ready to have it submitted to adjudication." "If anyone doubts the extent to which our presence is desired by the people of West Berlin, compared to East German feelings about their regime, we are ready to have that question submitted to a free vote in Berlin, and, if possible, among all the German people."

Kennedy declared that the world was not deceived by "the Communist attempt to label Berlin a hotbed of war." "There is peace in Berlin today. The source of world trouble and tension today is Moscow, not Berlin. And if war begins, it will have begun in Moscow, not Berlin," he said. The President cautioned, however, that the Soviet threat was "worldwide" and must be countered by measures "equally wide and strong." "We face a challenge in Berlin, but there is also ... a challenge in Southeast Asia," "in our own hemisphere and wherever else the freedom of human beings is at stake," he said.

A draft resolution requesting authority to call up the Ready Reserve and to extend armed forces' enlistments was sent to Congress by Kennedy July 26. Along with the resolution the President sent proposed amendments to the Defense Department's 1962 budget to cover his new arms proposals. The resolution asked for authority until July 1, 1962: (a) to order up to 250,000 Ready Reservists to active duty for a period up to one year; (b) to order the Defense Department to extend enlistments, including those of National Guardsmen, for a period up to one year. (The Ready Reserve currently numbered 2,415,000.)

The immediate reaction to the President's defense proposals was reported as generally favorable both in Congress and throughout the nation. Democratic and Republican Congressional leaders pledged to support the program. Senate minority leader Everett M. Dirksen (Ill.) said after a meeting of Senate GOP leaders July 26 that "this is an emergency situation" and that the President's requests would encounter "no difficulty." Senate GOP Policy Committee Chairman Styles Bridges (N.H.) said: "It is now clear to our enemies as well as to our friends the strong position we have taken." Conservatives of both parties backed the President's defense plans. An "unprecedented" and "overwhelmingly favorable" public response to the President's speech was reported July 26 by Presidential Press Secy. Salinger.

Khrushchev was reported Aug. 2 to have expressed the conviction that the Berlin crisis would end in renewed negotiations, rather than war, between East and West. Meeting in the Kremlin with Italian Premier Amintore Fanfani, Khrushchev was said to have declared: "We believe that there will be no war. A German peace treaty is necessary, and so are negotiations." The Khrushchev statement was reported by what were described as official Western sources. Khrushchev was said to have emphasized the USSR's proferred guarantees for the safety and freedom of a West Berlin transformed into a free city independent of East or West. He reportedly stressed the view that the Berlin problem was negotiable. In a farewell statement before Fanfani's departure Aug. 5, Khrushchev conceded their "different opinions" on the Berlin problem but again called for negotiations on a settlement. Moscow sources reported Aug. 6 that Khrushchev had warned Fanfani that both Italy and Britain were "hostage" to Soviet missiles and would be destroyed if nuclear war resulted from a Western resort to force in Berlin.

A Soviet reply to Kennedy's July 25 speech on Berlin was delivered by Khrushchev Aug. 7 in a televised address to the Russian people. Khrushchev reaffirmed the USSR's determination to sign a separate German peace treaty that would end Soviet occupation rights in East Germany and Western occupation rights in West Berlin. He declared again that the USSR opposed taking any military steps that might increase the danger of a new war, but he asserted that it might be compelled to begin moving troops westward in response to NATO pressures.

Khrushchev's warnings were coupled with this appeal for a negotiated settlement of the German problem: "The Soviet Union does not want to go to war with anyone. We do not need anyone's territories, anyone's wealth.... This is why we address ... the United States of America, Britain and France once more: Let us honestly meet at a roundtable conference; let us not create a war psychosis, let us clear the atmosphere, let us rely on reason and not on the power of thermonuclear weapons."

Khrushchev protested that Kennedy, in his July 25 speech, had resorted to threats and had presented the USSR with "something in the nature of an ultimatum." He said Kennedy had warned Americans that they faced "a challenge of some kind from the Soviet Union," "but he did not say a single word about the substance of the matter, ... that the Soviet Union proposes to conclude a peace treaty with Germany and that it strives to work out the terms of this treaty jointly with all states that took part in the war against Germany."

Khrushchev recalled that Kennedy had "said during our talks in Vienna that a balance of power had now been established between the 2 world camps and that a direct clash between the USSR and the United States must be prevented because such a clash would have the most disastrous consequences." Khrushchev said this was "a sober view ... and displayed a definite realism." But, he asserted, Kennedy had failed to support it with reasonable actions.

Khrushchev, describing the USSR's military response to Kennedy's speech, said:

● "It may be that we shall have to increase in the future the numerical strength of the army on the western frontiers by moving divisions from other parts of the Soviet Union." "In connection with this, we may have to call up a part of the reservists so that our divisions have a full complement ... ready for any eventuality." The USSR would not order new increases in its military budget because it had enough arms, including missiles with nuclear warheads.

● "It would be criminal thoughtlessness to expect ... that after unleashing war against the Socialist states it would be possible to keep it within certain bounds. If a clash does occur between the 2 giants ... neither would be ready to admit defeat without having used all weapons, including the most destructive ones."

● "We cannot view with indifference how the aggressive quarters of the Western powers, with Chancellor Adenauer's help, are mobilizing ... Western Germany for a 3d World War." West Germany had become an integral part of the NATO "military bloc spearheaded against the Soviet Union." "By will of the Western powers, more inflammable material has been stockpiled in the center of Europe.... It is here that the flame of a world war again threatens to break out."

The Soviet government's demand for Western participation in a conference on a German peace treaty and a settlement of central Europe's postwar frontiers was repeated in notes delivered to the U.S., Britain and France Aug. 4 and made public Aug. 5. The Soviet messages were in reply to the Western notes transmitted to the USSR July 17.

The 3 parallel Soviet notes repeated the cardinal points of Russia's recent policies toward Germany: (1) To preserve peace, there must be a settlement of the outstanding problems left by World War II in Berlin, Germany and central Europe. (2) The most feasible way to effect a settlement was by signing a German peace treaty under which West Berlin would be transformed into a demilitarized free city and the negotiation of Germany's reunification would be left to the East and West German governments. (3) If the West refused to join the USSR in an international conference on such a treaty, the USSR would sign a separate treaty with East Germany. (4) This treaty would terminate Western occupation rights in West Berlin and would force the Western powers to renegotiate the guarantees of their Berlin position with the East German government. (5) The entire Soviet bloc was ready to support East Germany if the West refused to accept a peaceful transformation of its Berlin position. (6) The USSR was prepared to begin negotiations with the West either on (a) a German peace treaty, or (b) guarantees to assure the freedom of West Berlin and its contacts with the West under a free-city statute.

Partial text of the Soviet note addressed to the U.S.:

"The Soviet government was willing to believe that the United States ... is sincerely prepared to assist in consolidating peace ..., as it was solemnly declared by the present [Kennedy] Administration.... However, in reply to the Soviet Union's call to begin settling jointly one of the most important and burning issues of our time, on whose solution peace and tranquility in Europe depends—conclusion of a peace treaty with Germany—the United States ... confined itself to setting forth ... [a] position ... which is far removed from true concern for peace....

"For many years the United States has been evading peaceful settlement with Germany, putting it off till the indefinite future. The American note shows that ... [it] apparently prefers to continue adhering to this line.

"... The entire content of the American note shows that the United States' ... main concern is to justify its policy ... and, as far as possible, avoid responsibility for the fact that no line has thus far been drawn under World War II and that there is no stability and international lawful order in the center of Europe while militarists and revanchists are again growing strong in Western Germany.

"Before everybody's eyes Western Germany is becoming a seat of war danger in Europe. A regular army headed by former Hitler generals and officers has sprung up there. Already, now, Western Germany has the largest army on the European Continent among all NATO member countries. [Its] representatives ... are capturing key posts in NATO headquarters one after another. The West German military are spoiling to get weapons of mass destruction into their possession. The Bundeswehr is being formed and trained as an army designed to wage a rocket-nuclear war....

"The United States, apparently, is inclined to belittle the significance of the war potential of [West Germany], ... proceeding from the fact that so far it is much inferior to the American. But it would be dangerous to overlook that [West Germany] ... already now has more than sufficient armed forces and armaments to provoke a general military conflict....

"No matter whether we proceed from the necessity of raising an obstacle to the growth of militarism and revanchism in Western Germany ... or from the interests of improving relations between the great powers ... the conclusion is unavoidable that a German peace treaty must be concluded.

"In its note the United States ... emphasizes that the question of a peace settlement with Germany cannot be settled until the reunification of Germany has been realized. But this is ... an unrealistic approach.... The problem of Germany's unification is a purely internal problem of the German people, and it can be solved only on the basis of agreement between the 2 German states....

"Manipulations with the slogan of self-determination of the German nation in the conditions when 2 independent German states exist are a rather cheap trick.... They are separated by deep-going differences in the internal way of life, in other words, by deep-going social differences.... Both these states have long since made their choice....

"The 4 powers can change nothing in the obtaining situation. Even if they agreed between themselves on the order of Germany's reunification desirable to them, they would have to impose their decision on the 2 German states by force....

"If the Western powers and [West Germany] ... refuse to sign a peace treaty with Germany, such a treaty will have to be signed without them. In this case a peace treaty will be concluded between the states which participated in the war against Hitler Germany, and which will be desirous to do so, and the [East] German Democratic Republic, which has already agreed to this.

"... This treaty will juridically seal the [postwar] frontiers of Germany....

"... By refusing to take part in a peace settlement, the United States ... would place itself in a position where the West Berlin question would be settled without it, with all consequences for the rights of the Western powers based on Germany's surrender.

"The proposal to turn West Berlin into a demilitarized free city means nothing other than the Soviet Union's readiness to settle, jointly with all sides concerned, the question of the status of West Berlin after the signing of a ... treaty....

"As regards the freedom of West Berlin, that is, the inalienable right of the city's population to settle the questions of internal life at their own discretion and to establish the political and social system in accordance with their own desire, this freedom is threatened by no one. On the contrary, the conclusion of a peace treaty, be it with one or both German states, will create a more solid basis for insuring freedom of West Berlin....

"The Soviet government has declared and declares again: It suggests conclusion of peace and a peace treaty with Germany. If this or that power or a group of powers take actions which will lead to dangerous consequences, it will not be the Soviet Union. Entire responsibility for the possible dangerous consequences ... will be borne by all those who will take steps directed against peace."

A similar Soviet message delivered to West Germany Aug. 4 warned that its people would not survive "even a few hours of the 3d world war if it is unleashed" over the Berlin crisis.

East & West Coordinate Berlin Policy

The heads of the Communist parties of the 8 Warsaw Pact countries Aug. 5 announced their determination to sign a peace treaty with East Germany by the year's end. The announcement was made in a joint communique issued by the 8 Communist leaders at the end of a 3-day Moscow meeting held "to discuss questions connected with ... a German peace treaty."

The communique said: "The meeting ... expressed readiness to contribute by every means to the attainment of a peaceful settlement with the 2 German states, coordinated with the Western powers"; "the German peace treaty should record the situation which has developed in Europe after the war, record in legal form the immutability of the present German frontiers, normalize the situation in West Berlin"; reliable and effective guarantees will be furnished by the peace treaty to insure strict nonintervention in the affairs of West Berlin and access to it"; "the meeting expressed the inflexible determination of all its participants to achieve a peace settlement with Germany before the end of this year."

U.S. State Secy. Rusk, French Foreign Min. Maurice Couve de Murville and the Earl of Home, British foreign secretary, conferred in Paris Aug. 5-7 on a coordinated Western response to the latest Soviet moves in the Berlin crisis. They were joined, for the first 2 days of talks, by West German Foreign Min. Heinrich von Brentano.

Official spokesmen declared Aug. 6 that the foreign ministers had reached agreement to affirm the West's readiness to negotiate a Berlin settlement on a "reasonable basis." They made it clear that such negotiations, if they took place, would have to be under "conditions of mutual respect and without preconditions." The 4 ministers were said to have decided against any rapid reply to Soviet calls for negotiating the Berlin crisis. This was described as a concession to French-West German views that a Western peace initiative, under current Soviet pressures, would be interpreted as a sign of weakness. The ministers' spokesmen declared that the 4 countries were agreed that they would not enter negotiations over Berlin under a threat of Soviet renunciation of wartime obligations in Germany or the signing of a Soviet-East German peace treaty. It was reported that, before entering such negotiations, the West planned to ask West Berlin to hold a plebiscite on the retention of Western troops in the city.

(The 3-day Paris meeting was divided into 2 phases: an initial series of sessions devoted to Berlin and Europe Aug. 5-6, and a final session centering on Asia and other problems Aug. 7.)

Coordinated policies worked out by the Western foreign ministers were presented to the NATO Permanent Council in Paris Aug. 8 by Rusk and were indorsed immediately by the alliance's 15 member states. A communique issued by the Council Aug. 8 said NATO would begin intensified consultations on the measures deemed necessary in view of the Berlin crisis. It reaffirmed a May 1961 NATO Ministerial Council statement that "a peaceful and just solution of the problem of Germany, including Berlin, is to be found only on the basis of self-determination."

Rusk's report was said to contain an appeal for NATO states to take rapid steps to fulfill their assigned military manpower and readiness commitments. (NATO forces were believed to total 21½ divisions; the alliance's long-range plans reportedly had provided for a current strength of 30 divisions. The *N.Y. Times* reported Aug. 9 that the U.S. was prepared to strengthen its 5 divisions in West Germany and to airlift up to 6 more Army divisions and 2 Marine divisions to Europe or elsewhere in the event of a sudden worsening of the crisis.)

The U.S.' intention to press other NATO states to fulfill their military commitments and take other steps to demonstrate Western firmness over Berlin had been disclosed by Pres. Kennedy at his press conference July 19. The President, conceding that other NATO states bore "particular burdens," said the U.S. "will ... have consultations with them about what we in common can do." He added: "If this alliance is going to move in concert, ... we have to improve our consultation" and "come to decisions ... quickly."

U.S. Defense Secy. Robert S. McNamara and Gen. Lyman L. Lemnitzer, chairman of the Joint Chiefs of Staff, flew to Europe July 22 to begin talks with NATO and European officials on strengthening Western defenses. They conferred in Paris July 23 with NATO Secy. Gen. Dirk U. Stikker and the NATO supreme commander, Gen. Lauris Norstad, and in London July 24 with British Defense Min. Harold Watkinson before returning to Washington. West German Defense Min. Franz Josef Strauss had met with McNamara in Washington July 14 during a visit to the U.S. to negotiate the purchase of $165 million worth of military equipment, including Pershing missiles and F-104 jet fighters. Strauss said at a press conference Aug. 1 that he believed the USSR might risk "city guerrilla warfare" in Berlin but not general nuclear war.

Stikker had conferred with Kennedy, Rusk and McNamara in Washington in June and then had told Washington newsmen June 16 that "Khrushchev made it abundantly clear that there is urgency" in the need for increased NATO strength. Stikker declared that NATO forces were sufficiently strong to halt "local incursions" but that a full-scale Communist attack on Europe could be stopped only with nuclear weapons.

Norstad, in testimony made public July 9 by the House Foreign Affairs Committee, had estimated that NATO faced a Communist force totaling 126 land divisions and 12,000 aircraft west of the Urals. Norstad said the far smaller NATO forces could "render a very good account of themselves" but still were inadequate to bear "the full burden of their responsibilities." He urged the beginning of a new long-range NATO buildup and the admission of Spain to the alliance.

(Orders for the transformation of 3 U.S. training divisions to combat units within the Strategic Army Force were made public by the Army Aug. 8. The 3 units were the First and 2d Infantry Divisions and the 2d Armored Division. Pentagon sources reported Aug. 4 that current Administration plans provided for the call-up of only 185,000 of the 225,227 men requested by Kennedy in his July 25 speech on Berlin.)

Miscellaneous Events

Among other developments relating to the Berlin crisis reported from Britain, France, East Germany, West Germany and the U.S.:

Britain —In a nationwide radio-TV address Aug. 4, Prime Min. Macmillan declared that Britain would honor its "responsibility to those 2 million people in Berlin" because "it would be neither prudent nor honorable to abandon them." He asserted that, "while we ... stand firm on our rights, there is perhaps the possibility of ... negotiation" on the Berlin problem. Macmillan had told Parliament June 27 that there could be "no question whatever of any modification of British commitments" in Berlin. He said the West was prepared to discuss the Berlin issue but that such talks must be "negotiations, and not ... blackmail." (Ex-Prime Min. Anthony Eden had called June 10 for the establishment of "a political general staff" to coordinate the West's response to Soviet policies.)

The Earl of Home, British foreign secretary, told the House of Lords July 19 that Britain had "never insisted on the *status quo*" in Berlin but that any change must be by "consent." He warned that "one false step over Berlin could easily plunge Europe into war." A Parliamentary statement made July 31 by Deputy Foreign Secy. Edward Heath asserted that the West "cannot prevent the signature of a separate peace treaty with East Germany, but neither can our rights in Berlin be affected by ... a peace treaty ... made unilaterally."

France —Pres. de Gaulle declared July 12 in a radio-TV report to the French people that there was "no chance" that the West would accept Soviet terms for the settlement of the Berlin crisis. De Gaulle accused Khrushchev of invoking "the peace of the world while posing demands that risk ... it." He warned the Soviet leader that his German policy could have serious consequences. De Gaulle emphasized that a Berlin settlement was possible only if the USSR halted its threats as a first step toward a relaxation of tensions. He said France planned to shorten its 27-month conscription term and to use the savings for modernizing its armed forces. De Gaulle had warned in a speech June 30 that the world was "on the eve of a serious ... crisis" because "in the East there exists a bloc and we do not definitely know whether it wants a war or peace."

East Germany —The East German government, in an attempt to stem the refugee flow: (1) Reinforced police controls on train traffic to East Berlin (reported July 22) and began army surveillance of truck and other highway traffic to the city (reported July 27). (2) Announced Aug. 1 that the East German Health Ministry had asked the government to "take steps in regard to travel between West Germany" and East Germany in view of an alleged West German polio epidemic. (3) Began alleged police harassment (reported Aug. 2) of the estimated 53,000 East Berliners who worked in West Berlin and crossed the city border daily. (43,000 East Germans were registered with the West Berlin currency equalization agency; another 10,000 were believed to work there without registration.) (4) Issued decrees (Aug. 4 by the East Berlin Governing Council) ordering all East Germans working in West Berlin to register and pay their rent and utilities in West German Deutschemarks, valued at 5 times the Eastmark.

The U.S., British and French military commandants in West Berlin protested to the Soviet commander Aug. 3 against the East German measures designed to "discriminate against and penalize" East Germans employed in West Berlin. Identical notes sent to Red Army Col. I. A. Solovyev by Maj. Gen. Albert Watson 2d of the U.S., Maj. Gen. Sir Rohan Delacombe of Britain and Brig. Gen. Jean Lacomme of France charged that the East German actions were in violation of the Berlin agreements signed during World War II and following the 1948 Berlin blockade.

(Decrees requiring all foreign aircraft equipped with radios to register with East German air control agencies had become effective July 31. The decrees were ignored by Western planes and were not enforced.)

East Berlin Mayor Friedrich Ebert called on West Berlin Mayor Willy Brandt Aug. 3 to cooperate in forming a joint committee to settle the "border crossing problem."

West Germany—A memo delivered to the Soviet government July 12 by West German Amb.-to-USSR Hans Kroll rejected proposals for direct Soviet-West German negotiations on a World War II peace treaty and the transformation of West Berlin into a free city. The West German memo, in reply to the Soviet note delivered Feb. 17, declared that a peace treaty could be signed only by a freely elected all-German government. It declared that any bilateral treaty signed by either the East German government or the West German government would be illegal. It based the Bonn government's views on this precept: "It is an indispensable fact that, despite all developments following World War II, the German people continued to exist as an entity."

Chancellor Adenauer had opened the West German election campaign July 6 with a speech in which he denounced any central European settlement based on the neutralization of Germany. Adenauer said: "He who has Germany has Western Europe and ... the upper hand in the ... dispute between East and West." "A country such as ... [West] Germany, ... a highly developed economy, lying between the Eastern and Western blocs, cannot remain neutral. Neutralization would not be honored in tense circumstances." Adenauer July 9 rejected a suggestion made the previous day by West Berlin Mayor Willy Brandt for a "super peace conference" of the 52 nations that fought Germany during World War II. Adenauer flew to West Berlin July 12 and conferred with Brandt, his Social Democratic opponent in the West German election campaign. Adenauer told newsmen before leaving Berlin July 13 that any German settlement based on neutralization would "mean the end of Germany" and an "immense increase of power for the Soviet Union."

Brandt, speaking June 17 at a West Berlin rally commemorating the 1953 East German uprising against Communist rule, had said his answer to renewed Communist pressure on the city was: "We shall never surrender." Brandt told newsmen Aug. 7 that he saw no need for a West Berlin plebiscite on the continued presence of Western occupation troops but that it would be held if requested by the Western powers. He noted that "every day more than 1,000 people are voting with their feet against the ridiculous government in East Germany."

(The 3d West German Bundestag had adjourned its final session June 30 after adopting a resolution calling for renewed U.S.-British-French-Soviet negotiations on a free all-German government and a German peace treaty.)

United States —State Secy. Rusk said at a Washington news conference July 27 that the West would seek "opportunities for a peaceful adjustment" of the Berlin problem without endangering the city's freedom. He asserted that the professed concern of the USSR for its security in central Europe was "unreal" because there had been no attempt "to change the *status quo* by force" in 16 years. Rusk, interviewed on ABC-TV's "Editor's Choice" program July 23, had asserted that the Western powers would take the Berlin problem to the UN General Assembly if "it develops into a situation of very high tension."

Sen. Hubert H. Humphrey (D., Minn.) had returned to Washington July 13 from visits to Geneva and Berlin and suggested that Khrushchev's renewed attack on the West in Berlin was "part of an effort to cover up the massive food problem in his wobbly empire."

Ex-Pres. Harry S. Truman told newsmen July 29 that he believed Khrushchev's threats against the West in Berlin were a bluff and that the USSR would not risk war because it feared Communist China.

Prelude to the Berlin Wall

Substantially increased numbers of East Germans—30,415—were registered at West Berlin refugee centers in July. The renewed exodus from East Germany was attributed to fears that the West Berlin escape route would be sealed off by the USSR and the East German government. It also was considered an indication of worsened living conditions in East Germany and of harsh coercive measures applied by the regime of East German Socialist Unity Party First Secy. Walter Ulbricht. The influx into West Berlin refugee centers reached a daily average of more than 1,500 in the beginning of August, and more than 16,000 East German refugees registered at the West Berlin center between Aug. 1 and Aug. 13. These figures were the highest reported since Mar. 1953. At least 2,000 of those registered in July were said to have come to West Berlin for the biennial *Kirchentag* rally of the German Evangelical Church July 19-23.

(East German refugees usually reached the West by going to East Berlin and then taking the elevated municipal railway to a station in West Berlin. Refugees also used several Berlin border points where pedestrians were able to cross from one zone to the other with minimum surveillance. The border between East and West Berlin was kept open under the wartime Allied agreement for joint occupation of the city. Refugees were flown from West Berlin to West Germany.)

West German Chancellor Adenauer declared July 13 that the large number of East Germans fleeing via West Berlin proved that "the people of East Germany have been gripped by ... fear and panic as a result of new restrictive measures by the Communist regime." All-German Affairs Min. Ernst Lemmer said July 22 that the exodus was a "catastrophe" for the Communist regime; he asserted that 3.5 million persons had fled East Germany since 1945.

Ulbricht told the East German Volkskammer (lower house) July 6 that "there will be no shooting" in Berlin but that the city "must cease being a bastion of the cold war" through a Soviet-East German peace treaty. Ulbricht said that such a treaty was "on history's calendar for 1961." He declared that the treaty "will apply to all of East Germany, including West Berlin. This means clearly that the Allied ... rights in West Berlin will be lifted."

East German Deputy Foreign Min. Otto Winzer July 10 rejected Western contentions that East German border police might be permitted to exercise a role in Berlin access control as "agents" of the USSR. Winzer asserted that East Germany had "full sovereignty, and its authorities will not act as the agents of any other power."

East Berlin food regulations made public July 14 tightened butter rationing and imposed new controls against food smuggling to and from West Berlin. (East German press dispatches reported July 14 that some East German farmers had begun a campaign for the breakup of collectives and a return to private farming.)

Columnist Joseph Alsop reported in the *N.Y. Herald Tribune* July 26 that U.S. Atty. Gen. Robert F. Kennedy had told Soviet Amb.-to-U.S. Mikhail A. Menshikov that Pres. Kennedy felt the Berlin issue was worth going to war over, if necessary. Alsop said: The warning was delivered in Washington in July at a private Soviet embassy meeting to which Menshikov had invited the attorney general; Atty. Gen. Kennedy received the President's approval before agreeing to meet Menshikov.

Premier Khrushchev warned in 2 major speeches Aug. 9 and 11 that the USSR had new weapons of frightening power and that hundreds of millions might die if a war resulted from the crisis over Berlin:

● In an impromptu address Aug. 9 at a Kremlin reception honoring Maj. Gherman S. Titov, Soviet cosmonaut, Khrushchev had declared that "scientists have suggested to the Soviet government that they can create a bomb equal to 100 million tons of TNT—only one bomb." Khrushchev asserted that the USSR had a rocket capable of delivering such a bomb, but it would prefer to "sink all these things [warheads] in the ocean" and use the rocket for scientific research. He asserted that "we do not want war" but that if war came and if it resulted from an attack by West Germany, "then there will be no German nation left after that; all Germany will be reduced to dust."

● Khrushchev said at a Soviet-Rumanian friendship meeting in the Kremlin Aug. 11 that he did not believe the West would "fight for the freedom of the Germans in West Germany if we sign a peace treaty." "This is a fairy tale," he declared. "They say they want to declare war for these 2,200,000 people [in West Berlin] and let hundreds of millions of people perish. What man of common sense can believe such nonsense?" Khrushchev said the fight for a German peace treaty was "not just literally for a

peace treaty" but a fight "for the recognition of our grandeur."
He said that "the roar of the British lion does not terrify
anybody anymore" and that the Egyptians "tugged him by the
tail and drove him away." Khrushchev said he had told Italian
Premier Amintore Fanfani and Greek Amb. George C.
Christopoulous recently that the NATO bases in their countries
would bring devastating Soviet attack there in case of war.

(The appointment of Marshal Ivan S. Konev, 64, as
commander of Soviet armed forces in East Germany was
announced Aug. 10. Konev, former commander of Warsaw
Pact forces, replaced Col. Gen. Ivan I. Jakubowski as head of
about 400,000 Soviet troops in East Germany.)

Berlin Wall Goes Up

The border between the Western and Soviet sectors of
Berlin was closed to East Germans Aug. 13 by troops, police,
and factory militia of the East German government. The
Communist action closed the principal escape route used by
East German refugees.

The border closure was applied only to East Germans;
West Germans, West Berliners and Allied military personnel
were permitted to enter and leave the Soviet sector. East
Berliners working in West Berlin were halted. Travel across
East Germany between West Berlin and West Germany was
not affected by the Communist action.

More than 4,100 East German refugees were registered in
the West Berlin refugee centers in the last 24 hours the border
was open.

A communique issued by the Warsaw Pact powers and
made public after midnight during the night of Aug. 12-13 by
the East German ADN news agency called on East Germany
to take temporary measures for the "protection and control" of
the border between East and West Berlin. The communique
charged that West Berlin had become a center for espionage
and subversion against the Soviet bloc. It said: "The ...
Warsaw Treaty member states address ... [the East German
government] with a proposal to establish such an order on the
borders of West Berlin which would securely block the way for
the subversive activity against the Socialist ... countries, so
that reliable safeguards and effective control can be established

around the whole territory of West Berlin including its border with Democratic [East] Berlin." "These measures must not affect the existing order of traffic and control on the ways of communication between West Berlin and Western Germany."

East German police and troops arrived at the Brandenburg Gate and other border crossing points and began erecting barricades at 3 a.m. Aug. 13.

The East German action was ordered in a government decree made public later Aug. 13. The decree said normal border controls would be instituted between the 2 sectors of Berlin on the basis of an East German cabinet decision made in response to the Warsaw Pact communique. It said specifically that East Germans would require a new special permit to enter West Berlin but that West Germans, West Berliners, foreign citizens and Allied military personnel could enter East Berlin as usual. It said that "this decree in no way revises former decisions on transit between West Berlin and West Germany via the [East] German Democratic Republic." The decree was to remain in force until "the conclusion of a German peace treaty."

The East Berlin city council Aug. 13 issued orders cancelling the passes held by the 53,000 East Berliners who worked in West Berlin.

West Berliners gathered near the closed border points Aug. 13 to jeer Communist police engaged in building barricades. West Berlin police prevented them from approaching the border at points where tension seemed high. Thousands passed the control points to make brief visits to East Berlin; all West Berliners were permitted to return to their own sector, but East Berliners were turned back. Several incidents were reported in which East German police were said to have used tear gas and high pressure water cannon to drive angered West Berliners back from the border. 5,000 West Berlin workers marched to the city hall early Aug. 14 to demand retaliation against the Communist measures.

West Berlin Mayor Willy Brandt appealed to West Berliners Aug. 13 to remain "calm and reasonable." He warned that "ill-considered actions do not help our city or our compatriots separated from us." Brandt met with the city's 3 Western military commandants and told the West Berlin parliament later Aug. 13 that he had urged them to ask their

governments for "energetic actions" to make the "Communists
... cancel their unlawful measures."

It was reported Aug. 13-14 that the border guard units
were supported by armored cars and that East German army
units containing 200 tanks had moved into the city. 2 Soviet
army divisions were said to have been deployed outside East
Berlin for use against any rebellion. East Germany announced
Aug. 14 that its Berlin border forces had been ordered to take
"counter-measures" against "hostile actions." The
Brandenburg Gate crossing was completely closed.

The isolation of East Berlin was intensified Aug. 14 with
the cutting of phone communications with West Berlin and
West Germany. The West German government disclosed later
the same day that all postal and telegraph service had been
interrupted between East and West Germany. The East
German Interior Ministry announced Aug. 15 that all West
Berlin vehicles would require special permits to enter East
Berlin. It said the new restrictions, the first to be applied to
West Berliners, were necessary because their freedom of access
to the Soviet sector had been abused for espionage purposes.

U.S. State Secy. Rusk charged Aug. 13 that the Berlin
border closing violated 2 international agreements. Rusk's
statement was issued in Washington after he had conferred by
telephone with Pres. Kennedy, who was spending the weekend
at Hyannis Port, Mass. "Limitation on travel within Berlin is a
violation of the 4-power status of Berlin and ... of the right of
free circulation throughout the city," Rusk declared in his
statement. "Restrictions on travel between East Germany and
Berlin are in direct contravention of the 4-power [Paris]
agreement" of June 20, 1949. But Rusk noted that the
Communist "measures taken thus far are aimed at residents of
East Berlin and East Germany and not at the Allied position in
West Berlin or access thereto."

Rusk's statement said: The German Communist moves "to
deny their own people access to West Berlin ... have doubtless
been prompted by the increased flow of refugees in recent
weeks. The refugees are not responding to persuasion or
propaganda from the West, but to the failures of communism
in East Germany.... Communist authorities are ... denying the
right of individuals to elect a world of free choice rather than a
world of coercion.... The refugees, more than half of whom are

less than 25 years of age, have 'voted with their feet' on whether communism is the wave of the future." (It was disclosed Sept. 20 that Prof. Ernst Bloch, 76, East Germany's leading Marxist philosopher, had been in Western Europe when the Berlin border was sealed and had decided not to return to East Berlin.)

Rusk's statement was indorsed by the British government, a British Foreign Office spokesman said in London Aug. 14, in the absence of Prime Min. Macmillan and the Earl of Home, British foreign secretary, who were on holiday. The Foreign Office official said Britain held the USSR responsible for the events in East Berlin.

The border closing apparently had surprised the Kennedy Administration. Rusk, returning from meetings with Western leaders in Europe, had said during a Paris stop-over Aug. 10, before the Communist move, that he thought there was agreement among the Allies that "there will be negotiations" with the USSR over Berlin and that "possibly some sort of initiative could be taken" by the West. Rusk added in Washington Aug. 11, after reporting to Kennedy, that the West was "determined to defend its vital interests" in Berlin. But he said immediate negotiations with the USSR were not desirable because chances of agreement were dim. "When great powers go into negotiations, there must be some prospect of success, because failure contributes to tension," he said.

East German workmen Aug. 15 began building a wall of 4-foot concrete blocks the length of the 25-mile East-West Berlin boundary to replace the barbed wire barricades originally strung along the border Aug. 13-14. Families were forced to move from some East Berlin houses along the border to prevent the use of the houses as an escape route to the West. In other border houses, doors opening into West Berlin were locked by police but the houses were not evacuated.

Warren Rogers Jr. reported in the *N.Y. Herald Tribune* Aug. 23 that the Communist plan to seal the border in this fashion had been known to the Allies since 1958 and had been dubbed "Operation Chinese Wall" by U.S. and West German intelligence agents. An East German government aide defecting to West Berlin in July 1958 had brought along a document describing the plan, which called initially for a barbed-wire barrier, then its replacement by a cement-block

fence and finally the erection of substantial "palisades." A copy
of the plan had been turned over to U.S. agents by Mayor
Brandt, who was reported to have given little weight to the
plan because (a) the defector had said the USSR had vetoed it
and (b) Brandt thought the Western Allies would be sure to
challenge such a violation of the 4-power occupation
agreement.

The East German Interior Ministry announced Aug. 22
that starting that midnight, "foreigners," including "members
of the occupation forces" (U.S., British and French), would be
allowed to cross the East-West Berlin border only at the
Friedrichstrasse crossing point. West Berliners and West
Germans were barred simultaneously from East Berlin unless
they bought special permits (at one Deutschemark each) in
advance from the East German travel agency. 4 crossing points
were designated for West Berliners, 2 points for West
Germans.

The East German announcement said the decree would be
effective "until the conclusion of a peace treaty." The new
curbs were ordered, the announcement said, because of
"provocations" and because East German "generosity" in not
barring West Berliners from East Berlin had been "abused" by
"agents of spying organizations." The announcement said all
people must stay at least 100 meters (328 feet) away from either
side of the border.

Phone connections between East and West Germany—but
not between East and West Berlin—were restored by East
Germany Aug. 22.

West Berliners, in retaliation for the Communist
restrictions, began to boycott the East German-run elevated
railway and thereby deprive East Germany of a source of West
German currency. East Berlin rail officials charged that West
Berliners also were breaking windows of the elevated trains and
tearing out seats.

After the Berlin Wall

A formal U.S.-British-French protest against the Berlin
border closings was made Aug. 15 in a message from the 3
Western commandants in Berlin to the Soviet commandant.
The note was rejected by the Soviet commandant Aug. 16.

"Not since the imposition of the Berlin blockade has there been such a flagrant violation of the 4-power agreements concerning Berlin," the Western message charged. "The agreement of June 20, 1949, in which the USSR pledged itself to facilitate freedom of movement within Berlin and between Berlin and the rest of Germany, has also been violated.... [Traffic between East and West Berlin] has been disrupted by the cutting of *S-bahn* [elevated] and *U-bahn* [subway] service, the tearing up of streets, the erection of road blocks and the stringing of barbed wire. In carrying out these illegal actions, military and paramilitary units, which were formed in violation of 4-power agreements and whose very presence in East Berlin is illegal, turned the Soviet sector of Berlin into an armed camp."

The Western message, addressed to Soviet Col. Andrei I. Solovyev, said: "We ... hold you responsible for the carrying out of the relevant agreements." It was signed by U.S. Maj. Gen. Albert Watson 2d, French Brig. Gen. Jean Lacomme and British Maj. Gen. Sir Rohan Delacombe.

Solovyev replied Aug. 16 that the protest was an attempt to interfere in matters that were the exclusive concern of the East German government. Rejecting the Western complaint about violation of the June 20, 1949 agreement, Solovyev's message said that "the necessary explications on this point" could be found in the Sept. 26, 1960 USSR note to the U.S. (which indicated that Allied rights in access routes to Berlin were limited to the supplying of Western garrisons in the city). Solovyev asserted that the "deterioration of the atmosphere in Berlin," of which the Allied commandants had complained, was a "result of the activity of those, who, supported by the occupation status which is still maintained in West Berlin, make use of West Berlin for illegal, provocative measures and subversion against the [East] German Democratic Republic and the Socialist states." In further notes to the 3 Western commandants Aug. 18, Solovyev reiterated that the border actions came "fully under the competence" of the East German government and that the Soviet commandant in Berlin "does not interfere in the affairs of the capital of the German Democratic Republic."

West German Chancellor Adenauer suggested in a political address in Regensburg Aug. 14 that the Western powers might retaliate for the Berlin border closing by imposing economic sanctions—including a possible total trade embargo on the Soviet bloc. The Bonn government was considering canceling the trade agreement between West and East Germany, he declared. Adenauer said U.S. State Secy. Rusk had indicated that he was "in favor" of economic countermeasures. "We shall not contribute to the economic build-up of the Soviet Union if Moscow does not agree to reasonable negotiations" with the NATO powers, he declared. Trade sanctions would be an excellent weapon, Adenauer asserted, because the USSR was "not as strong economically as the West is made to believe."

The East German Council of Ministers warned Bonn in a statement issued Aug. 15 that if Bonn canceled the trade agreements between East and West Germany, the East German government would start a new Berlin blockade and bar all surface freight to and from West Berlin. East German transport services for such freight were provided for under an annex to the trade agreements.

Mayor Brandt said at a rally of 250,000 West Berliners gathered in front of West Berlin's City Hall Aug. 16 that he had written to Pres. Kennedy to tell him that West Berlin expected "not merely words but political action" from the West in response to the construction of the wall. The rally appeared to be a forum for complaints of West Berliners that the West had failed to take strong action on the crisis. Signs displayed at the rally said: "Paper protests do not stop tanks." "Kennedy to Berlin." "Are we being betrayed by the West?"

Brandt declared that "the question at issue is that Berlin should not become a Munich." He warned that "if ... we do not pass this test, then the Communists will not stop at the Brandenburg Gate ... at the zonal border ... [or] on the Rhine."

Brandt's letter to Kennedy was published without authorization by the *Frankfurter Allgemeine Zeitung* Aug. 19. According to the published text, Brandt had proposed that the West "proclaim a 3-power status of West Berlin," "repeat the guarantee of their presence in Berlin until German reunification, and possibly have this supported through a referendum" in West Berlin and West Germany. Brandt warned in his letter that "inactivity and mere defensive tactics"

(a) "could bring about a crisis in confidence toward the West," and (b) "can lead to an overexaggerated self-assertion of the East Berlin regime, which is already boasting ... of the success of its military demonstration of power." Brandt said that "the legal sovereignty of the East Berlin government has been recognized by acceptance as far as the restrictions of the crossing points and access to the East sector are concerned." This development, he asserted, "was apt to arouse doubts about the Western powers' ability to react and about their determination." "The Soviet Union has achieved half of its free-city proposals," Brandt declared. One of Brandt's suggestions was that the U.S. garrison in West Berlin "demonstratively receive some reinforcement."

Kennedy's answer to Brandt's letter was delivered personally by U.S. Vice Pres. Lyndon B. Johnson Aug. 20. After reading the Kennedy reply and conferring with Johnson, Brandt said Aug. 20 that Johnson's visit had "erased any doubts among the people." The Johnson mission and the U.S. troop reinforcements had "made a deep impression on the Russians—and when they are impressed they are less likely to take risks," Brandt said.

Soviet Amb. Andrei A. Smirnov delivered to Adenauer in Bonn Aug. 16 an oral message from Premier Khrushchev assuring Adenauer that Khrushchev planned to do nothing that would make the Berlin situation worse. The message was delivered during a discussion of Soviet-West German relations attended by West German Foreign Min. Heinrich von Brentano, who then reported the conversation to the Bundestag's Foreign Policy and All-German Affairs committees.

Adenauer told the Bundestag Aug. 18 that although the Berlin border measures had been taken "with the consent" of the USSR, he hoped the Soviet government would disown the actions of "the authorities of the Soviet zone [East Germany]." He said the crisis would force West Germany to build up its defenses further but that it would do so "within the framework of the Atlantic defense organization." "We know and the Soviet Union knows that the total military potential of the West is superior to that of the Soviet Union," Adenauer said. "Hence the threats ... [against] NATO partners to the effect that it would devastate their territory by atomic bombs are dangerous. The Soviet government must know that by any such blow it would touch off a counterblow by which it would be annihilated."

During a campaign speech in Bonn Aug. 16, Adenauer had defended the behavior of the Western powers in Berlin. He said that the Berlin crisis was only beginning and that the West could be depended on "when an extraordinary crisis comes."

Adenauer visited West Berlin Aug. 22 and received a cold reception from many West Berliners, who felt he should have gone there as soon as the crisis started. Touring the Communist barricades at the East-West Berlin border, Adenauer was jeered at over loud speakers from the Communist side. Gerhard Eisler, East German propagandist who had jumped bail in the U.S., shouted to Adenauer at Potsdamer Platz: "There's only one way out, Konny. You'll have to deal with us." At the Brandenburg Gate, a voice shouted over Communist loud speakers: "We acted, but you did nothing."

U.S. Supports West Berliners

U.S. Vice Pres. Johnson had flown to Berlin Aug. 18-19 to deliver Pres. Kennedy's assurance to West Germans and West Berliners that the U.S. guaranteed their continued freedom and would give them full support in the crisis caused by the Communist closing of the borders between East and West Berlin. Speaking at a special meeting of the West Berlin Parliament Aug. 19, Johnson said:

". . . To the survival and to the creative future of this city we Americans have pledged, in effect, what our ancestors pledged in forming the United States—'our lives, our fortunes and our sacred honor'." "We must without fear seek peace always but be prepared now and ever more to defend freedom. This is a time . . . for faith in yourselves . . . [and] in your allies everywhere in the world. This island does not stand alone. You are a vital part of the whole free community of free men. Your lives . . . are linked with those who live in every town of Western Europe, Canada and the United States, and with those on every continent who live in freedom and are prepared to fight for it."

Johnson was accompanied by Gen. Lucius D. Clay, who had been U.S. military commander in Germany during the Berlin blockade, and by Charles E. Bohlen, State Department expert on German and Soviet affairs. En route to Berlin, the party stopped in Bonn Aug. 19 to confer with Adenauer and to change planes. It was reported that Johnson and Adenauer agreed on the need to forestall war and to arrive at a satisfactory settlement of disputes over Germany and Berlin by negotiation with the USSR.

Johnson told a crowd of welcoming Germans at the Bonn-Cologne airport that he was in Germany as Pres. Kennedy's representative "to express a conviction, to convey a pledge, to sound a warning and to reiterate a policy." Johnson said: "The American President and the American people are determined to fulfill all our obligations and to honor all our commitments"; "we urge the masters of the Soviet Union and East Germany who have manufactured this crisis to remember ... that a crime against peace will now be a crime against all humanity, and against that particular crime humanity's retribution will be swift and emphatic"; the American people were "not provocative, neither are we frightened; the American people have no genius for retreat, and we do not intend to retreat now."

Johnson and thousands of West Berliners greeted the first of 1,500 U.S. troops who arrived Aug. 20 by road convoy from West Germany to increase the U.S. garrison in West Berlin to 6,500 men. The reinforcements had been ordered to Berlin by Kennedy Aug. 18. They made the 110-mile *autobahn* trip through East Germany without incident.

Before leaving Berlin early Aug. 21, Johnson issued a statement saluting "with honor and gratitude the great-hearted people of West Berlin, the city of unconquerable freedom." "I am going home to tell the President and the people of America that the Western powers ... have never had better or braver allies than we have in the citizens of this city,"Johnson said."I shall tell my fellow Americans that I have seen the fruits of democracy in West Berlin and in Bonn."

Johnson reported to Kennedy in Washington Aug. 21. The President said later that Johnson's report "emphasizes the confidence and trust which the people of West Berlin have in this country and its commitments, and it places a heavy responsibility upon all of us to meet that responsibility." "We are going to pass through difficult weeks and months ... in maintaining the freedom of West Berlin, but maintain it we will," Kennedy declared.

U.S. State Secy. Rusk had predicted in a TV interview on NBC's "Meet the Press" program Aug. 20 that the Berlin problem as well as other problems of Germany and Central Europe would be solved by negotiations with the USSR. The Berlin issue "is a problem of the great worldwide confrontation between the Sino-Soviet bloc and the free world, and it is of great importance that we make our commitments clear," Rusk said. He pledged that the U.S. "will not be pushed out of West Berlin."

The U.S. State Department Aug. 21 abruptly canceled plans to sign a commercial airlines route agreement with the USSR. It said it did so "in view of the international [Berlin] situation, for which the U.S. government is not responsible." The pact was to have covered the sharing of Moscow-New York polar flights by Pan-American Airways and the USSR's Aeroflot. Washington talks on the pact had begun July 18 between teams headed by ex-CAB Chairman James M. Landis for the U.S. and by Col. Gen. Yevgeni F. Loginov, Soviet civil air director, for the USSR. According to observers, negotiations had been completed, and the agreement merely needed signature. (Plans for similar talks had been broken off in mid-1960 because of the U-2 incident and the shooting down of a U.S. RB-47 naval reconnaissance plane.)

(French Pres. Charles de Gaulle Aug. 17 ordered an undisclosed number of French ground and air units shifted from Algeria to France because of the Berlin crisis. British official sources in London reported Aug. 17 and 19, however, that Britain planned no immediate increase of its ground forces in Berlin.

(East Germany's Free German Youth organization, through its newspaper, *Young World,* called Aug. 17 on its 2 million members to volunteer for the armed forces in the Berlin crisis.)

West Attacks Border Curbs

The U.S., Britain and France Aug. 17 sent identic notes to

the Kremlin blaming the USSR for the Berlin border closings and demanding that the Soviet government "put an end to these illegal measures." The USSR, in an unprecedentedly quick reply Aug. 18, rejected the Western protest.

The Western notes, delivered by the ambassadors of the 3 protesting countries, charged that the boundary restrictions were "a flagrant, and particularly serious, violation of the quadripartite status of Berlin" as affirmed by the 4-power agreement of May 4, 1949 and by the 4 powers' foreign ministers June 29, 1949. Each Western power said in its note that it "holds the Soviet government responsible" for the Communist measures taken in Berlin.

The Western notes said: The Western powers had "never accepted that limitations can be imposed on freedom of movement within Berlin"; the boundary between the 2 sectors of Berlin "is not a state frontier"; the Western powers did "not accept the pretension that the Soviet sector of Berlin forms a part of the so-called 'German Democratic Republic' and that Berlin is situated on its territory"; "such a pretension is ... a violation of the solemnly pledged word of the USSR" in the agreement on German occupation zones and Berlin administration; the Western powers "cannot admit the right of the East German authorities to authorize their armed forces to enter the Soviet sector of Berlin"; the border closings were recommended by the Warsaw Treaty powers, who "are thus intervening in a domain in which they have no competence."

The Soviet Government rejected the Western notes Aug. 18. In parallel notes sent to the 3 Western governments, the USSR asserted that the quadripartite agreements had been "concluded for the period of Germany's occupation" and had been invalidated by repeated Western violations and by the creation of the "2 independent states" in Germany.

The USSR notes said: "The Soviet government fully understands and supports the action of the German Democratic Republic" in controlling the Berlin border "to block ... the subversive activities being conducted from West Berlin" against East Germany "and other countries of the Socialist Commonwealth"; East Germany "merely used the ordinary right of every sovereign state to defend its interests"; state frontier control was an internal question whose "settlement does not need recognition or approval by other governments";

Western attempts "to interfere" in East Germany's "internal affairs" by attacking the border measures "are absolutely groundless and irrelevant"; the Western powers were largely responsible for creating the situation that resulted in the Communist closings of the borders; West Germany, aided and encouraged by the Western powers, had turned West Berlin "into a center of subversive activities, sabotage and espionage, into a center of political and economic provocations" against East Germany and the Soviet bloc; the East German refugees were victims of a Western "army of recruiters," who used "deception, bribery and blackmail" to get them to leave East Germany.

The USSR charged in nearly identical notes to the U.S., British and French embassies in Moscow Aug. 23 that the 3 Western powers were abusing their air access to West Berlin by flying "revanchists, extremists, saboteurs and spies" and West German officials and politicians to West Berlin for "provocations" and "subversive activity" against East Germany "and other Socialist countries." The notes demanded that the Western powers end such "unlawful and provocative activities" of West Germany in Berlin.

The 3 Western powers Aug. 26 rejected the Soviet allegations as "false" and, in virtually identical notes delivered in Moscow, warned that "interference by the Soviet government or its East German regime with free access to Berlin would have the most serious consequences for which it would bear full responsibility." The Soviet notes of Aug. 23 charged that the Western use of air access to Berlin "represents a flagrant breach of the [1945] agreement ... under which ... air corridors were set aside for the 3 Western powers, on a temporary basis, to ensure the needs of their military garrisons. ..."

The Soviet notes said: Despite USSR complaints to the Western powers, "the unlawful and impermissible intervention by the Federal Republic of Germany (FRG) in the affairs of West Berlin ... has of late been sharply stepped up, especially in connection with the proposal for an immediate peace settlement with Germany and the solution of the West Berlin problem on this basis"; West German leaders "of late appear in West Berlin almost daily"; "right from the airport [they] go on demonstrative 'inspection' trips through the city, make provacative, hostile statements against the GDR [German Democratic Republic] and the Soviet Union"; this was part of a West German effort "to bring about a clash between the Western powers and the Soviet Union to the advantage of West German militarists and revenge-seekers"; "continuing to connive at [FRG] interference ... in the affairs of West Berlin and the use of the city's territory for international provacations," the Western powers assumed "full responsibility for the possible consequences."

The Western notes of Aug. 26 rejected "the suggestion that the purposes for which the Western Allies use the air corridors are within the competence of the Soviet Union."

The Western notes said: The 4-power Allied Control Council established the air corridors in 1945 "as the manner in which the unrestricted right of air access to Berlin would be exercised by the Western powers," and "there has never been any limitation whatsoever placed on their use" by the Western powers' planes; "if there are 'illegal and provocative activities'" taking place in Berlin, "they are certainly those of the authorities of East Germany" in clamping down the border restrictions; the Western powers did not understand the Soviet complaints against the presence of West German officials in West Berlin since "West Berlin has a wide variety of ties with the Federal Republic that are in no way incompatible with the 4-power status of Berlin"; furthermore, the USSR and East Germany "have been trying to integrate East Berlin completely into East Germany" despite the quadripartite status of all of Berlin.

The U.S. had warned Aug. 24, in a White House statement issued with the approval of Pres. Kennedy and State Secy. Rusk, that "any interference by the Soviet government or its East German regime with free access to West Berlin would be an aggressive act for the consequences of which the Soviet government would bear full responsibility." The U.S. statement described the Aug. 23 Soviet note as another "step in a deliberate campaign of deception and attempted intimidation designed to distract attention from failures of the Soviet government and to heighten world tension." The U.S. statement accused the USSR of "cynicism and irresponsibility" in making its "false" and "slanderous" charges "at the very moment when the Soviet government is sealing off the Eastern sector" of Berlin in "direct violation of the Soviet government's commitment to 'the economic and political unity of Germany'" and of its "pledged word ... to cooperate with the Allied governments 'to mitigate the effects of the administrative division of Germany and Berlin' by facilitation of the movement of persons and goods and the exchange of information 'throughout Germany, including Berlin'."

Soviet Amb.-to-West Germany Andrei A. Smirnov said in a speech at the American Club in Bad Godesberg Aug. 25 that the air corridor problem could be solved by transferring all civilian traffic from West Berlin's Templehof and Tegel airfields to East Berlin's Schoenfeld airfield. Otherwise, he said, "the same controls must be established for civilian air transport [currently controlled by the U.S., Britain, France and USSR] which now exist with the railway, the *autobahn* and the waterway transports [controlled by the East German police]."

All-German Affairs Min. Ernst Lemmer of West Germany, whose presence in West Berlin had been denounced specifically in the Aug. 23 Soviet notes, was ordered by Chancellor Adenauer Aug. 24 to remain in Berlin as an act of defiance and to cancel planned electioneering appearances in West Germany.

Identical letters protesting the tightening of border restrictions between East and West Berlin were sent by the U.S., British and French ambassadors in Bonn Aug. 26 to Soviet Amb. Mikhail G. Peruvkhin in East Berlin. "In addition to purporting to limit even more severely the crossing points" for West Berliners and West Germans, "these measures would limit foreigners, diplomats and ... members of the Allied forces to a single crossing point" and "warn all persons to remain 100 meters away from the sector boundary," the letters said. They insisted that Peruvkhin take "steps to insure continued unrestricted access to East Berlin without hindrance as to time and place." They urged him to "warn the East German authorities" that any attempt to enforce the "illegal" 100-meter requirement "could only have the most serious consequences."

West Berliners generally ignored the Communists' 100-meter limit and often crowded up to the border barriers to jeer at East German police and troops. U.S., British and French troops were ordered to patrol up to the border Aug. 23, and U.S. tanks and British and French armored cars were brought up to a short distance from the borders. The 3 Western commandants in Berlin, in a statement denouncing the new restrictions, said Aug. 23 that they were "taking the necessary action to insure the security and integrity of the sector borders."

A modification of the 100-meter curb was made public in the East Berlin newspaper *Neues Deutschland* Aug. 25. The statement indicated that the curb applied only to West Berliners, advised them to "keep away at the border from all gatherings of a provocative nature," but said that "there is no thought of interfering in any way with West Berlin citizens who live in the immediate vicinity of the border."

East German Socialist Unity Party First Secy. Walter Ulbricht said at a Communist rally in East Berlin's Sports Hall Aug. 25, that East Germany would not try to control Allied traffic in and out of West Berlin until a peace treaty had been signed. Until then, Ulbricht said, East Germany would "strictly adhere" to the Sept. 20, 1955 East German-Soviet agreement under which the USSR kept control of Allied traffic between West Germany and Berlin whereas East Germany received authority to control all other traffic. Ulbricht, directing part of his speech at Pres. Kennedy, said the Communists had "advance[d] the date" of the Berlin border closing because West Germany planned to attack East Germany after the Sept. 17 West German election. He said East-West negotiations on Berlin would have to take up the matters of: (a) East German control of Western land, air and water access to West Berlin, (b) the creation of a free city of West Berlin in which such provocative activities as the U.S.-owned RIAS radio would be banned, (c) the abandonment of West German demands for the recovery of the Oder-Neisse region and other eastern territory lost by Germany.

Soviet Premier Khrushchev said in an interview with U.S. columnist Drew Pearson that he was "ready at any moment" to negotiate with Western leaders on a "realistic settlement of the German problem on a mutually acceptable basis." In the interview, conducted at the Black Sea resort of Sochi (where Khrushchev was vacationing) and made public Aug. 27, Khrushchev repeated that the USSR was willing to guarantee free-city status for West Berlin and to station a token Soviet force there alongside U.S., British and French troops.

Khrushchev warned that unless the Western powers signed a peace treaty with East Germany, their access to West Berlin would depend on East Germany's permission. Should they use force to maintain access, "that means war," Khrushchev declared. He said: "Signing of a peace treaty ... will tie the hands of revenge-seekers and discourage them from indulging in gambles. In rejecting peaceful unification of the German nation, ... West Germany is contemplating the forcible seizure of the German Democratic Republic. Under these conditions, attack by West Germany against the German Democratic Republic ... would be the start of a thermonuclear war.... Are we to wait until Germany reunites—which ... can take place only by means of terrible war—or are we to sign a treaty with the actually existing states without further delay?..."

The office of Italian Premier Amintore Fanfani Aug. 27 sent Italian newspapers a note asserting that the Berlin border closings might have been averted if the Western powers had followed Fanfani's advice to negotiate with the Soviet Union. Fanfani said that when he visited Moscow Aug. 2-5 with Italian Foreign Min. Antonio Segni, he had urged Khrushchev to negotiate with the West and Khrushchev had agreed. The suggestion had been made after Khrushchev warned Fanfani that Italy and other Western nations faced nuclear destruction should war start. Fanfani, on returning to Rome, sent messages telling the Western governments of his conversations with Khrushchev. U.S. State Secy. Rusk and West German Chancellor Adenauer heard the story in person from Fanfani, but neither accepted Fanfani's proposal of East-West talks.

Ansa, the Italian news agency, reported Aug. 27 that Khrushchev, in a message delivered to Fanfani by Soviet Amb.-to-Italy Semyon P. Kozyrev Aug. 24, "confirmed in writing that he had accepted the invitation ... [of] Fanfani to hold negotiations [with the Allies] ... on the principal problems of the present moment." Fanfani, with Kremlin permission, sent copies of the Khrushchev letter to the U.S., British and West German governments. A new note from Khrushchev to Fanfani was delivered in Rome Sept. 2. A spokesman for Fanfani said the note reiterated Khrushchev's willingness to negotiate with the West and added that the USSR was prepared to receive Western proposals on the time and place of the talks.

West German Foreign Min. Heinrich von Brentano had said in Bonn Aug. 28 that the Western powers would soon invite the USSR to negotiate on Berlin but that Khrushchev would have to change his "negative" attitude if there was to be agreement. He suggested that the 2 sides start talks on a plan, proposed by the Western powers in 1959, that called for Germany's reunification by free elections and for putting all Berlin under a single elected council.

British Prime Min. Macmillan had told reporters Aug. 26 that the Berlin situation was "very worrying" but that "nobody is going to fight about it." Questioned on the golf course at Gleneagles, Scotland, where he was on holiday, Macmillan said: "We have to be very careful ... that nobody does anything foolish.... There would be much more danger of war if weapons were not so destructive.... But there is always the danger of folly." Macmillan conferred at Gleneagles Aug. 27 with the Earl of Home, British foreign secretary, who also was on holiday in Scotland. Macmillan then said he and Lord Home agreed "that negotiations should take place" but that they "must be held in the right atmosphere and at the right time." Lord Home said the Western powers were working on a "double-barreled policy" consisting of "building up the strength of NATO as part of the policy of finding a solution through negotiations." Strength was needed, he said, to convince the USSR that the West was able and determined to back up its insistence on these 3 conditions—"the freedom and viability of West Berlin, the presence of the Allies in the city to defend that freedom and the right of access to the city."

George Brown, British Labor Party deputy leader, speaking in the absence of Opposition leader Hugh Gaitskell (who was on holiday in Yugoslavia), had charged Aug. 26 that "the dither and delay of the last month" had jeopardized Western chances of a reasonable solution of the Berlin problem.

Indian Prime Min. Jawaharlal Nehru had told the Indian parliament Aug. 16 that he favored the "fullest facilities" for West German access to Berlin. This principle seemed to be accepted by all parties concerned, he declared. Nehru added Aug. 22 that he thought West Berlin must continue to live "in full freedom" and that its contacts with West Germany must be safeguarded. At least a "temporary solution" to any problem concerning Berlin and Germany could be found by negotiation, he said. In "any situation which might lead to war," military buildups and threats should be avoided, Nehru declared. He said he saw little use in a Soviet-East German peace treaty that other nations did not join. Nehru told the Indian parliament Aug. 23, however, that East Germany, as a sovereign state, had a legal right to close the East-West Berlin border "whether it was justifiable or not." He said the Western powers had obtained access to West Berlin "not as a right but as a concession from the Soviet authorities."

Nehru's Aug. 23 statement was attacked Aug. 24 by many U.S. Congress members, including such friends of India as Sen. John Sherman Cooper (R., Ky.), ex-ambassador to India, who called Nehru's assertion "incorrect"; Sen. Joseph S. Clark (D., Pa.), who said "the statement is most unfortunate, ill-timed and does not properly interpret the legalities"; Sen. Prescott Bush (R., Conn.), who called it "fantastic."

U.S. Amb.-to-India John Kenneth Galbraith discussed the issue with Nehru Aug. 25 and then said Nehru had authorized him to state that Nehru's remarks "should not be taken to mean that access to Berlin may be denied or impaired and to affirm his belief that it should not be changed." Nehru told the Indian parliament Aug. 28: "One thing should be accepted without reservation, and that is that access to West Berlin should be full and should continue as heretofore"; interference with Western access would have "the gravest consequences"; the disputants should not "stick too much to legal niceties" but should try to settle the issue peacefully.

Berlin Tensions Mount

Pres. Kennedy announced Aug. 30 that retired Gen. Lucius D. Clay, former military governor of the U.S. Zone of Germany, would return to West Berlin Sept. 15 as his personal representative with the rank of ambassador. The President expressed his "unusual confidence" that Clay would enhance the U.S.' "resources of judgment and action" in Berlin. Clay's appointment was believed to reflect Kennedy's dissatisfaction with U.S. military and political intelligence during the Berlin crisis.

Kennedy, meeting with Washington newsmen Aug. 30, expressed hope for the settlement of U.S.-Soviet differences in Berlin but made it clear that the U.S. would not agree to negotiate on the basis of Soviet demands for a free city of West Berlin and a German peace treaty. He said that the U.S. was prepared to join in "any exchange of views" on Germany through "all available channels" but that such talks must seek a solution for broad "problems in Europe and Germany" and must provide even "greater" guarantees of Berlin's freedom. He warned that "disaster" would result if either East or West attempted to settle the Berlin crisis by force.

Kennedy chided ex-Vice Pres. Richard M. Nixon for charging that the U.S. had exhibited weakness by sending 1,500 troops to reinforce its Berlin garrison. Nixon, interviewed Aug. 29 by CBS-TV, had said: "Any thought that moving a few ground troops into Berlin is going to have any effect on Mr. Khrushchev is a bunch of nonsense. I think it was an empty gesture and ... [one] which Mr. Khrushchev might well interpret as weakness rather than strength." Kennedy urged Republicans not to seek political advantage from the Berlin crisis.

The U.S.' determination to defend its Berlin position with nuclear weapons if necessary was stressed by Asst. Defense Secy. Paul H. Nitze in Washington Sept. 7 in an address at the convention of the U.S. Army Association. Nitze warned that, although the West had shown "great patience and forbearance" in the current crisis, "any interference with our essential rights in Berlin must be viewed by us as the straw that breaks the camel's back." He said the USSR faced "the certain prospect that we will back our non-nuclear forces by the use of our strategic capabilities should that be necessary."

Premier Khrushchev stated Sept. 7 that he was willing to meet Kennedy again in an effort "to find solutions for the major international issues now causing concern." "But the main thing is that such a meeting must be fruitful," Khrushchev noted. "And if Pres. Kennedy agrees to a meeting ..., it will be important that both sides display understanding of the need to resolve such important matters as the signing of a German peace treaty and the solution on this basis of the question of West Berlin."

The Khrushchev statement was given to C. L. Sulzberger of the *N. Y. Times* to clarify views expressed by Khrushchev Sept. 5 in a lengthy interview with Sulzberger. The statement and excerpts from the interview were printed Sept. 8 in the *Times* along with an article in which Sulzberger reported his impression that Khrushchev was (a) "supremely confident that he can win the present test of iron wills without recourse to war" and (b) "sure that the Western world will ... accept his basis for a new Berlin formula."

Among views Khrushchev stated during the Sulzberger interview: "I believe in the common sense of the Western statesmen. . . . They will draw the conclusion that a peace treaty must be signed with ... the 2 German states actually in existence, and they will give West Berlin the status of a free city. . . . It would be criminal to begin war over Berlin if West Berlin becomes a free city and if access to it is thereby insured not on the basis of the present occupation regime but on the basis of an agreement with ... the German Democratic Republic. The substance, after all, remains unchanged—access to West Berlin will be insured for all peoples and all countries who want it. . . . [We] declare that the political system of West Berlin will not be encroached upon and ... the Socialist countries will not interfere in the affairs of West Berlin." "I do not think the Western statesmen have lost their wits and are prepared to go to war over the signing of a peace treaty."

Khrushchev reiterated at a Soviet-Indian friendship meeting in the Kremlin Sept. 8 that he was prepared to negotiate with Kennedy, but he insisted that the talks take place soon and that they result in a German peace treaty. Recalling that Kennedy had said at his Aug. 30 press conference that the U.S. was ready for talks on solving the problems of Europe, Germany and Berlin, Khrushchev welcomed this attitude if it reflected "the real intentions of the Western powers, if they are ready for business-like negotiations." But he warned that any effort "to use the talk about negotiations in order to gain time, to mislead public opinion ... will not succeed." He promised that even if the USSR signed a unilateral peace treaty with East Germany, West Berlin would not be blockaded and the Communists would not interfere in West Berlin's internal affairs.

Decrees approved Aug. 24 by the East German cabinet and published Aug. 26 and 28 granted state agencies broad new powers to enforce economic and political discipline. Penalties included prison, forced labor and internal deportation. The decree on political discipline was aimed at persons "influenced by the [West's] psychological warfare" or whose behavior threatened public welfare or security. Courts were empowered to order "work education," controlled residence and deportation from "certain places" (presumably the East Berlin area) to other parts of East Germany. The economic decrees gave local councils power to draft people for farm work at night and on weekends and provided forced labor for work shirkers. In addition to some 300,000 persons drafted for weekend farm work, according to East German sources, a campaign for allegedly voluntary increases in work norms was instituted in East German factories Sept. 7.

Pres. Heinrich Luebke of West Germany flew to West Berlin Aug. 29 in a U.S. military plane for a 2-day visit to the city. Luebke, whose visit was disclosed only after he had landed in West Berlin, toured the city's border barrier, met with city officials and addressed a nationwide TV audience before returning to Bonn Aug. 31. His visit and the use of a U.S. plane were denounced as provocations by the East German government.

Chancellor Adenauer, speaking at an election rally in Hagen in the Ruhr Aug. 29, asserted that "everything that has happened since Aug. 13 [when the Berlin Wall was started] is an intentional help by Khrushchev to the Social Democratic Party." The allegation was denounced by West Berlin Mayor Brandt and most of the West German press and was retracted by Adenauer Aug. 14. Adenauer declared in a speech broadcast Sept. 6 that he doubted the current Berlin crisis would end in war despite mounting East-West tension over the city. Adenauer said that the tension could be dissipated only by negotiation but that talks could not be accepted on the basis of Soviet demands in Germany. He disclosed that he had received a personal letter from Kennedy reaffirming U.S.-West German ties.

In West Germany's general elections, held Sept. 17, Adenauer's Christian Democratic Union lost its absolute majority control of the West German Bundestag (lower house).

The election followed 3 months of campaigning marked by personal bitterness between Willy Brandt and Adenauer. Adenauer alluded frequently to Brandt's "alias," Herbert Karl Frahm. ("Frahm" was the surname of Brandt's unwed mother.) Adenauer also frequently referred to Brandt's having left Nazi Germany during World War II to fight in the Norwegian resistance. Brandt, on the other hand, criticized Adenauer for not having come quickly to West Berlin after the borders between East and West Berlin were sealed Aug. 13. Brandt charged that Adenauer had withheld vital information on the Berlin crisis from the German people. West Berlin, though not legally part of West Germany in the view of the Western allies, elected Brandt and 21 other non-legislating delegates to the Bundestag. (Berlin delegates were generally permitted to vote in Bundestag committees but not on the floor).

A number of incidents in Berlin itself arose from Communist efforts to restrict the Berlin movements of Western military personnel, from clashes between West Berliners and Communist police and from escape attempts by East German refugees despite the Wall. Among the reported incidents:

● The closing of all Communist Party offices in West Berlin was ordered Aug. 24 by West Berlin Mayor Brandt. The party, a branch of East Germany's ruling Socialist Unity (Communist) Party, operated in West Berlin under the 4-power agreements guaranteeing freedom of political activity in all sectors.

● East German police halted 3 busloads of U.S. soldiers Aug. 24 as they crossed the sector border to tour East Berlin. The buses drove on without interference after drivers refused to submit their documents to East German inspection. The incident occurred at the Friedrichstrasse crossing point, the only one remaining open to foreigners except for crossing points on the municipal transit system.

● West Berlin police Aug. 26 closed 2 offices that East German authorities had opened at municipal railway stations to process applications by West Berliners to visit East Berlin. An East Berlin request for permission to open such offices in West Berlin had been denied by Brandt Aug. 24.

● A U.S. Army car was halted and detained by Communist police in East Berlin Aug. 30 but was released after a tank and armored infantry unit were sent to the nearby border crossing.

● 2 East Germans were shot and killed by Communist police as they sought to swim to West Berlin—the first Aug. 24 at the edge of the British sector and the 2d Aug. 29 in the Teltow Canal bordering the U.S. sector. A 3d eluded Communist gunfire and swam across the Teltow Canal to West Berlin Aug. 30.

● Maj. Gen. Albert E. Watson 2d, U.S. commander in Berlin, protested to the Soviet commandant Sept. 1 against the border violations committed by East German guards when they fired into West Berlin while attempting to kill escapees. He warned that U.S. personnel might return such fire.

● 3 cases were reported of East Berliners who escaped to West Berlin by ramming trucks through the border barriers Sept. 8, 10 and 11. Other escapes were made by East Berliners who slid down ropes from apartments overlooking West Berlin streets, climbed through sewers and swam border canals and rivers.

● Soviet threats to hamper work of the 4-power Berlin Air Safety Center were transmitted to the U.S. commander in Berlin Sept. 5 by Col. Andrei I. Solovyev, the Soviet commander. He protested to Maj. Gen. Albert E. Watson 2d that West Berlin "rowdies" and U.S. soldiers had interfered with Soviet officers on their way to the center, in West Berlin. He warned that such incidents could disrupt the center's coordination of air traffic. (U.S. and British airline pilots complained Sept. 9 that East German searchlights had been focused on their planes, endangering their landings at West Berlin airfields.)

● Patrolling U.S. soldiers hurled tear gas grenades at East German police twice Sept. 5 after they had been sprayed by water hoses operated by the police on Treptowerstrasse.

● The Rev. Dr. Kurt Scharf, chairman of the Council of the Evangelical Church in Germany, was barred by Communist police as he sought to return to his East Berlin home Sept. 1 from a visit to West Berlin. Scharf, who had lived in East Berlin since 1952, had succeeded Bishop Otto Dibelius in the church post.

French Pres. de Gaulle declared Sept. 5 that the West should be prepared to defend with force its positions in Berlin and Germany even if this led to general war. At a Paris news conference, de Gaulle said: "If the Soviets want by force to reduce the positions and cut the communications of the Allies in

Berlin, the Allies must maintain [these] by force.... Clearly one
thing leads to another ... and ... we may end up with a general
war. But then, this would be what the Soviets deliberately
want.... Admittedly, the Soviets possess terrible nuclear
weapons, but the Western powers also possess some formidable
ones. If the world conflict were to break out ..., [it would
bring] the complete disruption of Russia and the countries
which are a prey to communism" and would destroy the Soviet
regime. De Gaulle suggested specifically that any Soviet
interference with Allied traffic to Berlin be resisted in Berlin
and be answered with Western attacks on Soviet air and sea
traffic anywhere in the world.

'War of the Notes'

Soviet and East German efforts to seal off East Berlin and
to reduce or hamper air communications between West Berlin
and West Germany were discussed in a series of notes and
statements exchanged by the USSR and the Western Allies
Sept. 1-12.

The U.S. State Department Sept. 1 made public the text of
a Feb. 5, 1947 Soviet document that the U.S. contended gave
sanction to the unrestricted use of the Berlin air corridors from
West Germany by both civil and military aircraft of the U.S.,
Britain and France. The document, a Soviet report submitted
via the Allied Control Council for Germany at a Big 4 foreign
ministers' conference in Moscow, was largely devoted to a
rejection of Western suggestions that other friendly powers be
granted the right to use the air corridors for civil flights
between Berlin and the Western-occupied zones of Germany.
The State Department contended that the Soviet document
contained an implicit recognition of the Western powers' rights
to unrestricted civil flights in the Berlin air corridors.

Soviet notes delivered to the U.S., Britain and France Sept.
2 and made public the next day insisted that the West had never
been granted unlimited civil use of the Berlin air corridors and
that the West had violated the Berlin air access agreements by
using the corridors to transport "militarists," "spies,"
"saboteurs" and West German officials to West Berlin. The
Soviet note to the U.S. said: The air corridors "were
temporarily assigned exclusively for supplying the needs of

United States, British and French military garrisons in West Berlin"; "no quadripartite decisions on uncontrolled commercial air transportation over air corridors or on transportation over them of any German personnel or persons not in the service of the ... 3 powers ... had been taken by the [Allied] Control Council, and no such decisions exist in fact." The Soviet note warned the U.S. against abetting any alleged West German subversion in Berlin.

Parallel U.S., British and French notes transmitted to the USSR and made public Sept. 8 rejected the Sept. 2 Soviet messages and warned that interference with Western Air traffic to Berlin would be regarded as "aggressive action." The U.S. note pointed out that Western allied civil flights to Berlin had been made on an unrestricted basis since 1945 and that the free air movement of persons and goods, especially those of German origin, was necessary to maintain West Berlin as a viable community. The U.S. note said that the West's juridical right to such flights derived from the conquest of Nazi Germany and from Allied Control Council decisions of Nov. 22 and 30, 1945. It cited the Council's Nov. 22, 1945 approval of proposals for the establishment of the Berlin air corridors for flights that "will be conducted without previous notice being given by aircraft of the nations governing Germany." The U.S. note condemned the Communist sealing off of East Berlin as a violation of all past agreements on the city's quadripartite status and of Berliners' freedom of movement.

Notes transmitted to the U.S., British and French ambassadors in Bonn Sept. 11 by Soviet Amb.-to-East Germany Mikhail G. Pervukhin rejected protests made by the Western Allies Aug. 26 against the sealing off of East Berlin, against restrictions on travel to the sector by foreigners and Allied personnel and against the consequent violation of Berlin's 4-power occupation statute. The Soviet note to the U.S. said: "The occupation government exists only in West Berlin as a remnant eaten away by gangrene"; "visits to the German Democratic Republic, which is known to be an independent sovereign state, and to its capital by citizens of foreign states, will be regulated by the government of the German Democratic Republic"; if the Western powers had "any wishes in this connection," they should communicate them directly to the East German government. The note renewed charges that

Western military forces had staged "provocative" actions in the access routes to West Berlin and on the East Berlin border.

A special statement issued Sept. 12 by the U.S. State Department rejected the contents of the Sept. 11 Soviet note. The U.S. statement said: "We cannot ... accept any unilateral transfer by the Soviets of their responsibilities in Berlin to the puppet East German regime. We continue to hold the Soviets responsible for any actions taken by the Communist East German authorities which violate the quadripartite status of Berlin, or which result in a further increase of tension." (The State Department had advised Americans Sept. 2 against travel to East Berlin or East Germany except for compelling reasons. It had been reported that the several thousand West European and U.S. citizens living in East Berlin had been informed by Communist authorities that they were temporarily forbidden to cross the sector border.)

East Germany announced Sept. 2 that it had protested formally to the U.S. against the sending of 1,500 soldiers to reinforce the U.S.' West Berlin garrison. The East German note said that the U.S. action was "provocative" and a misuse of the land routes to West Berlin that would complicate negotiations over the future of the routes. The East German protest was ignored by the U.S.

(Among military moves related to the Berlin crisis: NATO forces throughout Europe carried out a 2-day field exercise Sept. 12-13; British Defense Min. Harold Watkinson announced Sept. 9 that a British reserve division would be activated to prepare for duty in West Germany; Canadian Prime Min. John G. Diefenbaker announced Sept. 7 that Canada would assign 2,000 more men to NATO; the West German Defense Ministry Sept. 12 ordered the retention of 6,000 officers and specialists beyond their tours of duty.)

East & West Resume Negotiations

The terms for a possible resumption of East-West negotiations on the future of Berlin were discussed by State Secy. Rusk and Soviet Foreign Min. Gromyko at a series of exploratory talks held in New York Sept. 21, 27 and 30. The first 2 meetings were attended by Adlai E. Stevenson and Valerian A. Zorin, U.S. and Soviet envoys to the UN.

The Rusk-Gromyko talks were the first formal attempts to renew negotiations on Berlin since the Communists sealed the Berlin border Aug. 13. The discussions were arranged after Pres. Kennedy had commented Sept. 13 that such talks would be feasible in connection with the New York visits of Rusk and Gromyko for the UN General Assembly. In a Foreign Ministry statement issued Sept. 14, the USSR accepted the suggestion that the 2 men meet for an "exchange of opinions."

Rusk and Gromyko each characterized their meetings as useful, but neither would say progress had been made on substantive questions. Gromyko was said to have insisted that the USSR would enter new East-West negotiations only on condition they were devoted to working out a German peace treaty and the establishment of a free city of West Berlin.

Rusk's talks with Gromyko had been indorsed at a Western foreign ministers' meeting held in Washington Sept. 14-16. The meeting was attended by Rusk, Lord Home of Britain, Maurice Couve de Murville of France and Heinrich von Brentano of West Germany. It opened with a broad discussion of East-West problems in Europe, Asia and Africa Sept. 14 and culminated in a detailed examination of the Berlin crisis Sept. 15-16.

In a final communique issued Sept. 15, the Western ministers charged that the current "dangerous heightening of world tension" was due solely to the "Soviet unilateral actions in Berlin" and "the Soviet decision to resume extensive nuclear testing in the atmosphere." The statement said: "The ministers agreed that a peaceful solution to the problem of Germany and Berlin can be achieved if both sides are prepared to undertake discussions which take account of the rights and interests of all concerned. They agreed that an effort should be made to ascertain if there exists reasonable basis for [such] negotiations" with the USSR.

(The *N.Y. Times* reported Sept. 17 that French objections to any negotiations with the USSR under current conditions had been conveyed to Kennedy Sept. 15 by Couve de Murville. The French were said to feel that the Berlin crisis could be settled only by a Soviet retreat or by war.)

Lord Home, on returning to London Oct. 1 after addressing the UN Assembly, told newsmen that he and Rusk had "made Gromyko and the Russians understand that the

Berlin situation was extremely dangerous and, if they went right ahead with their proposals to make a treaty with East Germany, it might be extremely dangerous also."

An immediate, insufficiently prepared summit conference was rejected by Kennedy Sept. 12-13 in discussions with Presidents Sukarno of Indonesia and Modibo Keita of Mali, both of whom had come to Washington to deliver an appeal of the Belgrade conference for "direct negotiations," *i.e.,* a summit conference between Kennedy and Khrushchev to avoid war. In a letter given to his 2 visitors Sept. 13 Mr. Kennedy noted:

"... We believe it is incumbent upon all responsible governments to explore all possible avenues, including negotiations at the highest levels, for mutually acceptable solutions of current international problems. However, ... [we] feel that at a time of great tension it is particularly necessary that negotiations of the kind proposed by the Belgrade conference not only have careful preparation but also a reasonable chance of success.

"We see no reason why eventual negotiations should not be successful in coping with the present crisis. However, we do not intend to enter into negotiations under ultimata or threats.... We do not propose to discuss either abdication of our responsibility or renunciation of the modalities for carrying [them] out....

"... We endorse the [Belgrade] declaration's reference to the rights of all nations to unity, self-determination and independence, and its condemnation of intimidation, intervention, and interference in the right of self-determination. We presume that these principles apply equally to the people of Germany and Berlin.

"... We are determined to honor our commitments [in Berlin and Germany] and are prepared to meet force with force if it is used against us.

"While the United States and its allies are all agreed that there must be negotiations on the problem, the Soviet Union must give indication of a readiness to engage in discussion based on mutual respect. The only conditions it has yet exhibited any willingness to consider are conditions which involve the surrender of Western rights...."

Keita told newsmen Sept. 13 that he considered Berlin "a minor problem" inflated out of proportion to its importance. In answer to a question, he said the right of self-determination did not apply to the German problem because "the German people have their independence."

Khrushchev, replying to the Belgrade conference's call for a Khrushchev-Kennedy meeting, said in a letter (dated Sept. 16 and made public Sept. 22) to Indian Prime Min. Jawaharlal Nehru that "in the name of insuring peace, we are ready for talks any time, any place and at any level." But, he warned, negotiations could be doomed to failure by the insistence of West German and other Western leaders that the West take "a tough position."

Belgian Foreign Min. Paul-Henri Spaak conferred with Khrushchev for 5 hours in the Kremlin Sept. 19 and then reported to the NATO Council in Paris Sept. 21 that Khrushchev was willing to let the projected East-West negotiations cover issues in addition to the Berlin and German problems. Spaak said Khrushchev had denied that he had limited the date for such negotiations or had set a year-end deadline for them. It was reported that Khrushchev was uncompromising only in his insistence that there be no negotiations on East Berlin since the USSR considered the city to be East Germany's capital. He was reported to have suggested that, since the Western powers refused to sign a peace treaty with East Germany, they could sign one with West Germany and let the 2 Germanies take responsibility for negotiating their future reunification.

Ex-French Premier Paul Reynaud, reporting in a copyrighted article in *Le Figaro* Sept. 23 on his conversation with Khrushchev in the Kremlin the previous week, said Khrushchev had told him: He (Khrushchev) was not willing to start war over Berlin; the Communists did not consider West Berlin of major importance in the East-West struggle and did not want the city; West Berlin's freedom and Western access to it must be guaranteed through an agreement between East and West Germany and not under any 4-power occupation statute.

East German Recognition Under Review?

A series of statements by leading American policy makers

sparked rumors of a U.S. policy reversal regarding recognition of East Germany as well as the general firmness of the U.S. commitment to West Berlin.

Sen. Hubert H. Humphrey (D., Minn.), in a Senate speech reported to have Administration indorsement, said Sept. 23 that genuine East-West negotiations on Berlin would require "give and take on both sides" that it would be "mischievous folly" to call "appeasement." Humphrey asserted that Kennedy had no intention of "agreeing to anything which will adversely affect our national security" but felt that "to remain adamant on points which do not affect our vital interests ..., [and] could promote constructive negotiations, would be irresponsible."

Chairman J. W. Fulbright (D., Ark.) of the Senate Foreign Relations Committee told reporters in London Sept. 30 that he supported moves to explore the meaning of the Soviet Union's offers of guaranteed access to a free city of West Berlin. He agreed with a questioner that nuclear weapons should not be given to West Germany if this denial would contribute to reaching a settlement over Berlin. Fulbright asserted that the postwar Berlin situation "was not just the fault of the Russians" but that "we bear a very heavy responsibility for the stupidity of that situation."

Fulbright's comments were considered by some observers to have been partially an answer to a letter by ex-Pres. Eisenhower. In his letter, made public Sept. 18, Eisenhower denied suggestions contained in a State Department pamphlet that U.S. troops could have taken Berlin in 1945. Eisenhower asserted that it was a "venturesome military critic who would now contend that the Western forces might have taken Berlin before the Soviets could or did." Eisenhower recalled that the West's troops were 250 miles from Berlin at the time the Soviet forces reached a point 35 miles from the city. He denied that the Allies' final military positions had been politically dictated.

Remarks made Sept. 22 by Gen. Lucius D. Clay, Pres. Kennedy's personal representative in West Berlin, were interpreted by some observers as indicating a reversal of the established U.S. policy against recognizing East Germany. In a statement issued Sept. 23, however, Clay denied any alteration in U.S. policy toward Berlin and German reunification. (Thousands of West Berliners had accorded Clay an enthusiastic welcome Sept. 19 when he returned to Berlin to take up his duties as Presidential representative in the city.)

Clay's remarks on East German recognition, initially attributed to an authoritative American source, were made off the record at a reception for newsmen in West Berlin. Clay was reported to have said: West Germany should accept the "reality" of East Germany's existence because the best chance for achieving German reunification ultimately lay in "talking to the East Germans" rather than in ignoring them; the continued entrenchment of the East German government and the signing of a Soviet-East German peace treaty may make "some form of dealings necessary with East Germany," particularly on the question of traffic documents on the access routes to Berlin; however, "no real interferences will be tolerated" in Western access rights to Berlin—the "showing of identification papers does not mean granting them the right of control"; regarding the division of the city: "it may take 3 or 4 years, but the wall will fall."

Clay's formal statement on the controversy, issued Sept. 23, did not comment on the accuracy of the quoted remarks. It said: "There is no change in United States policy, and no change was announced by any ... spokesman in Berlin.... [U.S. policy] is made in Washington and not in West Berlin.... American policy remains that we are in Berlin by right of victory. We will maintain our rights of ground access to Berlin completely free for Allied personnel and our rights in the air corridors completely free. We ... support the reunification of Germany."

The remarks reportedly made by Clay aroused strong criticism in the West German press and were the subject of a series of statements by Bonn leaders. West German critics especially condemned what they termed the U.S.' apparent readiness to ease East-West tension at Bonn's expense by accepting limited recognition of East Germany and the settlement of the German reunification issue by the 2 German states.

West German Pres. Heinrich Luebke assured West Germans Sept. 24 that they could "rely firmly on our American, British and French allies" to defend "the freedom of West Berlin and its links with the free world." Speaking at the opening of the new West Berlin Opera, Luebke asserted that

"Gen. Clay has not come here to surrender West Berlin but to defend it as in 1948."

West German Foreign Min. Heinrich von Brentano said in a radio talk Sept. 26 that "the 4 [Western] governments are in complete agreement on all essential questions ... on Germany and Berlin." He declared, however, that Bonn never would recognize East Germany.

A formal assurance that there had been no change in American policy on Germany was delivered to the West German Foreign Ministry in Bonn Sept. 26 by U.S. Amb.-to-West Germany Walter C. Dowling.

Incidents Add to Tensions

2 West German Air Force F-84 jet fighters landed at Tegel Airport in the French sector of West Berlin Sept. 24 after allegedly straying over East Germany during what was described as a training flight. The 2 West German pilots, who were taken temporarily into custody by the French, asserted that they had been directed to Tegel by the Templehof Airport control tower after running short of fuel. The flight, which did not take place in the air corridors to Berlin, was in violation of the prohibition on any West German flights over East Germany or to Berlin. West Germany apologized for the incident in messages delivered to the U.S., British, French and Soviet embassies in Bonn.

The USSR protested that the flight was a deliberate West German attempt to hamper an East-West settlement on Berlin. Parallel Soviet notes delivered to the U.S., Britain, France and West Germany warned that any further violations of East German airspace by West German aircraft would result in the intruders' destruction. An East German Foreign Ministry statement denounced the air violation the same day and demanded the 2 pilots be handed over for questioning.

The 4 Western nations rejected the Soviet protest Sept. 26 in separate but similar notes. The U.S. message reiterated that the incident had been unintentional, and it cautioned the USSR not to overemphasize all such events.

The 25-mile-long border barrier between the Western and Soviet sectors of Berlin was strengthened by the East German regime beginning Sept. 16 to halt a continuing trickle of refugees attempting to run, jump, swim and batter their way into West Berlin. Additional walls and concrete barriers were installed behind 4 of the 7 Berlin crossing points Sept. 16 to force drivers to zigzag at low speeds when approaching the barrier from the Communist side. 5 cases had been reported of escapees who rammed through the barrier in trucks.

The removal of the occupants of houses bordering on West Berlin was begun by East German police Sept. 20. (Many refugees had escaped by jumping from windows of border houses into West Berlin.) In suburban Berlin areas, bulldozers, aided by workmen, militia and youth organization members, began levelling homes and garden plots to create an open no-man's-land of 50 to 100 yards behind the multiple barbed wire barriers along the border. (The *N.Y. Herald Tribune* reported Sept. 30 that 3,000 forced laborers had been put to work on razing the border area.)

Toward the end of September, after spokesmen from both East and West had presented their positions, Pres. Kennedy addressed the UN General Assembly. In a 38-minute address at UN headquarters in New York Sept. 25, Kennedy stated that the West was ready to defend its obligations in West Berlin, "by whatever means are forced" on it, but preferred to settle the issue through negotiations. The President told the Assembly: "The events and decisions of the next 10 months may well decide the fate of man for the next 10,000 years.... We shall be remembered either as the generation that turned this planet into a flaming pyre or as the generation that met its vow 'to save succeeding generations from the scourge of war.' In the endeavor to meet that vow, I pledge you every effort this nation possesses. I pledge you that we shall neither commit nor provoke aggression, that we shall neither flee nor invoke the threat of force, that we shall never negotiate out of fear and never fear to negotiate."

Kennedy made these specific comments on Berlin:

"It is absurd to allege that we are threatening a war merely to prevent the Soviet Union and East Germany from signing a so-called 'treaty' of peace." The "dangerous crisis in Berlin" was caused by "threats against the vital interests and the deep commitments of the Western powers and the freedom of West Berlin. We cannot yield these interests. We cannot fail these commitments. We cannot surrender the freedom of people for whom we are responsible. A 'peace treaty' which would destroy the peace would be a fraud. A 'free city' which would suffocate freedom would be an infamy.... If anyone doubts the extent to which our presence is desired by the people of West Berlin, we are ready to have that question submitted to a free vote in all Berlin and ... among all [Germans]....

"The Western powers have calmly resolved to defend, by whatever means are forced upon them, their obligations and their access to the free citizens of West Berlin and the self-determination of those citizens."

"We are committed to no rigid formula. We see no perfect solution.... But we believe that a peaceful agreement is possible which protects the freedom of West Berlin and allied presence and access, while recognizing the historic and legitimate interests of others in assuring European security.... There is no need for a crisis over Berlin—and if those who created this crisis desire peace, there will always be peace in Berlin."

Berlin Negotiations Start

Pres. Kennedy and Soviet Foreign Min. Gromyko held a 2-hour exploratory conference at the White House Oct. 6 in an effort to determine whether an acceptable basis could be found for East-West negotiations on Berlin, Germany and other issues. Gromyko told reporters after the session that the conversation had been "useful," but Kennedy was reported to have said the results were "zero." State Secy. Dean Rusk and Asst. State Secy. Foy D. Kohler assisted the President at the meeting, and Rusk described the session as "interesting." Gromyko was aided at the conference by Soviet Deputy Foreign Min. Vladimir S. Semyonov and Soviet Amb.-to-U.S. Mikhail A. Menshikov.

It was reported that Gromyko opened the session by reading a memo that largely reiterated positions previously enunciated by himself and Soviet Premier Khrushchev. He told reporters he had stressed the "importance the Soviet Union attaches to a peace treaty with East Germany." It was reported that Gromyko repeated USSR suggestions that Soviet troops join those of the West in policing a free city of West Berlin but that he rejected similar Western rights in East Berlin. Gromyko reiterated a Soviet hint that the USSR might extend the year-end deadline it had set for an East German peace treaty. He was reported to have said that if the U.S. accepted the USSR's stand on Berlin, the Soviets might discuss Germany's eastern boundaries and similar issues.

Kennedy interrupted Gromyko at this point to say: "You have offered to trade us an apple for an orchard. We don't do that in this country."

Gromyko proposed that an East-West agreement should be of limited duration and that a free city of West Berlin should have no organic ties with West Germany. Kennedy was unable to get Gromyko to explain how the USSR planned to fulfill its promises of "access" to West Berlin and "guarantees" of West Berlin's freedom. The President emphatically reiterated the Western determination to defend the right of access and the freedom of the city.

Following the White House conference, Gromyko flew to London Oct. 9-10 for a discussion Oct. 10 with British Prime Min. Macmillan, who strongly supported the U.S. stand on Berlin. Macmillan warned Gromyko that unilateral Soviet action curbing Western access to West Berlin would involve "grave dangers." Macmillan emphasized the need to negotiate a Berlin settlement but said he saw no basis for negotiations in any of Gromyko's remarks in the U.S. or in London.

West Berlin Mayor Willy Brandt flew to New York Oct. 5 for an Oct. 6 ceremony at which Freedom House gave him its Freedom Award for 1961. Accepting the award, Brandt asserted that the Communist wall dividing Berlin was a brazen challenge to the West. "That wall in Berlin must come down," he declared. Aug. 13, the day the Communists started building the wall, was a "Black Sunday" that marked a turning point in East-West relations, Brandt said. He called it "a day of annexation" on which East German Communist leader Walter Ulbricht "received a green light from Khrushchev and the Warsaw Pact powers, permitting him to occupy East Berlin by military force." Brandt assured the free world that it need not worry about West Berlin morale. He said: "We shall carry on fully aware that we are the keepers of the torch of freedom."

Kennedy phoned Brandt Oct. 8 and praised Brandt's speech.

Brandt told West Berliners on flying home Oct. 8 that he was convinced that the U.S. government and people "are fully determined that Berlin shall remain free" and that anybody who underestimated this determination "is playing with fire."

East German Socialist Unity Party First Secy. Walter Ulbricht had declared Oct. 6 that a Soviet-East German peace treaty could contain special guarantees for "a peaceful settlement of the West Berlin issue" and other East-West differences over Germany's future. Ulbricht made his suggestion in a speech at a rally marking the 12th anniversary of the (East) German Democratic Republic. Soviet Premier Khrushchev, in a congratulatory message delivered to Ulbricht and made public earlier Oct. 6, said the USSR intended to sign a separate East German peace treaty "within a very short time." This Soviet assertion was repeated in addresses delivered at an East Berlin rally Oct. 7 by Soviet First Deputy Premier Anastas I. Mikoyan and Marshal Ho Lung, Communist Chinese deputy premier. Ho assured East Germans that "the whole 650 million people of China stand at your side."

Proposals for a withdrawal of Soviet and Western armed forces from their borderline positions in Central Europe were reiterated by Khrushchev. His renewal of the plan was contained in a letter written to British leftist Emanuel Shinwell and other Laborite MPs. The letter, made public Oct. 12, proposed this 5-point agreement for settling East-West differences on Germany: (1) "Disengagement of NATO and Warsaw Treaty armed forces"; (2) a ban on the supply of nuclear weapons to both East and West Germany; (3) an agreement on "guaranteed access" to Berlin; (4) recognition of the Oder-Neisse boundary between East Germany and Poland; (5) recognition of East and West Germany and their entry into the UN.

Sen. Hubert H. Humphrey (D., Minn.), visiting Poland, told a Warsaw TV audience Oct. 16 that the disengagement plan proposed by Polish Foreign Min. Adam Rapacki in 1957 was being given "very thoughtful and serious study" by U.S. officials. Humphrey said the U.S. looked on "the Rapacki plan and others as part of our general program for ... disarmament." A special statement issued Oct. 17 by the State Department, however, said that the U.S. considered the Rapacki plan and other disengagement proposals "transparent devices intended to weaken and ultimately destroy the Atlantic alliance."

The Soviet Union's foreign and domestic policies were given a major restatement by Khrushchev Oct. 17 in a 6½-hour address at the opening session of the 23d Soviet Communist Party Congress. The address made 2 major points regarding Berlin and Germany:

● The USSR was willing to withdraw its year-end deadline for the signing of a separate peace treaty between Russia and East Germany if the Western powers demonstrated willingness to negotiate on the future of Berlin and Germany.

● As a result of the talks held by Soviet Foreign Min. Gromyko with Pres. Kennedy and State Secy. Rusk, "we have the impression that the Western powers were displaying a certain understanding of the situation and that they were inclined to seek a solution for the German problem and for the West Berlin issue on a mutually acceptable basis." "If the Western powers show readiness to settle the German problem, the question of a deadline for the signing of a German peace treaty will not be of such importance. Then we shall not insist on the signing of the peace treaty before Dec. 31, 1961." The USSR's aims, however, remained the transformation of West Berlin into a "demilitarized free city" and the signature of a German peace treaty which would "do away with the vestiges" of World War II.

Khrushchev indicated his belief that peaceful coexistence was possible and that despite the current crisis, war was not inevitable. "The indications are that it may actually be feasible to banish world war from the life of society even before the complete triumph of socialism on earth, with capitalism surviving in part of the world," Khrushchev said.

In a Sept. 20 interview in *Pravda,* Khrushchev indorsed a Sept. 10 appeal by Pope John XXIII to world leaders to use negotiation as a means of averting war over the Berlin issue. Khrushchev called the appeal "a tribute to common sense" and said: "We can only welcome a call for talks in the interest of peace, no matter where it comes from."

2 left-wing British Labor Party members of Parliament, Sir Leslie Plummer and Konni Zilliacus, interviewed Khrushchev at his Black Sea summer home near Yalta Aug. 31. Plummer said Sept. 1 that Khrushchev had indicated that he

had decided to resume nuclear testing to shock the Western powers into negotiating on Germany and disarmament.

Khrushchev's apparent offer to relax Soviet pressure on Berlin was welcomed Oct. 18 by State Secy. Rusk. But Rusk made it clear that Khrushchev had not altered the USSR's unacceptable proposals for a German peace treaty and European disengagement. Speaking at a Washington news conference, Rusk declared that Khrushchev's remarks on Germany "confirmed publicly" what Gromyko had said in his recent exploratory talks in the U.S. Rusk said that Khrushchev's speech, "indicating that he does not assert an ultimatum [on Germany] with respect to time, may serve to reduce tension somewhat. But his general observations about the Berlin problems show little if any change" from his earlier stand.

Rusk called the USSR's terms for full-scale negotiations on Germany "too narrow." He said the Soviet demand for "a peace treaty with Germany and a solution of the problem of West Berlin on that basis is too restrictive" for serious talks. He denied "that the idea of disengagement has any future in it because disengagement implies the abandonment of responsibilities and implies the creation of perhaps a vacuum which would not itself be conducive to stability and peace." Disengagement would be acceptable to the U.S. only as part of a disarmament agreement, he said.

Kennedy Oct. 11 expressed doubt that the exploratory talks held by himself, Rusk, and Gromyko had contributed any substantive progress toward a Berlin settlement. The President, speaking at his press conference in Washington before Khrushchev's CP Congress speech, asserted that the Gromyko talks had been preliminary and devoted to determining the USSR's exact position on precise aspects of the Berlin problem. He said: "I don't think that we can come to any conclusion as to what the ultimate conclusion will be, though the talks which we had with ... Gromyko did not give us immediate hope" of an easy settlement.

Asked for his view of the U.S.' refusal to oppose with force the Communist wall on the Berlin border, the President said: "... Eastern Berlin and East Germany have been under the control of the Soviet Union, really, since 1947 and '48.... There are many things that happen in Eastern Europe ... which we consider to be wholly unsatisfactory—the denial of liberties, the denial of political freedom, national independence, and all the rest."

Kennedy rejected Republican charges that the current defense buildup had weakened the U.S.' "nuclear credibility" (the belief that the U.S. actually would use its nuclear weapons) and had persuaded the USSR that the West would not defend with force its Berlin commitments. He said that "we have indicated that we will meet our commitments with whatever resources are necessary to meet them." He added, however, that, given the power of nuclear weapons, "anyone would be reluctant, unless all else had failed, to destroy so much of the world." The U.S., he said, sought accords which would "protect the interests and freedom of the people involved without having to go to . . . these extreme weapons."

Reports of Western differences on the terms and timetable for projected German talks with the USSR were confirmed Oct. 15 with the apparent cancellation of a planned London meeting of senior Western foreign service officials. Arrangements for the meeting were first reported Oct. 11, in connection with West German requests for discussion of its views on the U.S. and British talks with Soviet Foreign Min. Gromyko. (Bonn was said to have reiterated its opposition to any East-West negotiations involving plans for the neutralization of West Germany or recognition of the East German government in its current form.) The British Foreign Office confirmed Oct. 13 that a meeting was planned for London, but a French Foreign Ministry statement said Oct. 14 that such a meeting would be "premature." The State Department said Oct. 14 that the London talks would be held as planned, but department officials conceded the next day that the meeting had been canceled.

The *N.Y. Times* reported Oct. 16 that Lord Home, British foreign secretary, had informed French Amb.-to-Britain Jean Chauvel of the Macmillan government's irritation at French refusal even to discuss unified Western terms for eventual negotiations over the German problem. French and West German opposition to any Western concessions on Berlin or the German problem was conveyed to Kennedy in personal letters from Pres. de Gaulle Oct. 23 and Chancellor Adenauer Oct. 24. De Gaulle's message was said to have reiterated his objection to entering any Berlin negotiations under the current Soviet threats and to have warned that the West weakened its position by repeated declarations of willingness to participate in such negotiations. West German Amb.-to-U.S. Wilhelm Grewe, meeting reporters Oct. 24 after delivering the Adenauer letter to Kennedy, said that "the German evaluation of the situation is very close to the French position" but that Bonn was not opposed to exploratory talks seeking "common ground" for possible negotiations.

Opening a 2-day Parliamentary foreign affairs debate Oct. 17, Lord Home told the British House of Lords that the question of Germany's future—whether the country should be reunified under new East-West agreement or remain partitioned—should be decided by a "free vote, internationally supervised," in both parts of Germany. Home had said Oct. 11 that Pres. Kennedy and Prime Min. Macmillan had convinced Soviet Foreign Min. Gromyko that the USSR was risking a "head-on collision" and nuclear war over Berlin.

Macmillan, addressing the British House of Commons Oct. 18, asserted that "some parts" of Khrushchev's CP Congress speech had "showed that the Russians do realize the Allies are unwilling to surrender over the issue of Berlin." Macmillan said: The West was preparing for talks on Germany, but "we must not be led too soon into too extensive a negotiation."

Kennedy, in a letter to British ex-Defense Min. Emanuel Shinwell and 71 other Laborite MPs, declared Oct. 23 that the U.S. was "committed to no rigid formulas" and was "prepared to explore every reasonable avenue of approach" to a settlement on the Berlin question.

De Gaulle had said at a rally in Rodez, France Sept. 21 that the West would be risking "disaster" if it sought hasty negotiations on Germany. He said that to negotiate on Soviet terms, "you start out giving your hat, then you give your coat, then your shirt, then your skin, and finally your soul." De Gaulle, in a radio-TV address to the French people Oct. 2, said France's "duty" was "to stand firm and erect in the face of demands from the totalitarian bloc and to urge our allies to do the same." He added: "... Nothing would be more dangerous to our cause ... than to retreat step by step before those who are menacing us. But, should the threats stop ... and should relations between East and West return to normal, then France will be ready to enter into constructive negotiations ... on world problems."

UN sources told the *N.Y. Times* Oct. 5 that the U.S. had urged West Germany to reconsider its past refusal to negotiate directly with East Germany on the question of guaranteed Western access to West Berlin. According to the UN informants, the U.S. believed that if a detailed Berlin access accord would be reached by East and West Germany, it then could be guaranteed by the U.S., Britain, France and the USSR. The U.S. plan reportedly was linked to Gen. Clay's statement urging Bonn to recognize the existence of an East German regime. The *Times* report was denied by the State Department Oct. 6 as untrue. But West German Foreign Min. Heinrich von Brentano said at a meeting of the Christian Democratic Union parliamentary group Oct. 12 that West Germany might be willing to begin limited talks with East Germany provided this did not constitute *de facto* recognition of the Communist regime. Adenauer, at a Bonn meeting Oct. 13 with his foreign policy advisers, was reported to have ruled out any concessions for a German settlement beyond those offered at the 1959 Geneva foreign ministers conference on Germany. Adenauer Oct. 14 received a letter from Pres. Kennedy in which the President was said to have renewed assurances that the U.S. would not seek an East-West settlement at West Germany's expense.

A proposal for the internationalization of Berlin under the UN had been advanced Sept. 11 by Canadian Prime Min. John G. Diefenbaker. He said UN action on Berlin might include: (a) the sponsorship of a new 4-power agreement on the city's future; (b) the supervision of an East-West Berlin pact; (c) the establishment of an "international regime in Berlin"; (d) the supervision of Western access.

A front-page editorial published Sept. 19 by the Soviet government newspaper *Izvestia* suggested that the UN General Assembly consider moving the entire UN headquarters from New York to a site in a free city of West Berlin. State Secy. Rusk Dec. 3 expressed support for suggestions that West Berlin's future freedom could be assured more easily if "certain of the agencies of the United Nations" were transferred to the city. But he opposed the idea of "moving this mammoth headquarters that is now in New York" to Berlin. (His remarks were made in a taped TV interview.)

Berlin 'Incidents' Increase

Armed U.S. military police entered East Berlin Oct. 22 to protect and insure the right of passage of an American official who had been halted by East German border police when he refused to show them identity papers. The official was E. Allan Lightner Jr., assistant chief of the U.S. mission in Berlin. He had driven to the Friedrichstrasse checkpoint on the Berlin border in a private car carrying a U.S. armed forces license. When halted by the East Germans and asked to prove his identity, Lightner refused to show his papers to any but a Russian officer.

After 1½ hours, a 9-man U.S. MP patrol accompanied Lightner a few yards into East Berlin and then back to the border. The East German police did not interfere with this. Lightner then attempted to enter East Berlin a 2d time, was halted by the East Germans and again was escorted a short way beyond the checkpoint and back to the border by the MP patrol. In a 3d attempt, made the same day after a protest had been given a Soviet officer at the post, Lightner, accompanied by a convoy of British and French cars, was permitted to take a brief drive in East Berlin.

The stopping of Lightner was protested in a note delivered to Soviet military authorities Oct. 22 by Maj. Gen. Albert E. Watson 2d, U.S. commandant in West Berlin, and in a statement issued Oct. 23 by Gen. Lucius D. Clay, Pres. Kennedy's personal representative in the city.

Harassment of American personnel had started Oct. 15, when East Berlin border police halted 4 private cars containing 11 civilians attached to U.S. military and diplomatic offices in West Berlin. The officials were turned back when they refused to show identity papers to the East German guards. Gens. Watson and Clay then tested the new Communist measure by driving into East Berlin in their official cars in civilian clothes. They were unmolested. An East German Interior Ministry decree published Oct. 23 by the ADN news agency said: "Civilians traveling into the DDR [East Germany] will have to identify themselves in every case as is customary in the DDR and according to international law."

The U.S. had instructed its personnel not to show identity papers to East Berlin border police. It held that the government registration plates carried by cars of military and government personnel were sufficient to classify passengers as officials whose access to all parts of Berlin was guaranteed by the 4-power occupation statutes. Military vehicles and private cars carrying uniformed U.S. personnel had not been halted by East Berlin guards. Occupants of government-licensed cars halted by East Berlin police were ordered to demand that a Soviet officer be called to confirm their status and protect their rights of access.

U.S. authorities at the Friedrichstrasse checkpoint stopped American civilians from attempting private trips to East Berlin Oct. 23 but rescinded the ban the next day. U.S. authorities claimed that American tourists and other civilians ordinarily had submitted to East German passport controls on entering and leaving East Berlin, but these authorities did not consider this any recognition of the East German government.

U.S. spokesmen in West Berlin had confirmed Sept. 20 that Col. Andrei I. Solovyev, the USSR's Berlin commandant, had protested an increase in U.S. military police patrols on the 100-mile *autobahn* corridor linking West Berlin with West Germany. The spokesmen disclosed that the MP patrols had been increased Sept. 22 to 6 each day. The U.S. action was in response to the halting and detention of 2 American soldiers on the road by East German police Sept. 21. The 2, dressed in civilian clothes, were released after a Soviet officer had been summoned at their demand.

U.S. military sources in Berlin reported Oct. 7 that Army patrols, carried out on a 24-hour basis since Aug. 23 along the border between East and West Berlin, had been reduced and replaced by MP patrols. This change, opposed by West Berlin newspapers, was intended to return control of the border to West Berlin police and to remove U.S. troops from areas in which they might become involved in minor border incidents or shooting.

An East Berlin court Sept. 26 had sentenced 2 U.S. students to 2 years of prison each. The students, Victor S. Pankey, 20, and Gilbert P. Ferrey, 18, both of California, were charged with attempting to smuggle an East Berlin girl into West Berlin in the trunk of their car. Their arrest, together with that of 4 other foreigners, had been reported by East Germany Sept. 13.

2 U.S. Army battle groups comprising ½ of the 6,000-man American garrison in West Berlin staged maneuvers in the city's Grunewald Forest area Oct. 18-20. The closing exercises were attended by Gens. Clay and Watson.

West Berlin police were armed Oct. 24 with automatic rifles, tear-gas grenades and Sten submachineguns. The step had been threatened by Mayor Brandt Oct. 9 in view of the arms used by East Berlin police, who often fired on refugees attempting to flee into the city's Western sectors. The arms were supplied by the U.S. and Britain.

The U.S. State Department, in a statement issued in Washington Oct. 5, had warned Soviet authorities in Berlin that further shootings by East Berlin guards could "jeopardize peace."

Among incidents reported along the Berlin and German borders:

● East German border guards and civilian laborers began Oct. 2 to fortify outlying sections of the wall and barbed wire barrier encircling West Berlin. Communist officials said trenches and bunkers were being built because "the wall around Berlin is to be permanent." (West German officials reported Oct. 2 that nearly 300 East Berlin border police had fled to West Berlin since the border was closed Aug. 13.)

● A mass escape into West Germany in the Goettingen area was carried out Oct. 3 by 55 members of 16 East German families whose homes lay near the border and were to be torn down to create a no-man's-land for the capture of would-be refugees.

● West Berlin police fired on East Berlin border guards for the first time Oct. 4 and wounded one of them in an attempt to aid the escape of 2 men being pursued over rooftops near the border. The East Berlin police had fired into Western territory. One refugee fell to his death, the other was captured. East Berlin police fired at Western guards at the same spot Oct. 5 but missed.

● 4 West Berliners were forced at gunpoint to crawl through the barrier into East Berlin Oct. 7 after they had approached a section of the fence on East German territory. 4 more West Berliners were arrested on Eastern territory Oct. 8 when they ran to help East Berlin policemen staging a mock escape.

● Kurt Lichtenstein, 49, reporter for the *Westfaelische Rundschau* of Dortmund, was wounded fatally by East German police Oct. 12 when he stepped over the border to talk to a farmer.

● 16 refugees escaped to West Berlin Oct. 16 despite a hail of gunfire from East sector police. 5 of the escapees jumped from an East Berlin house into a West Berlin truck filled with fine gravel.

● 3 East German youths rammed through the border into West Berlin's Staaken district Oct. 17 in a truck they had armored.

● Eastern and Western border police exchanged a barrage of tear gas grenades Oct. 24 after the East Berlin guards had thrown them at a loudspeaker van near the Eastern sector wall.

● East Berlin police fired more than 300 shots into Western territory Oct. 31 in an unsuccessful attempt to halt 9 youths who rammed their way through the border barrier on the outskirts of West Berlin in a stolen truck. The shooting was protested the next day by Gen. Watson, U.S. commandant in Berlin.

Military Buildup by Both Sides

As tensions over the Berlin situation mounted, both the Western and Communist sides made it plain that they were continuing to strengthen their military forces. But Vice Pres. Lyndon B. Johnson met with Gen. Lauris Norstad, NATO supreme commander, in Paris Sept. 30 and told newsmen later that day that the U.S. and its allies "have not done everything we would like to do" to increase NATO military strength. He indicated dissatisfaction with some NATO countries' failure to emulate the U.S. build-up.

The U.S. Air Force had announced Sept. 27 that 8 tactical fighter squadrons had been assigned temporarily to the 17th Air Force, centered in Ramstein, West Germany, for extended overseas training. 4 of the squadrons already were in Europe for NATO air defense exercises. The Air Force announced Oct.

19-20 that 4 of its French air bases—at Chaumont, Chambley, Etain and Phalsbourg—would be reactivated. The 4 bases had been placed on housekeeping status in 1958 when Pres. de Gaulle refused to allow nuclear weapons for U.S. planes to be stockpiled in France. Paris sources had reported Oct. 3 that 2 of the U.S. fighter-bomber squadrons withdrawn from France during the nuclear storage controversy had returned to bases there. U.S. Air Force Secy. Eugene M. Zuckert had disclosed Oct. 3 that the shutdown of 4 of the U.S.' 16 air bases in Britain had been "postponed indefinitely." Zuckert said the 7 squadrons of B-66 and RB-66 bombers based at the 4 fields would remain in Britain.

The first contingent of a previously announced movement of 40,000 U.S. troops to Europe reached Cherbourg, France Oct. 11.

U.S. Deputy Defense Secy. Roswell L. Gilpatric warned Oct. 21 that the U.S. nuclear retaliatory force had "such lethal power that an enemy move which brought it into play would be an act of self-destruction on his part." Speaking at a Hot Springs, Va. meeting of the Business Council, Gilpatric said: "The United States has today hundreds of manned intercontinental bombers capable of reaching the Soviet Union, including 600 heavy bombers and many more medium bombers capable of intercontinental operations.... [The U.S.] also has 6 Polaris submarines at sea carrying a total of 96 missiles, and dozens of intercontinental ballistic missiles. Our carrier strike forces and land-based ... forces could deliver additional hundreds of megatons. The total number of our nuclear delivery vehicles, tactical as well as strategic, is in the 10s of thousands; and of course, we have more than one warhead for each vehicle.... Therefore, we are confident that the Soviets will not provoke a major nuclear conflict."

State Secy. Rusk disclosed Oct. 22 that he had reviewed the Gilpatric statement before its release. Rusk told ABC—TV's "Issues & Answers" interviewers that the U.S. did not fear negotiations on any subject with the USSR because "we are not dealing ... from a position of weakness." He added, however, that he did not believe "immediate negotiations in the usual sense of that word" were likely over the German problem. He conceded that the Western Big 3 differed on the question of terms and timing for eventual East-West talks on Germany.

Gilpatric arrived in Bonn Oct. 23 to begin a series of talks with NATO defense ministers intended to persuade Britain, France and West Germany to duplicate the military buildup begun by the U.S. A communique issued Oct. 24 by Gilpatric and Defense Min. Franz Josef Strauss declared their "complete agreement with respect to the equipping of the Bundeswehr," presumably with missiles capable of carrying nuclear warheads. Gilpatric was said to have assured Strauss the U.S.' opposed any policy dependent on European disengagement and Germany's neutralization.

British Prime Min. Macmillan told Parliament Oct. 30 that his government would seek authority to recall some reservists and to extend for 6 months the duty of the last 15,000 draftees called before the end of conscription in 1960. He declared, however, that the world situation did not require a mobilization or resumption of conscription. Defense Min. Harold Watkinson Nov. 3 rejected Laborite charges that the Army of the Rhine was dangerously undermanned.

The long-term demobilization of Russian military manpower announced by Khrushchev in 1960 was revealed to have been halted Aug. 29. A statement issued by the Soviet cabinet and the Communist Party Central Committee said that Marshal Rodion Y. Malinovsky, Soviet defense minister, had been ordered to halt the demobilization of all personnel scheduled for release in 1961 "until the conclusion of a peace treaty with Germany" and the cessation of Western war threats.

A general build-up of Soviet-bloc armed forces was approved at a 2-day meeting of Warsaw Pact defense ministers and general staff chiefs in Warsaw Sept. 8-9. The decision was disclosed in a joint communique reported by Tass from Moscow Sept. 9.

Polish CP First Secy. Wladyslaw Gomulka announced in a Warsaw speech Sept. 10 that new measures had been taken to raise the "combat readiness of the Polish army." It was reported that a partial mobilization of reserves and the retention of all men on active service had been ordered for the army, estimated to comprise 225,000 men in 12-14 divisions.

Thousands of Russian, Polish and Czechoslovak troops were reported to be entering East Germany Oct. 10 to take part in the largest joint military maneuvers in the history of the

Warsaw Treaty. West Berlin sources reported that at least 50,000 new Soviet troops and 10,000 Polish servicemen, mainly in parachute, airborne and other combat units, already had arrived at East German maneuver areas. The new arrivals were said to have increased Russian forces in East Germany to 300,000. Plans for the maneuvers, to continue into November, had been announced by the Warsaw Pact powers Sept. 25.

The *N.Y. Times* reported Oct. 20 that Czech industry was recruiting pensioners and women to replace thousands of men recalled in an unannounced military mobilization.

A report published in London Nov. 21 by the Institute for Strategic Studies held that the Western powers were superior to the Soviet bloc in every vital index of military strength.

U.S.-Soviet Tank Confrontation

U.S. and Soviet tanks were brought to the border between East and West Berlin Oct. 27 but were withdrawn without incident 16 hours later. The tank confrontation was a direct outgrowth of an East German decree ordering all foreigners—including U.S. officials and military personnel in civilian clothes—to submit to identity controls on entering East Berlin. A U.S. protest against the East German order had been delivered Oct. 25 to Col. Andrei I. Solovyev, Soviet commander in Berlin, by Maj. Gen. Albert Watson 2d, the U.S. commandant. Solovyev rejected the protest and, according to a U.S. statement on the meeting, told Watson that "the decrees of the Soviet zone regime are binding on access to East Berlin." Watson made it clear that U.S. personnel would not submit to East German controls.

The protest was repeated in Moscow Oct. 27 by U.S. Amb.-to-USSR Llewellyn E. Thompson Jr. at a meeting with Soviet Foreign Min. Gromyko. Thompson demanded that the USSR take steps to restore the freedom of access to East Berlin guaranteed by the 4-power occupation statute. Gromyko rejected the protest and complained of sorties made into East Berlin by U.S. troops sent to protect Americans halted by Communist police.

This was the sequence of events at the Friedrichstrasse border crossing point in Berlin:

Oct. 25 —East Berlin police passed a first private car without control but halted a 2d, which returned to the Western sector after its occupants refused to show papers to anyone but a Soviet officer. 12 U.S. MPs crossed the border to escort a 3d private car on a brief trip into East Berlin after it had been halted and its occupants had refused to show their papers. 10 U.S. M-48 tanks and 3 British Centurion tanks were moved to the border but were withdrawn later in the day.

Oct. 26 —The USSR's Berlin command was informed that an American in civilian clothes would enter East Berlin without showing papers to the East German police. 10 U.S. tanks were brought to the border and an unidentified American drove to the East German border point in a private car bearing an official U.S. license. Halted when he refused to show the East Germans his papers, he returned to the Western sector and drove back to the East German post accompanied by 3 jeeploads of armed U.S. soldiers. His car, escorted through the border point, made a brief circuit, unaccompanied, in East Berlin. It was halted by East German police on its return to the border point but was escorted back to the Western sector by the jeep convoy, summoned by the car's driver with headlight signals after he again refused to submit to the East German identity check.

33 Soviet T-54 medium tanks manned by Russian-speaking crews entered East Berlin from East Germany and parked a mile from the border point later in the day. The tanks' markings were covered with tape, but they were identified as belonging to the USSR's 20th Guards Division. They were the first Soviet-manned tanks to enter East Berlin in years.

Oct. 27 —10 U.S. tanks were brought to the Western sector border point, and a private car was escorted by 5 jeeploads of soldiers on a brief sortie in East Berlin after its driver and the East Berlin police had repeated their actions of the previous day. The U.S. tanks then left the border. 10 Soviet T-54s then appeared on the Eastern side of the border but withdrew shortly afterward. The U.S. tanks, summoned when the Soviet force had first appeared, then reappeared at the Western border point; the Soviet tanks reappeared at the Eastern check point 30 minutes later. The 2 formations were deployed in field order, with the lead tanks facing each other 100 yards apart.

Lt. Gen Lucius D. Clay, Pres. Kennedy's personal representative in Berlin, declared in a statement issued Oct. 27 that the appearance of Soviet tanks at the sector border had destroyed the "fiction" that East Germany, not the USSR, exercised authority in East Berlin. He said it proved that recent Berlin harassments "were not those of the self-styled East German government but ordered by its Soviet masters."

Oct. 28 —The 2 tank formations were withdrawn from the Berlin border after facing each other for 16 hours. The Soviet tanks, the first to leave, rejoined the other Soviet vehicles a mile from the border. The U.S. M-48s were recalled to a parking area 600 yards behind the Western checkpoint. The U.S. made no effort to repeat its private car sorties into East Berlin while the Soviet tanks were at the border. It also stopped all American civilians except newsmen from attempting to enter East Berlin during the period. Other normal civil and military traffic generally was maintained during the tank confrontation.

It was reported in Washington Oct. 28 that Pres. Kennedy had ordered a halt to the test sorties into East Berlin. Administration officials were said to feel that the U.S.' position had succeeded in bringing direct Soviet intervention. It was felt that negotiations on the checkpoint dispute were possible with the Russians but could not take place with the East Germans without constituting a form of recognition of the East German regime.

It was reported from Berlin Oct. 30 that East German police had turned back several groups of State Department personnel when they sought to enter East Berlin without showing their passports. U.S. officials in Berlin confirmed that the State Department had canceled trips to East Berlin by its personnel after the 4th group was halted.

West Berlin police began Nov. 1 to check the identity papers of civilians entering West Berlin in cars bearing Soviet-bloc diplomatic licenses. Soviet military vehicles or military-licensed cars were permitted to pass the border unmolested. The West Berlin Senate was said to have requested Allied permission for the identity check on the ground that East German Communists were using the diplomatic cars to enter and leave West Berlin.

East German police tightened their Berlin border controls Nov. 3 by requiring occupants of an official British car to hand their identity cards to police rather than merely to show them through the car windows. The East Germans detained 2 U.S. State Department employes briefly Nov. 4 when they refused to show their passports after being stopped for an identity check in East Berlin. 4 U.S. military vehicles driven by soldiers were pursued by East German police cars and detained briefly in East Berlin the same day.

The *N.Y. Times* reported from Bonn Nov. 6 that a majority of NATO member states had expressed alarm to the U.S. over its use of troops to force civilian entry into East Berlin. The protesting NATO states—not named—were said to have informed Thomas K. Finletter, U.S. representative to the NATO Permanent Council in Paris, that their governments opposed risking war over identification procedures for U.S. officials entering East Berlin in officially-licensed civilian cars. They reportedly pointed out that British personnel partly had accepted the East German identity checks and that U.S.

personnel showed their papers to East German police when traveling in East Berlin by subway.

Soviet Premier Khrushchev said Nov. 7 that the USSR was prepared to permit a relaxation of East-West tensions in Berlin "for the time being." Chatting with Western newsmen at a Kremlin reception marking the 44th anniversary of the Bolshevik revolution, Khrushchev was asked whether the USSR would take any new action in Berlin or would await new East-West negotiations. He said: "It is a difficult question. For the moment we shall wait. We still have patience.... It is not good for the time being to press one another." Similar views had been expressed by Khrushchev Nov. 3 in an interview with IPU Council Pres. Giuseppe Codacci Pisanelli. Codacci Pisanelli reported that Khrushchev had told him that he had never intended the Dec. 31 Soviet deadline for a German peace treaty as an ultimatum and that he did not intend to act hastily in Germany.

East German Socialist Unity Party First Secy. Walter Ulbricht had said Nov. 3, on his return to Berlin from the 22d Soviet CP Congress, that preliminary U.S.-Soviet talks had created "the possibility" of negotiations on Germany. (U.S. Amb.-to-USSR Llewellyn E. Thompson Jr. had returned to Moscow Oct. 24 to seek preliminary talks.)

U.S. Army "assistance patrols" on the *autobahn* connecting Berlin and West Germany had been ended Oct. 30 after Soviet Army officers halted patrol cars identified by U.S. military police markings. The assistance patrols along the *autobahn* had been started in 1952 after the USSR had forced the U.S. to end regular MP patrols on the road. They were increased in Sept. 1961 after 2 U.S. soldiers had been halted on the highway by East German police. 2 patrols were stopped by Soviet officers as they sought to pass through the Babelsberg checkpoint outside West Berlin Oct. 29. The patrols were dropped by the U.S. after Soviet officers turned back 2 assistance cars Oct. 30.

A company of U.S. motorized infantry went to West Berlin without incident via the *autobahn* Nov. 10 on what officials said was an exercise in "convoy procedures." The infantrymen traveled in full combat dress. Soviet officials had been notified of the trip in advance, as was customary for troop movements.

East-West Berlin Detente?

It was reported from Moscow Nov. 9 that the USSR had advanced new and possibly more acceptable terms for settling the Berlin dispute. The reports were denied by the Western embassies in Moscow, and the West German government confirmed Nov. 13 that they were the result of an "unauthorized initiative" taken by West German Amb.-to-USSR Hans A. Kroll at a private meeting with Soviet Premier Khrushchev.

The Kroll-Khrushchev proposals initially were reported by all major Western news agencies in Moscow. Attributed to unnamed but "authoritative" Western diplomatic sources, they were said to call for:

● A new Berlin statute, guaranteeing the city's freedom and the West's access to it, signed by the U.S., Britain, France and the USSR.

● East German commitments to respect and abide by the new Berlin statute, signed separately by East Germany and the USSR.

● The Western governments' agreement, with the participation of West Germany, to respect East German sovereignty.

Some versions of the proposals contained a 4th point providing for East and West to agree to begin negotiations on a German peace treaty and general disarmament after the settlement of the Berlin question. But Western newsmen noted that the proposals apparently contained these Soviet concessions to the West's position: (1) they did not appear to commit the West in advance to negotiations on a German peace treaty; (2) in the absence of a peace treaty, the partition of Germany would not (in the West's view) be recognized as permanent, and the West would retain its postwar occupation rights in Berlin; (3) the Soviet-East German agreement on a new Berlin statute would eliminate previous Soviet demands that the West negotiate new Berlin access guarantees directly with East Germany and thus give de facto recognition to the Communist East German regime.

Kroll's connection with the reported proposals was indicated by the State Department spokesmen. They said Nov. 9 that the U.S. had received no new Soviet offers on Germany but that Kroll had met earlier that day with Khrushchev and would report on the meeting to the U.S., British and French ambassadors. The State Department confirmed Nov. 10 that the proposals had been raised at the Kroll-Khrushchev meeting and had been transmitted by Kroll to the other Western ambassadors—Llewellyn E. Thompson Jr. of the U.S., Sir Frank Roberts of Britain and Maurice Dejean of France.

West German government sources confirmed this version of the story Nov. 11. They emphasized that Kroll had done most of the talking at his meeting with Khrushchev but had spoken as an individual and without authorization to begin any kind of bilateral West German-Soviet talks on Berlin. West German government spokesman Felix von Eckardt declared Nov. 13 that Kroll had taken an "unauthorized initiative" in his discussion with Khrushchev and would return to Bonn to explain his action. Von Eckardt said that Kroll had suggested the first 2 points of the proposal and Khrushchev the point concerning "respect" for East Germany.

Kroll returned to Bonn Nov. 15 and reported to Chancellor Adenauer.

Seymour Topping, Moscow correspondent for the *N.Y. Times,* gave the following account of Kroll's action in a dispatch published Nov. 14: Soviet Foreign Min. Gromyko mentioned several of the proposals in a conversation with Kroll and the other Western ambassadors Nov. 7 at a Kremlin reception on the 44th anniversary of the Bolshevik revolution. Although several of these points had been brought up by Gromyko in earlier talks with State Secy. Rusk and U.S. Amb. Thompson, Kroll appeared interested in them and arranged a private meeting with Khrushchev at which they were further discussed. The day of the Kroll-Khrushchev meeting (Nov. 9), the contents of the Nov. 7 Gromyko conversation were leaked to newsmen by Western sources as a serious Soviet approach. This view was encouraged by Communist newsmen, apparently at Soviet government behest. Western foreign ministries, seeking an explanation for the Soviet proposals (which had not been communicated except in the press), mistakenly connected reports of the Gromyko conversation with the similar discussion held by Kroll and Khrushchev 2 days later. No restatement of the proposals had come from Soviet officials by Nov. 15.

The *N.Y. Times* reported from Bonn Nov. 17 that Kroll had been responsible for nearly all of the proposals discussed in his meeting with Khrushchev. Kroll also was said to have advanced the idea of a "grand reconciliation" between the USSR and West Germany.

The West German government ultimately withdrew its charge that Kroll's conversation with Khrushchev constituted an "unauthorized initiative" on a major foreign policy matter. Bonn sources indicated that a close inquiry had proven that Kroll had made no policy proposals to Khrushchev, although he had explored a number of suggestions that were raised during his meeting with the Soviet premier. According to these sources, it was Khrushchev who sought the meeting and who presumably brought up the topics for discussion.

Kroll returned to Moscow Nov. 20 after being absolved of charges that he had initiated proposals for a Berlin settlement. At a meeting Nov. 16 with U.S. newsmen, Adenauer had denied that Kroll had committed an "indiscretion" in his talks with Khrushchev. He added that Kroll would have been remiss if he had rebuffed Khrushchev's request for a meeting or if he failed to take advantage of the interview to discuss a possible settlement.

(State Secy. Rusk, in a Voice of America broadcast recorded Oct. 24 and made public Oct. 28, had reiterated the U.S.' rejection of the disengagement concept. He said: The Soviet bloc's stated intention to probe and infiltrate neutral zones made it "extremely difficult" to acquiesce in the creation of such zones; the West would not accept disengagement while "the policy of the Sino-Soviet bloc is to press ... world revolution.")

A new West German coalition cabinet of Christian Democratic Union (CDU) and Free Democratic Party (FDP) members was sworn in before the Bundestag (lower house) Nov. 14. Chancellor Adenauer remained as head of the government while Dr. Erich Mende, leader of the FDP, agreed to the coalition cabinet Nov. 3. The Adenauer-Mende agreement, approved by the CDU's Bundestag deputies Nov. 4, called for West Germany to insist on several points. Those relating to Berlin included: (1) A greater share of NATO command posts for West German officers. (2) A "modern" nuclear weapon-delivery system for all NATO members and "a voice for [all European members of NATO] in decisions about atomic warheads." (3) Opposition to the following concessions in negotiations with the USSR on a Berlin settlement: (a) the cutting or easing of West Berlin ties with the Bonn government; (b) West German *de facto* or *de jure* recognition of East Germany; (c) recognition of the Communist sealing of the Berlin border or recognition of Soviet or East German control of civilian traffic to and from Berlin; (d) a German-Polish border settlement before a peace treaty unifying Germany. (4) West Germany's right to approve or disapprove any German peace treaty by the USSR and the Western powers. (5) An increase in the period of compulsory military service from 12 to 18 months.

Berlin & the Wall

Gen. Lucius D. Clay, Pres. Kennedy's personal representative in Berlin, demanded Nov. 13 that the restoration of free movement between East and West Berlin be made a major issue in any East-West negotiations on Germany. Clay outlined his views in an interview given the West German DPA news agency 3 months after East Germany had begun building the Berlin Wall. Clay said he was convinced that ways could be found to restore the free movement halted by the Communists Aug. 13. He denied that Administration officials in Washington had criticized his use of troops to test East German control of access to East Berlin, but he said no decision had been reached to reverse the halt in U.S. civilian officials' trips to the eastern sector.

West Berlin city officials had disclosed Oct. 31 that an average of 1,700 persons had left the city for West Germany each week since Aug. 13.

The West German Press & Information Office *Bulletin,* in the issue for Nov. 14, said that West Berlin Mayor Willy Brandt had reported 268 "incidents" involving refugees escaping over the wall since Aug. 13. 8 refugees were killed and 69 wounded in the incidents. Brandt reported that 201 members of the East German army and East Berlin police had fled to West Berlin during the period. Among Berlin incidents reported recently: East Berlin police fired on several groups of refugees attempting to cross the border barrier Oct. 31 and recaptured 6 persons; gunfire halted 21 of 30 East Berliners who attempted a mass escape Nov. 5; West Berlin and East Berlin police engaged in the biggest tear gas duel yet reported when workmen Nov. 6 began tearing down a portion of the border fence that had been erected on West Berlin territory; 3 more heavy tear gas duels broke out Nov. 11 when East Berlin police sought to prevent TV photography of the wall. (Despite the border gunfire an estimated 10-20 East Berliners were escaping to the West each night.)

East German troops and workmen began fortifying the Berlin Wall Nov. 19. Crews of up to 500 men worked by searchlight to install heavy anti-tank barriers and dig deep ditches behind the existing wall at 7 key points in East Berlin, among them the Friedrichstrasse crossing point open to Western officials. The fortifications were designed to protect major East Berlin entrance points most likely to be targets of any Western tank sortie. The Brandenburg Gate was sealed with a barrier 250 yards long, 8 feet high and 6 feet thick.

Deputy Mayor Franz Amrehn of West Berlin inspected the new construction Nov. 20 and said: "That is a wall for 1,000 years."

The East German CP newspaper *Neues Deutschland* said Nov. 21 that the fortified wall was intended to discourage a Western tank thrust that "could well bring the outbreak of a worldwide war of nuclear weapons and rockets."

It was reported Nov. 20 that Khrushchev, at his meeting with West German Amb. Kroll, had agreed that the Berlin wall was an "ugly thing" but that it would remain until a "general understanding" had been reached between East and West Germany. Khrushchev reportedly disclosed that the wall had been ordered built by East German Socialist Unity Party First Secy. Walter Ulbricht for "well-known reasons." This presumably referred to the flight of refugees from East Germany. Ulbricht, in a party Central Committee report published Nov. 26 by the East German newspaper *Neues Deutschland,* declared that the East Berlin wall would "become unnecessary" only after West Germany quit NATO and dismissed its "Hitler generals." Ulbricht said that East Germany would reject any Western proposals that accorded it only de facto recognition. He asserted that the 4-power occupation statute applied to West Berlin only and not to East

Berlin, which was, he said, within East Germany's state territory.

1,000 demonstrating West Berlin students attempted Nov. 20 to storm the wall at the Zimmerstrasse crossing point but were driven back and dispersed by West Berlin police. 6,000 students were halted and dispersed by police a mile from the border as they marched toward the Brandenburg Gate. The 2 groups had formed after a student protest rally, attended by an estimated 40,000 persons, marking the 100th day since the start of the Berlin Wall. East Berlin police threw tear gas grenades over the wall to halt the students.

The Soviet government newspaper *Izvestia* Nov. 28 published the full text of an interview in which Pres. Kennedy outlined for the Russian people his views on major world problems. Kennedy repeated that none of these problems was insoluble if the USSR were prepared to abandon its drive to communize the world and were ready to deal honestly with the West. His remarks concerning Berlin, either directly or indirectly, included:

"Where we feel the difficulty comes is the effort by the Soviet Union to communize, in a sense, the entire world. If the Soviet Union were merely seeking to protect its own national interests, to protect its own national security, and would permit other countries to live as they wish—to live in peace—then I believe that the problems which now cause so much tension would fade away. We want the people of the Soviet Union to live in peace—we want the same for our own people. It is this effort to push outward the Communist system, on to country after country, that represents, I think, the great threat to peace." "If the people of any country choose to follow a Communist system in a free election, after a fair opportunity for a number of views to be presented, the United States would accept that. What we find to be objectionable, and a threat to the peace, is when a system is imposed by a small militant group by subversion, infiltration, and all the rest."

"We had been under the impression that the Yalta Agreement and the Potsdam Agreement provided for a free choice for the peoples of Eastern Europe. They do not, in our opinion, today, have a free choice. You may argue that they may want to live under communism, but if they do not, they are not given the opportunity to change."

"I am hopeful that, in the conversations and negotiations which we hope to have with the Soviet Union, assurances will be given which will permit us to continue to exercise the rights which we now have in West Berlin, as a result of the existing 4-power agreement, and will permit free access in and out of the city. We do not want to stay in West Berlin if the people there do not want us to stay. But they want us to stay...."

"... In attempting to work out a solution of the problems which came about as a result of World War II, we don't want to increase the chances of World War III. All we wish to do is maintain a very limited—and they are a very limited—number of troops of the 3 powers in West Berlin and to have for example, an international administration on the *autobahn* so that goods and people can move freely in and out.... But if East Germany is going to exercise the right of authority over that access, we are going to have continued tension there...."

"... West Germany now has only 9 divisions, which is a fraction of the Soviet forces.... It has no nuclear weapons of its own. It has a very small air force—almost no navy.... So that I do not see that this country represents a military threat now to the Soviet Union, even though I recognize how bitter was the struggle in World War II...."

"... The United States, as a matter of national policy, will not give nuclear· weapons to any country, and I would be extremely reluctant to see West Germany acquire a nuclear capacity of its own. Chancellor Adenauer stated that they would not, in 1954. That is still the policy of that government, and I think that is the wise policy."

"I think, if we look at it realistically, we should be able to reach an accord which protects the interests of our 2 great countries, and permits us both to go ahead with increasing our standard of living and meeting other problems. In the United States in the last 14 years our living standard has increased 40%. In the Soviet Union it has gone up sharply. Nobody can benefit more from peace than the Soviet Union and the United States."

Izvestia Dec. 3 rebutted the major views expressed by Kennedy in his interview. The *Izvestia* response was made in an unsigned article believed to have been written by one or more high Soviet officials. The article applauded Kennedy's expression of hope for the settlement of East-West problems, but it rejected most of his specific suggestions for solving those problems, especially with respect to Germany. *Izvestia* said: The U.S.' "big stick" foreign policy matched "the intentions of Bonn's revanchists, who are dreaming ... of seizing the GDR [East German] communications and then all of her territory." Kennedy's insistence on Western occupation rights in Berlin was an "outlived approach" because World War II had ended 16 years ago and "preservation [of the occupation rights] leads not to the improvement but to the aggravation of the situation in central Europe." The Soviet Union welcomed Kennedy's opposition to West Germany's acquisition of nuclear weapons, but the USSR knew Bonn was attempting "to acquire nuclear weapons by the round-about way" through NATO. Kennedy's charge that the USSR "hoped to communize all the world" was a "cock and bull story" that failed to take into account "the powerful social forces" changing people's lives.

At a Moscow reception, Khrushchev commented Dec. 6 on the Kennedy interview. He said: "Interesting, ... but I cannot agree with everything said. When Mr. Kennedy becomes a Communist we shall then speak a common language, but that will not happen for a very long time."

West Divided on Berlin?

West German Chancellor Adenauer flew to the U.S. Nov. 19 to confer with Pres. Kennedy on a coordinated Western policy toward negotiations on the future of Berlin and Germany. The 2 leaders Nov. 22 announced their full agreement on Western terms for the negotiations and on military measures to resist continued Soviet pressures in Germany. The communique issued by the 2 men claimed that their talks had dispelled reported U.S.-West German mistrust and differences over the West's response to Soviet actions in Berlin.

The communique said: "The President and the chancellor reaffirmed their clear determination to insure ... a free and vigorous life for the population of Berlin. They are in accord on the basic elements which will permit a peaceful resolution of this crisis through negotiation if there is reasonableness on the part of the Soviet Union.... They also agreed on the necessity for ... increasing the ability of ... [NATO] to cope with any military developments."

The communique branded as "false and unwarranted" the USSR's charges of NATO and West German aggressive intent. It said: (1) NATO was "an alliance for defense against aggression which abides fully by the requirements of the [UN] Charter." (2) West Germany had "demonstrated that it looks to its legitimate security interests entirely within [NATO] ... and has integrated its entire effective defense establishment into the multinational NATO framework."

Washington sources reported Nov. 22 that Kennedy had assured Adenauer that the U.S. was not considering any solution that would weaken West Berlin's ties with West Germany or diminish Western occupation rights in the city. He reportedly pledged the U.S. to oppose any settlement based on military disengagement or recognition of East Germany's Communist regime. Adenauer was said to have promised an intensified West German arms buildup.

Adenauer, meeting Nov. 16 with U.S. newsmen before his trip to see Kennedy, had called for ending the U.S. President's exclusive authority to order the use of NATO nuclear weapons. He said that NATO could face a situation in which an "immediate decision had to be taken when the fate of all could be decided in one hour and the President ... cannot be reached...." Therefore, he continued, "we must arrange within NATO that a decision can be taken to use atomic weapons even before the President is heard from."

Kennedy Nov. 8 had denied Soviet charges that Adenauer and the Bonn government were militarists. He said at his press conference in Washington that East Germany, although smaller than West Germany, had "substantially larger ground forces."

French Pres. de Gaulle visited British Prime Min. Macmillan privately Nov. 24-26 for talks on reconciling British–French differences over the need for East–West negotiations on the Berlin question. No joint statement was issued on their talks. But British and French sources reported Nov. 26 that de Gaulle had agreed not to obstruct preliminary steps toward new Berlin negotiations. De Gaulle was said to have remained unenthusiastic about the value of such talks with the USSR, but he reportedly accepted Macmillan's view that

France should take part in formulating coordinated Western terms for negotiations. De Gaulle was said to have refused to promise that France would participate in East–West talks on Germany. But he reportedly retreated from his prior position that the Berlin crisis had been begun unilaterally by the USSR and should be ended by it.

State Secy. Rusk indicated Nov. 17 that the U.S. considered the removal of the Berlin Wall to be a goal of future East-West negotiations rather than a precondition for talks. Rusk refused to make a clear statement of U.S. policy on the matter but said: "The wall certainly ought not be a permanent feature of the European landscape"; "I see no reason why the Soviet Union should think that it is to their advantage ... to leave ... that monument to Communist failure in East Berlin and East Germany, that prison wall...."

Rusk's remarks were in answer to questions concerning a statement Nov. 16 by Chancellor Adenauer that the wall was "non-negotiable" and its destruction should be made a prior condition for any East-West talks on Germany. Gerhard Schroeder, the new West German foreign minister, declared Nov. 18, however, that Bonn had not made the wall's removal a precondition for East-West talks so long as such talks were not held under Soviet pressure.

Rusk, in an address Nov. 28 at a New York meeting of the Academy of Political Science, declared that the U.S. was prepared to continue negotiations with the USSR in the hope that "the raw edges of our basic conflict in objectives may be ... dulled." He suggested that East-West negotiations might best be devoted to these 4 areas: (1) arms control, particularly agreements to prevent "war by accident and miscalculation"; (2) resolution of "specific crises which have reached the point of clear and present danger"; (3) prevention of "future crises" by "continuous communications between ourselves and the Communists"; (4) cooperation serving "the interests of both sides" in the field of health, science, space exploration and nuclear energy. Rusk added: Khrushchev's "program for an eventual total Communist victory does not exclude the use of force and threats—it seems to exclude only the great war which would destroy the Soviet Union."

U.S. Defense Secy. Robert S. McNamara had said Nov. 17 that the military buildup in the Berlin crisis was proceeding "very satisfactorily" and that there were "no present plans" to call up more reservists. McNamara said U.S. armed manpower had been increased in recent months by 300,000 men, including 45,000 sent to Europe.

The foreign ministers of the U.S., Britain, France and West Germany conferred in Paris Dec. 11-12 but failed to agree on a unified Western position on negotiations with the USSR over Berlin. It was reported that the major obstacle to Western agreement was France's refusal to accept such negotiations as wise or necessary. The French reportedly felt that the Berlin crisis was solely a Soviet creation and that the West's position was not negotiable. The foreign ministers— Dean Rusk of the U.S., Lord Home of Britain, Maurice Couve de Murville of France and Gerhard Schroeder of West Germany—did not issue a joint communique. Western officials reported that the 4 ministers had agreed only to continue exploratory diplomatic talks with the Russians to find out whether a reasonable basis existed for full negotiations on Berlin.

The U.S. and Britain had let it be known that they expected the Paris meetings to produce agreement on terms for a more formal approach to the Soviet Union on Berlin negotiations. The French, however, refused to join in the diplomatic soundings under way in Moscow but did agree not to disavow them publicly. They did not promise to join in any East-West negotiations resulting from the Moscow soundings, but they did agree to the soundings being conducted by U.S. Amb.-to-USSR Thompson.

The 4 foreign ministers reported the results of their talks to the NATO Ministerial Council at a meeting convened in Paris Dec. 13. The 11 other NATO foreign ministers were said to have expressed dissatisfaction with their failure to achieve a formula for a negotiated end to the Berlin tension. Replying to Couve de Murville's defense of the French position, Belgian Foreign Min. Paul-Henri Spaak told the Council: "We have probed enough; it is time to negotiate." Couve de Murville had warned that Soviet behavior in Berlin was aimed at the ultimate neutralization and detachment of West Germany and the Scandinavian countries from NATO. It was France's view, he said, that the only proper Western response was a military preparedness program designed to face the Soviet threat with "firmness and dignity." Opening the Council session, Rusk had declared that the U.S. did not regard readiness to negotiate as a sign of weakness.

France's refusal to negotiate on Berlin had been explained by Pres. de Gaulle during a 5-hour meeting with West German Chancellor Adenauer in Paris Dec. 9. It was generally believed that Adenauer had gone to Paris to urge de Gaulle to accept some of the terms for Berlin negotiations worked out by Adenauer and Pres. Kennedy in their talks in Washington Nov. 19-22. A joint communique issued by de Gaulle and Adenauer Dec. 9 declared their agreement on the need for Western solidarity but said nothing about a negotiated Berlin settlement. Bonn sources claimed, however, that Adenauer had persuaded de Gaulle to accept continued Western diplomatic probing of the USSR's position. The French position on negotiations had been explained to the French Senate Dec. 5 by Couve de Murville. France had "never accepted the idea that it should be possible to negotiate under threats, be it even the supreme threat ... of atomic destruction," Couve de Murville said.

British officials suggested Dec. 6 that the West might have to consider East-West negotiations on Berlin without French participation. They asserted that Britain considered itself virtually committed to open such negotiations early in 1962.

Pres. Kennedy Nov. 29 had stressed the U.S. view that the world's most pressing need was for effective East-West negotiations on Berlin and other problems. At his press conference Kennedy had said: "I think that the important thing now is to attempt to work out a solution to the difficult problems which disturb our relations." "We cannot have ... an increase in harmony between the 2 blocs until we have come to some negotiated and mutually satisfactory agreement in regard to Berlin and Germany." Such an agreement should provide for " an international administration on the *autobahn* [to Berlin] so that goods and people can move freely in and out."

Kennedy's suggestion of international control of the *autobahn* to Berlin was rejected as "useless speculation" Dec. 2 by East German Communist chief Ulbricht. It was rejected again by Soviet Amb.-to-U.S. Mikhail A. Menshikov, who told the National Press Club Dec. 11 that "if the purpose of the Western powers in the [proposed Berlin] negotiations is to get confirmation of their occupation rights, then ... there will be nothing to talk about."

The foreign ministers of the 15 NATO countries met again in Paris Dec. 13-15 and approved the U.S.-British-French-West German agreement to probe the possibility of full-scale East-West negotiations on the Berlin problem. Meeting in the semiannual ministerial session of the NATO Council, the 15 ministers reached an agreed position only after France again made clear its opposition to such negotiations so long as the USSR maintained its current pressure against the Western position in Berlin. The French stand and the limited 4-power Western agreement to seek further diplomatic contacts with the USSR were communicated to the Council at its opening session Dec. 13 by French Foreign Min. Couve de Murville and his opposite numbers from the U.S., Britain, and West Germany.

The NATO Council said in a final communique issued Dec. 15: "Their [other] colleagues approved the resumption of diplomatic contacts and expressed the hope that a negotiated settlement could be achieved." The communique stressed, however, NATO's "determination to protect and defend the liberties of West Berlin and insure to its people the conditions for a free and prosperous life." It "reaffirmed the responsibilities which each member state has assumed in regard to the security and welfare of Berlin and the maintenance of the position of the 3 powers in that city."

Tough Stances Adopted

Armed U.S. infantrymen were deployed at the U.S.-sector border between East and West Berlin Dec. 3 after workmen began building additional tank barriers on the Communist side of the wall. The U.S. troops took positions behind sandbags after East German troops armed with submachineguns had moved to the border to shield workmen building tank traps at the Friedrichstrasse crossing point used by Western military traffic. Similar work was begun at Berlin's 6 other crossing points. The Communist action was protested in a note to the Soviet commandant from Maj. Gen. Albert Watson 2d, U.S.

commandant in West Berlin. The opposing troops were withdrawn from the border Dec. 4.

East German customs posts were erected Dec. 8 at each of the 7 crossing points between East and West Berlin. Persons crossing the border were subjected to the usual identity check. Western military personnel and vehicles continued to use the Friedrichstrasse crossing freely.

East Germany protested Dec. 16 against what it said were "illegal, provocative troop movements" by the U.S. along the *autobahn* linking West Berlin with West Germany. The East German protest was made in a note transmitted to the U.S. through the Czechoslovak government. It was directed specifically against the exchange of 2 1,500-man infantry battle groups between garrisons in West Berlin and West Germany. The movement, involving 500 vehicles, was carried out in a series of *autobahn* convoys Dec. 7-15. The U.S., ignoring the note, sent an infantry company from Berlin to West Germany Dec. 18. The U.S. had begun emphasizing its rights to military use of the *autobahn* by heavier traffic in November. A U.S. military train had been halted for 15 hours Nov. 23 at the Soviet checkpoint in Marienborn, East Germany. It was released only after U.S. authorities had turned over to Soviet officers an East German who had broken into the train and hidden during its trip across East Germany. The train was one of 4 run daily between Frankfurt and West Berlin. East Germany said the stowaway was fleeing arrest as a burglar. (East German border police had detained and interrogated 4 Britons Nov. 15. 2 were released after they promised to spy on West Berlin troop dispositions in order to get back their air tickets home. They reported the incident on their release.)

In the first response to U.S. demands that other NATO allies share the burden of the current Western build-up, West German Defense Min. Franz-Jozef Strauss disclosed Nov. 30 that Bonn had agreed to buy $700 million worth of U.S. military equipment in 1961-2. The French were said to have promised U.S. Deputy Defense Secy. Roswell L. Gilpatric that 2 army divisions withdrawn from Algeria would be sent to join the 2 French divisions currently serving in West Germany. Britain's response reportedly was limited to a pledge to reinforce the German-based British Army of the Rhine. French

Armed Forces Min. Pierre Messmer said at a Washington news conference Nov. 30 that France had agreed to buy $50 million worth of military equipment in the U.S. that it ordinarily would have bought elsewhere. Messmer said, however, that France would not reverse its prohibition on the use of French bases by nuclear-armed U.S. aircraft. U.S. administration officials made it clear that the U.S. considered the new French military effort an adequate response to NATO's current needs.

The West Berlin Social Democratic Party called on the Western powers Dec. 3 to seize the initiative in the German problem by summoning a peace conference of all 52 nations that fought Germany in World War II. The West Berlin party rejected any German settlement that would alter West Berlin's constitutional relationship with West Germany or reduce freedoms guaranteed by the Western allies.

Among continuing incidents reported in Berlin:

● 25 East German refugees escaped to West Berlin Dec. 5 aboard a commuter train in which they sped into the British sector from East Berlin. The train was driven by refugee Harry Deterling, 28.

● East German border guards fired across the barrier twice Dec. 9, killing a West Berlin student who had entered East German territory. (The barrier was set back from the actual frontier in most places.) More shots were fired Dec. 10; East German officials said they were aimed at "provocateurs" who sought to breach the border barriers.

● East and West Berlin police dueled with tear gas grenades Dec. 21 after Communist police had stoned Christmas trees erected on the Western side of the Berlin wall. Bernard J. Collett, a Briton, was freed by East Germany Dec. 26 after 16 weeks' detention on charges of trying to smuggle refugees to the West.

● East German border guards barred Howard Trivers, chief political officer of the U.S. State Department mission in Berlin, from entering East Berlin Dec. 22 for a meeting with his Soviet counterpart. Trivers, who had passed the border freely in the past, was refused entry unless he showed identity papers. Trivers was driven to the East Berlin checkpoint Dec. 23 in a car with Maj. Gen. Albert Watson 2d, U.S. commandant in Berlin, but again was barred. Watson cancelled an appointment with the Soviet commandant to return to the Western zone with Trivers. The incident was protested by U.S. Amb.-to-West Germany Walter C. Dowling Dec. 24 in a note to Soviet Amb.-to-East Germany Mikhail G. Pervukhin.

● The U.S. mission in West Berlin disclosed Dec. 29 that Col. Andrei I. Solovyev, the USSR's Berlin commandant, had been barred from the U.S. sector of West Berlin. The action was in retaliation for the barring of Trivers. Occupants of all Soviet military vehicles entering the U.S. sector were subjected to identity checks beginning Dec. 31.

(The West German Ministry for All-German Affairs announced Dec. 23 that nearly 10,000 East Germans had managed to flee to West Germany since Aug. 13, when the Communists began building barriers along the borders between East and West Berlin and between East and West Germany.)

U.S. intentions to safeguard West Berlin's freedom "for many years to come" were reaffirmed by Pres. Kennedy in a taped TV Christmas message broadcast in the city Dec. 25. The President told West Berliners that "the bonds which tie us have been tested before: we are at your side now, as before. We shall stay." Kennedy's remarks were echoed in a similar message broadcast to West Berliners the same day by Gen. Lucius D. Clay, the President's personal representative in the city. Clay reminded West Berliners that despite "this shameful wall," their city was "the showcase of the West."

A personal assessment by Kennedy of the results of his first year in office was published prominently by U.S. newspapers Dec. 31. Kennedy was said to feel that 1961 had produced no major alteration of the power balance and that the U.S. had maintained a narrow military and political lead over the USSR. He also reportedly felt that cold-war tensions had not declined, but a 3d world war was less likely. He also felt that there had been no significant progress toward settlement of major East-West difference.